DATE DUE

DEMCO 38-296

LUKAS FOSS

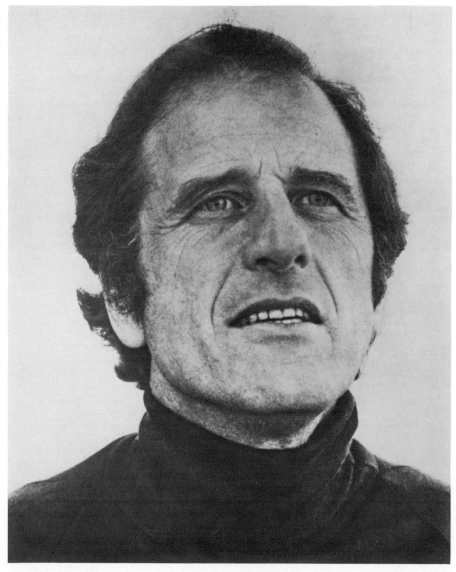

Lukas Foss

LUKAS FOSS
A BIO-BIBLIOGRAPHY

KAREN L. PERONE

Bio-Bibliographies in Music, Number 37
Donald L. Hixon, Series Adviser

GREENWOOD PRESS
New York • Westport, Connecticut • London

Library of Congress Cataloging-in-Publication Data

Perone, Karen L.
  Lukas Foss : a bio-bibliography / Karen L. Perone.
      p.   cm.—(Bio-bibliographies in music, ISSN 0742-6968 ; no.
  37)
  Includes discographies and index.
  ISBN 0-313-26811-8 (alk. paper)
  1. Foss, Lukas, 1922- —Bibliography. 2. Foss, Lukas, 1922- —
Discography. I. Title. II. Series.
ML134.F59P47   1991
016.78′092—dc20
  [B]   90-29280

British Library Cataloguing in Publication Data is available.

Library of Congress Catalog Card Number: 90-29280
ISBN: 0-313-26811-8
ISSN: 0742-6968

First published in 1991

Greenwood Press, 88 Post Road West, Westport, CT   06881
An imprint of Greenwood Publishing Group, Inc.

Printed in the United States of America

The paper used in this book complies with the
Permanent Paper Standard issued by the National
Information Standards Organization (Z39.48-1984).

10 9 8 7 6 5 4 3 2 1

CONTENTS

PREFACE

While following the general format of the other volumes in Greenwood's *Bio-Bibliographies in Music* series, I have opted to a slight variance in style. Relevant reviews and analyses of performances and the works themselves follow the main descriptive entry of each work in the Works and Performances section and a separate Discography Bibliography section has been utilized to list reviews of recordings near their discographical citations and to separate them from the General Bibliography. Thus, the volume is divided into the following sections: 1) Biography; 2) Works and Performances (with bibliographical references); 3) Discography; 4) Discography Bibliography; 5) General Bibliography; and 6) Appendices listing Foss's many awards and honors, and his compositions, first chronologically and then alphabetically.

Within the Works and Performances section, the compositions have been arranged first by genre (Theater, Operas, Ballets, Choral Music, Music for Solo Voice, Orchestral Music, Chamber Music, Music for Solo Instruments, and Adaptations by Foss of Works by other composers) and then chronologically within each category by the date of the composition. Each composition is designated by the mnemonic "W" for "Work" followed by a sequential number. Details pertaining to date of composition, publisher availability, contents, commissioning information, manuscript location, author of text, related works, and other information are listed with each work.

First performances and other significant performances are listed after the descriptive details of each work. The performances are listed chronologically and are notated by works number followed by sequential lower case letters. Each performance listing includes as many details as possible regarding date, location, and performers. Related performances (i.e., other works by Foss on the same program) and bibliographical or discographical entry numbers are listed in each entry as a "See" or "See also" note.

Following the listings of performances for each work are bibliographical references to the performances and the works themselves. The bibliographical references are numbered sequentially with the mnemonic "WB" for "Works Bibliography" and the entries are listed in chronological order. Appropriate references are made to the performances reviewed or to other citations for a more detailed annotation.

Since Foss is an active conductor and pianist as well as a composer, I have divided the Discography section into three parts. First are recordings of Foss's compositions. The order of these works follows the order of the compositions in the Works and Performances section: first by genre, and then chronologically. The second section lists recordings conducted by Foss in chronological order. The third section lists recordings on which Foss performs as pianist, again listed in chronological order. Appropriate references are made in all sections to related recordings, and reviews in the Discography Bibliography section. Each recording is numbered sequentially and contains the mnemonic "D" for "Discography." Details pertaining to record label (if commercially available) or archival location, date of release/recording, performers, and other works on the recording are listed for each entry.

The Discography Bibliography contains annotated references to reviews of recordings in the Discography section. The arrangement of entries follows that of the Discography section. Again the entries are listed in chronological order and numbered sequentially. Each entry number contains the mnemonic "DB" for "Discography Bibliography." "See" references are provided to refer the reader to the appropriate recording listing in the Discography section.

The final major section is that of general bibliographical citations. These entries are listed in chronological order and are sequentially numbered with the mnemonic "B" for "Bibliography." This section includes significant citations to books, dissertations, and journal and newspaper articles which refer to Foss's personal life, his career, and reviews of Foss's performances as a conductor or pianist.

Throughout the volume, extensive use of citations from the *New York Times* and Buffalo newspapers have been made. Many citations from these sources were not included due to space limitations. Insignificant journal articles (primarily those listing or announcing performances) have also been omitted due to their brevity.

Accuracy has been assured by the close readings of the manuscript drafts by Mr. Foss himself. Many reviews and details could not have been included if he had not been so patient and helpful.

ACKNOWLEDGMENTS

This work could not have been completed without the help of several very important people. First of all, I would like to thank **Lukas Foss** for all of the time that he devoted to reading the manuscript and his advisement along the way regarding the compositions, performances, and reviews. Only with Foss's help and interest in this project have I been able to accurately represent his vast career.

Second, I would like to thank **Jack Schweigel** of the Canisius College Computer Center for all of his programming help and computer expertise. Without his help, this book would still be hopelessly lost inside my computer.

This project was begun under the direction of Carol June **Bradley** and James **Coover**, both of the Music Library, State University of New York at Buffalo. Without their graduate school project, this bio-bibliography would have never seen daylight.

Numerous other persons have gone above and beyond the call of duty to help this work become a reality. They are: Mary **Blair**, Greenwood Press; Karen **Bordonaro**, Canisius College Library; Marilyn **Brownstein**, Greenwood Press; **the Staff of the Music Department, Buffalo and Erie County Public Library**; Arthur **Cohn**, Carl Fischer, Inc.; Sally **DiCarlo**, Canisius College Library; Alena **Hajdu**, Canisius College Library; Don **Hixon**, University of California at Irvine; Dale L. **Hudson**, Florida State University Music Library; Pat **McCarty**, Carl Fischer, Inc.; Michael **Nascimben; the staff of the New York Public Library Music Research Division**; James **Perone**, Canisius College; Laura **Piantini**, Theodore Presser Co.; Sally **Scott**, Greenwood Press; **the staff of the State University of New York at Buffalo Music Library**; Leslie **Troutman**, University of Illinois at Urbana-Champaign Music Library; Joseph **Umhauer**, Nioga Library System; Carol **Wincenc**.

BIOGRAPHY

Always gracious, enthusiastic, curious, and energetic, Lukas Foss has been referred to both as the "eternal Wunderkind" and an "Enfant Terrible." Stravinsky had once told him, "Lukas, soyez rosse. (Lukas, be fierce.)" (Wright 1982, 12. See: B182) His conducting has always involved the interpretation of the masters "as if the ink were hardly dry," and the playing of "new music with the same awe, respect and distance we usually accord to the classics." (Foss 1963, 52. See: B54) His performance skills as a pianist were cultivated at an early age and allowed him to become the staff pianist for the Boston Symphony Orchestra at age 22. A 1961 Tanglewood piano performance by Foss earned the review that "[Foss] is capable of a slow-burning crescendo, which burst into flame at the cadenza and blazed through the finale." (Dumm 1961, 61. See: B36) Foss is equally accomplished as a "composer, conductor, pianist, teacher, impressario-organizer, and tireless proponent of the newest new music." (Salzman 1967, 73. See: B93)

On August 15, 1922, Lukas Foss was born in Berlin as Lukas Fuchs to Martin Fuchs, a lawyer, who later became a professor of philosophy at Haverford College in Pennsylvania and Hilda Schindler Fuchs, a painter. The family changed its name to Foss after coming to America in 1937. He has a brother, Oliver Ulric Foss, who, like his mother, is a painter. He resides in Paris.

Foss is a naturally gifted musician. He received an accordion as a gift at the age of five and began to accompany the German folk songs that his mother had taught him. Foss did not formally begin piano lessons until the age of seven, when he studied piano and theory with Julius Goldstein Herford. He continued to study with Herford until age 11. He quickly became quite accomplished on the piano, but did not tour as a child prodigy; his parents wanted him to have a normal childhood. At the age of eight, Foss's mother told him the story of the little devil who came to earth on his birthday to cause trouble for a day. Young Foss asked his mother to write a libretto based on the story so that he could compose an opera on it. This first operatic attempt was abandoned in favor of more "mature" ventures shortly after it was begun. It was not until 1953 that Foss returned to this story and composed the opera *Griffelkin* for NBC-TV (See: W4). *Griffelkin* is lovingly dedicated to Foss's mother. It remains one of his favorite compositions today, and is a high point of his adventure with an American type of Neo-Classicism.

When Foss was nine, he heard a performance of Mozart's *Le Nozze de Figaro* that caused him to decide that music would be his vocation. He soon memorized the score to the finale of act 2 and could perform all the parts, becoming quite a hit at family gatherings.

In 1933, the Foss family moved to Paris to escape the Nazis, living there until 1937. Here, he studied piano with Lazare Lévy and composition with Noël Gallon, both teachers at the Conservatoire de Paris. He also studied orchestration with Felix Wolfes and flute with Louis Moyse. All of Foss's academic schooling was at the Lyceé Pasteur in Paris since he was too young to officially attend the Conservatory.

Soon after the Foss family's move to New York City in 1937, Lukas auditioned for Fritz Reiner in Philadelphia, who was recruiting promising students in Europe for the Curtis Institute. Reiner put a score for the slow movement of Beethoven's *Fourth Symphony* in front of Foss, which he correctly identified. Duly impressed, Reiner accepted Foss immediately for the school.

Foss continued his piano studies with Isabelle Vengerova, a teacher at the Curtis Institute. He studied composition with Rosario Scalero (who, as Foss relates, was too old to offer much inside training), orchestration with Randall Thompson, and conducting with Fritz Reiner at the Curtis Institute in Philadelphia. Foss wrote *Four Two-Part Inventions* (See: W97) and *Grotesque Dance* (See: W98) while commuting on the New York subway trains to his music lessons at age 15. Foss was invited to audition these works before Carl Engel, head of G. Schirmer who accepted and subsequently published the compositions in 1938. In 1940, he graduated with honors from Curtis, receiving diplomas in all the above mentioned disciplines.

When the new Berkshire Music Center in Tanglewood, Massachusetts opened in 1940, Foss was one of the first registered students. Here, he spent his summers until 1943 studying composition with Paul Hindemith and conducting with Serge Koussevitzky. One of the rules of the Center was that students could only enroll in either the conducting or composition programs but not both. Serge Koussevitzky made an exception to this rule after observing Foss's conducting of the student orchestra in *Till Eulenspiegel's Merry Pranks* by Richard Strauss. Foss had never conducted an orchestra before, but thought he knew how. Impressing Koussevitzky, Foss was soon taken on as Koussevitzky's protégé and assistant.

At age 15, Foss's compositional style was beginning to take on the characteristics of Hindemith's music. However, when he finally was able to study composition at Tanglewood and Yale University with Hindemith from 1940-41, Foss had discovered Stravinsky. (See: B13) Hindemith threw Foss out of class twice because of his rebelliousness, resulting from this newly found compositional style. Hindemith had once told Koussevitzky,

"Foss wants to know everything but not to follow." (Kupferberg 1984, 14. See: B196)

Foss was awarded a commission on the recommendation of Samuel Barber and Gian Carlo Menotti to write incidental music for a children's production of Shakespeare's *The Tempest* in 1940. (See: W1) "[Foss] wrote the music in a month...[and] turned in a remarkably workmanlike score." (*Time* 1940, 60. See: WB1) This score resulted in the awarding of a Pulitzer Traveling Scholarship to Foss.

In 1942, Foss became a naturalized citizen of the United States and fell in love with his new homeland. He composed *The Prairie* (See: W11) based on the Carl Sandburg poem "Cornhuskers" and established his own brand of American music "through broad, sweeping melodies and sonorities suggestive of vast open spaces." (Ewen 1982, 234. See: B183) In 1943, Serge Koussevitzky asked Foss to prepare a suite of the music from *The Prairie* that would be premiered by the Boston Symphony Orchestra. This was the first time an orchestral work by Foss was performed by a major symphony orchestra. (See: W40a) As a result, Foss became the youngest composer to have a work performed by the Boston Symphony Orchestra. The New York Music Critics' Circle Citation was awarded to Foss for *The Prairie* as the most important new American choral work of 1944.

Having performed as piano soloist with a number of major American orchestras, Foss gained a growing reputation for his pianistic abilities. After performing his *Concerto No. 1 for Piano* as soloist with the Boston Symphony Orchestra in 1944 (See: W38b), Foss became the official pianist of the Boston Symphony Orchestra, succeeding Jesús Maria Sanromá. He retained this post until 1950. On September 3, 1944, Foss premiered Hindemith's *Theme and Variations According to the Four Temperaments* as piano soloist with the Boston Symphony Orchestra, Richard Burgin, conductor. (See: B1)

The summer of 1944 was spent at the MacDowell Artists Colony where Foss wrote *Symphony No. 1 in G* (See: W39). A productive year, Foss also completed *Ode* (See: W41) and three ballets: *The Heart Remembers* (See: W6), *Within These Walls* (See: W7), and *The Gift of the Magi*. (See: W8)

In 1945, at the age of 23, Foss became the youngest composer to ever receive a Guggenheim Fellowship. This allowed him to devote his time to composing. During this Fellowship, he composed the two biblical solo cantatas, *Song of Anguish* (See: W28) and *Song of Songs* (See: W29). "Both biblical cantatas are songful, sensuous in style, with page upon page of great emotional intensity." (Ewen 1982, 234. See: B183) Koussevitzky was so impressed by *Song of Songs* that he programmed it for an unprecedented eight performances in nine days by the Boston Symphony Orchestra. The Columbia recording of this work (See: D23) received the Naumburg Recording Award in 1957.

With Koussevitzky's increasing interest in Foss, Koussevitzky appointed Foss to be his assistant and a member of the Berkshire teaching faculty in 1946. This marked the beginning of Foss's teaching career. He returned to Berkshire for numerous summers in this capacity.

Foss received more awards in the years that followed: a citation from the Society for the Publication of American Music for *String Quartet No. 1 in G* (See: W72) in 1948; the Prix de Rome which allowed Foss to become a Fellow of the American Academy in Rome from 1950 to 1951; his first Fulbright Scholarship from 1950 to 1952; and the Mark M. Horblit/Boston Symphony Award awarded to Foss in 1952 for his *Concerto No. 2 for Piano*. (See: W46)

Foss, as piano soloist, premiered his *Concerto No. 2 for Piano* in Venice on October 7, 1951 (See: W46a), thus enhancing his international musical reputation. He returned to Boston in November 1951 to perform the American premiere performance of the work (See: W46b). After revising the *Concerto* in 1953, Foss was awarded the New York Music Critics' Circle Citation in 1954 for the best new instrumental work of the season. The *Concerto* has been described as "a modern version of the grand virtuoso concerto of the past." (Machlis 1963, 195. See: B46)

In October 1951, Foss married painter Cornelia Brendel. The couple has two children: Christopher, a writer, and Eliza, an actress.

After the death of Arnold Schoenberg, Foss became a member of the music faculty at the University of California at Los Angeles in 1953. Here, Foss, the youngest full professor ever hired at UCLA, taught composition and conducting until 1962, gaining much practical experience, both in teaching and conducting. In 1956, Foss received an honorary LL.D. from the Los Angeles Conservatory of Music.

He became the director of the Ojai (California) Festival from 1955 to 1957, repeating this honor again in the 1960s. (See: B35) He also conducted the first six-hour marathon concerts at the Hollywood Bowl with the Los Angeles Philharmonic Orchestra while in California. These concerts featured performances of works by a single composer or style (e.g., Bach, Mozart, Beethoven, contemporary, Romantic) by various combinations of instruments from the Orchestra in a setting that allowed audience members to come and go as they pleased. The results were overwhelmingly successful and attracted large audiences, including many young people. This procedure was later used in New York and Israel for a total of 16 concerts, each with equally great success. (See: B134, B135, B138, B144-B146)

1956-61 became a transitional composition period as Foss began his experiments in ensemble improvisation. He worked on the development of controlled ensemble improvisation venturing into atonality and serialism and into aleatoric music before the expression "aleatoric" had been coined.

Foss received a Creative Music Grant from the National Institute of Arts and Letters in 1957. This same year, Foss founded the Improvisation Chamber Ensemble with Richard Dufallo (clarinet) and Charles DeLancey (percussion). Howard Colf (violoncello) joined to round out the quartet in 1959. The group originally began as an experiment for Foss's students at UCLA and employed Bob Drasnin (flute), William Malm (bass clarinet), Eugene Wilson (violoncello), and Douglas Davis (violoncello) at various times. "'It all started very modestly as a means of helping the students,' Foss recalls, 'but suddenly a door opened for me and I saw a vast new

territory to explore.'" (Ewen 1982, 235. See: B183) Foss felt that
through ensemble improvisation he could allow his students a freedom that
they would not be able to explore through the printed score and also as a
way to bridge the gap between composer and performer. The reviewer at
an early performance noted, "The tedious score-bound performances, which
have become so sterile in our modern concert halls, might be set free if our
contemporary musicians were alerted to group improvisations of this type."
(Faulkner 1959, 70. See: B19)

The Improvisation Chamber Ensemble performed its first national
concert tour in 1960, performing *Concerto for Improvising Instruments and
Orchestra* with the Philadelphia Orchestra in Philadelphia and New York City.
(See: W48a, W48b) Reviews for the performances varied greatly, ranging
from "unreviewable music" (See: WB205) to music that "both fascinated
and frustrated many listeners." (See: WB207)

The concept of ensemble improvisation became a highly publicized
topic and generated much interest from the press. (See: B17, B19, B22-
B25, B37, B38, B40, B41, B43, B49, B52) Foss became very intrigued and
motivated by his new style of "composition" and had even planned to write
a textbook on ensemble improvisation to be used in colleges and
universities. In his liner notes to the album *Studies in Improvisation*, Foss
stated, "At the risk of being proven wrong, I should like to predict that in
due time, ensemble improvisation, in one form or another, will be studied in
conservatories and universities." (Foss 1961. See: WB324, D61)

More works for the combination of instruments in the Improvisation
Chamber Ensemble followed involving the use of diagrams and charts
instead of traditionally notated music scores. This allowed the members to
improvise within specific guidelines. These works include *Studies in
Improvisation* (See: W73) and the interludes from *Time Cycle* (See: W31),
among others. Only Foss's composition *MAP* (See: W80) is not notated
and relies solely on the improvisational talents of the performers. *Time
Cycle* and *Echoi* (See: W74), written for this combination of instruments,
have been erroneously referred to as improvisational works. Neither of
these works contain any improvisations but are completely notated. *Time
Cycle* received the New York Music Critics' Circle Award in 1961. *Echoi*
received the New York Music Critics' Circle Award in 1964 as the best new
chamber music work. It is Foss's major chamber music work and one of the
most difficult pieces ever written.

Time Cycle was the piece most responsible for the transition into
Foss's experimental period and the first piece which brought him to the
foreground of leading contemporary composers. The improvisations
between movements which were performed in the early orchestral
performances were not originally intended to be included. Instead, they
were offered as a "commedia dell'arte" and remained with the performances
of this version. (Gagne and Caras 1982, 196-197. See: B180) Bernstein
performed *Time Cycle* an unprecedented second time at the premiere
performance because of the artistic significance of the work. Foss also
made a chamber version of the composition in 1961 (See: W32) which
does not include the improvisational interludes so that the work could better
stand on its own merits.

The Improvisation Chamber Ensemble disbanded after Foss moved to Buffalo, New York in 1963. After *Non-Improvisation* (See: W75), Foss felt that group improvisations were no longer adventurous--that the music had become "safe." Foss states, "Improvisation that works is improvisation made safe....When I found this out, I dissolved my improvisation ensemble and returned to composition, incorporating techniques I developed during my five years of improvising." (Austin 1968, 17. See: B102) The performers began to improvise only what they felt comfortable with, the danger that the jazz artist faces by falling into an improvising "routine." At this point, Foss abandoned improvisation as a compositional tool, leaving the idea for the use of his students and other composers, such as John Cage, Larry Austin, Cornelius Cardew, and others. He felt that he "could be more adventurous in the solitude of composition in his own chamber" by leaving this technique behind. (Foss 1990. See: B223)

1960 was a momentous year for Foss's career. He received his second Guggenheim Fellowship and was selected along with Aaron Copland to tour the Soviet Union under the auspices of the U.S. State Department's Cultural Exchange Program. (See: B27-B31) The two musical ambassadors performed with and conducted the Leningrad Symphony Orchestra for a series of four concerts, becoming the first Americans to conduct this orchestra. From Russia, Foss continued alone to Poland for more performances before returning to the United States.

In 1962, Foss was elected to the National Institute of Arts and Letters. After returning home from a concert tour that year, he was greeted by his wife Cornelia and their two small children with the bad news that their home in Bel Air, California had burned to the ground, a victim of the 1962 Bel Air fire. Returning to the site where their home had once stood, all that remained was the chimney. In the fire, all their personal belongings as well as musical manuscripts and valuable art works by Mrs. Foss and other prominent artists were destroyed. (See: B64)

The years in Buffalo (1963-70) were important to Foss, the Buffalo Philharmonic Orchestra, the State University of New York at Buffalo, and the city of Buffalo. Earlier, in 1957, Foss had turned down an offer from his former teacher Fritz Reiner to become the Associate Conductor of the Chicago Symphony. He felt that a full-time conducting position such as this would interfere with his time for composing. Copland informed him that by holding such a conducting position, he could "write his own ticket" as far as scheduling time to compose. In 1962, Foss was approved unanimously by the 42 directors of the Buffalo Philharmonic Orchestra's Board and Foss accepted the post of Conductor and Music Director. He signed a two-year contract with the orchestra on December 28, 1962 to begin his appointment with the 1963-64 season. (See: B44-B45) He renewed this contract in 1964 to continue his directing through the 1967-68 season. (See: B67)

He initially agreed with the Buffalo Philharmonic Orchestra's Board of Directors that the programming should include mostly classical standard orchestral works. As Robert I. Millonzi told the press, "He is not here to play bizarre music or to conduct just his own music." (Reeves 1962, 1. See: B44) However, Foss was becoming a growing proponent of the newly established avant garde group of composers and began what "one observer's description in the *New York Times* [as Foss's] 'reign of terror' [in

Buffalo]." (Kupferberg 1984, 13. See: B196) He began by programming a mixture of both new and classic music. His first Philharmonic concert on October 26, 1963 was greeted by standing ovations at the beginning, intermission, and conclusion of the concert. Performed were the Buffalo premieres of Ives's *The Unanswered Question* and Stravinsky's *Le Sacre du Printemps* as well as Brahms's *First Symphony*. (See: B55) More premieres, including American and world premieres, of works by Diamond (See: B56), Smit, Xenakis, Stockhausen (See: B62, B63), Webern (See: B88), Penderecki, and others, followed during Foss's tenure with the orchestra. Foss and the Buffalo Philharmonic Orchestra also became important factors in the planning and implementing of the two Festivals of the Arts Today in Buffalo (See: B75, B77, B95, B96, B104), recording major new works for the Nonesuch label. (See: B103, D47, D111, D112) With coverage in *Time*, the Festivals received more publicity than anything else Foss had done to that time.

At a performance by the Buffalo Philharmonic Orchestra during the 1965 3rd Inter-American Festival in Washington, D.C., Foss staged a protest over the auditorium air-conditioning fans and the noise they produced. It was a hot May evening and the fans were essential for the comfort of everyone in the theater. Foss had asked for the fans to be turned off prior to the performance so that the pianissimos of the new works to be performed could be heard and was told that they would be. When the fans were not silenced, Foss stopped the performance and sat silently on the podium in protest. An intermission was called finally, after which the performance continued with the noise of the fans. Foss's protest was staged to prove that new music deserved a fair hearing and was applauded by the press. (See: B79, B80, B82)

On October 30, 1966, Foss, conducting the Buffalo Philharmonic Orchestra, premiered Anton Webern's *Three Orchestral Songs* posthumously at the 3rd International Webern Festival with Marni Nixon as soprano soloist. Though Buffalonians shunned the performances, "scholars and musicians from principal universities and cultural centers of Europe were present." (Dwyer 1966, 34. See: B88) Through performances such as this, Buffalo and the Buffalo Philharmonic Orchestra gained an international reputation under Foss's direction.

In 1963, Foss and Allen Sapp founded and became co-directors of the Center for Creative and Performing Arts at the State University of New York at Buffalo with funds from a Rockefeller Foundation Grant. The Center was designed as a vehicle for musicians who had degrees in music (primarily young performers) and were still new enough in their careers to be "coaxed" into the pursuit of avant garde music as a useful outlet for their talents. As an outgrowth of this project, the Evenings for New Music concerts (first in Buffalo and subsequently in New York City) were begun in 1964, serving as a stage for adventurous programming and the newest music of the avant garde movement. These progams greatly divided the residents of Buffalo and became a highly controversial topic.

On one side were the avant garde enthusiasts who greeted the programs with open arms, and on the other were the opponents of the avant garde who proceeded to equate Foss's name with experimental music. At one point, Foss had to go on Buffalo television to defend his musical position to the community. (See: B72) Also, the mixed programming on the orchestra's concerts which had worked at first began to work against Foss. The Buffalo audiences didn't appreciate having new works forced on them. The charismatic conductor who had brought Buffalo and the Buffalo Philharmonic Orchestra to international prominence began to lose his popularity.

The merger that never happened between the Buffalo Philharmonic Orchestra and the Rochester Philharmonic Orchestra (See: B117-B122) is considered by Foss to be the only "lowlight" of his tenure in Buffalo. This event caused Foss to resign his post from the Buffalo Philharmonic Orchestra. He feels that his resignation may have actually prevented the merger from happening. Overall, he states, "Buffalo was a very good experience for me." (Foss 1990. See: B223)

Though Foss's time in Buffalo was always busy, he continued to pursue activities in other locales. He taught composition at the Berkshire Music Center at Tanglewood, Massachusetts during the summer of 1964. Notable students here included William Albright and Toshi Ichiyanagi. In 1965, along with Elliott Carter and Leon Fleischer, Foss was elected to the Board of Directors of the Walter W. Naumburg Foundation. Foreign travel included a European tour in June 1965 when Foss guest conducted the Berlin Philharmonic Orchestra and attended the Zagreb Festival in Yugoslavia in the same capacity.

In July 1965, Foss was the artistic director and conductor for the New York Philharmonic Orchestra's three-week French-American Festival. (See: B69, B81) He returned to New York City in July 1966 to direct and conduct the Orchestra's Stravinsky Festival. (See: B84-B86, WB335) Both festivals were held in conjunction with Lincoln Center.

Although Foss had composed three operas, he had never conducted one. He debuted on February 11, 1967 in this capacity when he took to the podium of the New York City Opera in a production of Mozart's *Le Nozze de Figaro*. Foss's performance was spectacular as noted in the *New York Times* and *High Fidelity/Musical America* reviews. (See: B92, B94)

Throughout Foss's experimental composition period, which continued through the early 1970s, the composer developed new techniques for the performance of his music, shedding indeterminate notation in favor of controlled compositions which were fully notated. "Haphazard, accidental music is seldom Foss's intention. He has created a notation that reveals his compositional desires. The composer's control of the music is essential." (Bassin 1987, 22. See: B216)

One of the techniques with which Foss is credited is that of *niente* playing, the technique of inaudible music performance. The performer continues to finger or mouth the pitches or words, but no sound is produced. This technique was used prominently in *Geod* (See: W53), *Elytres* (See: W49), *Fragments of Archilochos* (See: W17), and *Baroque Variations*. (See: W52) In these works, the conductor has control over the performance outcome by cueing the various performers into and out of audibility. (See: B140)

With the tumultuous Buffalo years behind him, the opportunity to become the Music Advisor and Conductor of the Brooklyn Philharmonia in 1971 (which changed its name to the Brooklyn Philharmonic Orchestra in 1982) arose. As one German critic noted, "Foss [was] named conductor...of a previously insignificant orchestra, a part of New York City known more for its slums and gangster shootings than for symphony concerts." (Heinsheimer 1971, 607. See: B136) His early programming in Brooklyn included marathon concerts like the ones he had conducted in California. Beginning in 1976, more traditional programming was undertaken. This programming evolved into the two subscription series of the Orchestra, the "Majors" and "Meet the Moderns."

Originally, the orchestra was like a community ensemble. Foss had to shape the group into a professional orchestra and make its programs so different that New Yorkers would come to Brooklyn to see it perform. (See: B134) Foss refers to the ensemble as "an orchestra of 80 soloists and chamber musicians" and it consists of freelance performers and excellent teachers from the Metropolitan New York area. As a "virtuoso orchestra," it has no peers and is unique in that its membership is drawn from a large metropolitan area that only New York City can offer.

With the Brooklyn Philharmonic Orchestra, Foss conducted the premieres of many works. On November 13, 1973, the Orchestra gave the first performance of Darius Milhaud's *Ani Ma Amin--Un Chant Perdu et Retrouvé* at Carnegie Hall. Ned Rorem's *Six Songs for High Voice and Orchestra* was premiered by Foss and the Brooklyn Philharmonic Orchestra with Geanie Faulkner as soprano soloist on April 28, 1978. The United States premiere of Friedrich Nietzche's *Hymn to Life* was given by the Brooklyn Philharmonic Orchestra and the Grace Choral Society of Brooklyn on January 2, 1987. (See: B208, B215) William Bolcom's *Songs of Innocence and of Experience*, settings of William Blake's poetry, was premiered shortly thereafter on January 9, 1987. This work took Bolcom 26 years to compose and the performance lasted two hours and twenty minutes. (See: B209-B211)

Another premiere conducted by Foss during this time is the first performance of Joseph Schwantner's *Aftertones of Infinity* on January 29, 1979. It was performed by the American Composers' Alliance Orchestra in Alice Tully Hall at Lincoln Center. (See: WB270)

Foss continued to develop as a teacher, serving as a visiting professor of music at Harvard University from 1969 to 1971. From 1972 to 1973, Foss became a visiting professor of music at the Manhattan School of Music in New York City. He was also the Composer-In-Residence at the University of Cincinnati Conservatory of Music in 1975.

Foss became the recipient of numerous awards during this time, including the Alice Ditson Award in 1974 for the "conductor who has done the most for American music," the New York City Award for special contributions to the arts in 1976, a 1979 award from the American Society of Composers, Authors, and Publishers (ASCAP) for "adventurous programming," the American Composers Alliance Laurel Leaf Award in 1980, and the Brandeis University Creative Arts Award in Music in 1982. In

1983, Foss was elected to the Academy of the American Academy and Institute of Arts and Letters.

Always exploring new avenues for his musical expression, Foss became the Music Advisor and Conductor of the Kol Israel Orchestra of Jerusalem from 1972 to 1976. This orchestra was renamed the Jerusalem Symphony through the efforts of Foss. Foss commuted to Jerusalem up to seven times per year during these four years while still maintaining his conducting position with the Brooklyn Philharmonic Orchestra. "Jerusalem was relaxing in those days and was an enjoyable and interesting experience," reflects Foss. (Foss 1990. See: B223) His composition *Fanfare* (See: W55), which was written during this time, baffled the Turks for whom it was written. "[They felt threatened by the work, they] thought I was writing a normal fanfare--they were shocked." (Foss 1990. See: B223)

Becoming the Music Director of the Milwaukee Symphony Orchestra in 1981, a position he held until 1986, once again had Foss conducting two orchestras. The Milwaukee Symphony Orchestra, previously under the 10-year direction of Kenneth Schermerhorn, had developed into a fine ensemble. Foss has said of this group, "The Milwaukee Symphony is...underrated.... [Milwaukee] was culture-starved for too long. Milwaukee's claim to fame no longer is only beer; now it's the orchestra." (Kupferberg 1984, 13. See: B196)

Foss was chosen to be the director after he directed an energetic performance of Tchaikovsky's *Pathetique* Symphony as guest conductor. Under his direction, subscription concert sales rose dramatically, the orchestra continued to improve musically, and in 1986, the group embarked on its first and only European tour to date. "The Orchestra won rave reviews for its energy and technical virtuosity, and received cheers and occasional catcalls for daring to bring his new visionary and stringent interpretations of Beethoven and Brahms to the composers' very birthplaces." (Shuman Associates 1987, 7. See: B206)

Several recordings were produced by the Milwaukee Symphony Orchestra under Foss's direction including the orchestrated version of his *Psalms* (See: D14) and the only recordings of *Ode* (See: D36) and *With Music Strong*. (See: D22)

In 1984, Foss planned the citywide Milwaukee Festival of American Sacred Music which included performances of instrumental and choral works of all idioms, including jazz, classical, gospel, and American Indian. The performances were held thoughout the city in concert halls, churches, and synagogues. Performed were world premieres of *The Last Gospel* by David Del Tredici, *Cosmic Cycle* by Dane Rudyhar, and *Creations* by John Corigliano. (See: B198, B199) Other premieres by the Milwaukee Symphony include the January 31, 1986 performance of *The Chairman Dances* by John Adams. (See: B205)

Foss has spoken on numerous occasions about the place of the symphony orchestra in the 20th century. In 1968, he spoke on a panel regarding the new approach orchestras take in performing the classics after studying and performing new music (See: B105) and on how to "successfully" program new music. (See: B106) He discussed the concept of the symphony orchestra as a museum during a 1968 symposium broadcast by the Eastern Educational Network. (See: B110) In a 1979 interview, Foss explained his reasons for the two series of concerts presented by the Brooklyn Philharmonic Orchestra, the "Majors" and "Meet the Moderns." He again referred to the "symphony" orchestra as a museum, not a living art form. (See: B163) Foss added to this in a 1982 interview by stating that he no longer "[wants] to shock people anymore" by programming new works on the same concerts as the classics. (See: B188) Perhaps Foss's feelings toward conducting an orchestra can best be summed up with a statement he made in 1984: "Composing is like going to a no-man's land. Conducting is like coming home." (Kupferberg 1984, 17. See: B196)

In the fall of 1990, Foss will relinquish the Music Directorship of the Brooklyn Philharmonic Orchestra and become its Conductor Laureate, a title he also holds with the Milwaukee Symphony. His future plans are to compose a major orchestral work for the Chicago Symphony's 100th anniversary and a left-hand concerto for the Boston Symphony Orchestra and Leon Fleischer, pianist. He will continue to conduct regularly around the world.

WORKS AND
PERFORMANCES

THEATER MUSIC

W1. **Incidental Music for Shakespeare's Tempest** (1939-40; manuscript.)

For voices and chamber orchestra.
Prizes: Pulitzer Traveling Scholarship.
Manuscript and reproduction of manuscript (7 leaves, 24-31 cm.)
+ typescript ed. of play (24 leaves) laid in, has caption title:
The Tempest, by William Shakespeare; an acting version for
children in two acts, located in the New York Public Library.
Duration: 15 minutes.
Written as incidental music for a children's production of *The
Tempest* at the King-Coit School in Manhattan (See also:
Where the Bee Sucks, W26).

FIRST PERFORMANCE

W1a.   April 1940. King-Coit School, Manhattan.

BIBLIOGRAPHY

WB1.   "Seventeen-Year-Old." *Time* 35:60 (April 22, 1940)
            Brief biographical information and review of the
incidental music to *The Tempest*. "He wrote the music
in a month...[and] turned in a remarkably workmanlike
score."

W2.   **Music for Antigone** (1978?; lost.)

Written for the Beaumont Theatre.

OPERAS

W3.   **The Jumping Frog of Calaveras County (Der Held von Calaveras)** (1949; VOCAL SCORE: New York: Carl Fischer, 1951. Pub. pl. no. 30807, N1692. Pub. no. O3720. Revised edition: New York: Carl Fischer, c1968. Orchestral score and parts available on rental.)

Cast: Lulu, mezzo soprano; Smiley, tenor; Uncle Henry, baritone; Stranger, bass; Guitar Player, baritone; 1st Crap Shooter, tenor; 2nd Crap Shooter, bass; optional chorus (SATB) and orchestra (flute/piccolo, oboe, 2 clarinets, bassoon, horn, 2 trumpets, trombone, tuba, percussion (snare drum, bass drum, cymbal, high woodblock, triangle), piano, strings/string quintet (2-1-1-1))
Dedication: "To Ellie."
Duration: 45-50 minutes.
Opera in two scenes. Libretto by Jean Karsavina after the story *The Celebrated Jumping Frog of Calaveras County* by Mark Twain.
The 1968 revised edition published by Carl Fischer includes the addition of "Lulu's Song" written for Anne Brown (Lulu) at the Venice Festival performance in 1952.
The finale on the rental score has this note: "For television or movie production, it is suggested that Daniel gathers himself up for a great jump, swells as he takes a gargantuan breath and sails right into the camera, looming larger and larger until he fills the screen."

FIRST PERFORMANCE

W3a.   May 18, 1950. Indiana University Opera Department, East Hall, Bloomington, Indiana. Alton E. Wilder; Lou Herber; Charles Campbell; Hans Busch, stage director; Ernst Hoffman, musical director and conductor; Walter S. Russell, technical director. Televised May 26, 1950 on WTTV, Bloomington, Indiana. (See: WB2, WB5, WB6)

OTHER PERFORMANCES

W3b.   1949. Radio premiere.

W3c.   June 7, 1950. Master Theatre, New York City. After Dinner Opera Company (Burton Trimble, tenor; Tina Prescott; Paul Ukena, bass-baritone; Richard Flusser, artistic and stage director; Lukas Foss, piano). New York premiere. Piano was used as the accompaniment. (See: WB3, WB4)

W3d.   March 28, 1952. Los Angeles City College, Los
       Angeles, California. Los Angeles City College; Adolph
       Heller, music director; Henry Reese, stage director. Los
       Angeles premiere. (See: WB9)

W3e.   1953. Venice, Italy. Anne Brown, Lulu. European
       premiere. (See: WB11)

W3f.   April 23, 1955. University of Alabama. University
       Opera Workshop (Ronnie Freeman, Calvin Coots, Paul
       Doster, Forrest Wilson, Anna Cate Blackmon, Dewey
       Camp, Richard Armstrong, cast); Roland Johnson,
       conductor; Howard Goodson, sets. (See: WB12; See
       also: W15d)

W3g.   1958. Kolner Opera Haus. German premiere.

W3h.   February 25, 1984. Jacksonville, Florida. Opera-à-la-
       Carte. (See: WB16)

BIBLIOGRAPHY

WB2.   Nettl, Paul. "Indiana University Presents New Foss and
       Rogers Works." *Musical America* 70:11 (June 1950)
            Review of the May 18, 1950 premiere
       performance of *The Jumping Frog of Calaveras County*
       and *The Veil* (Bernard Rogers). "Foss's score manifests
       considerable rhythmic force and orchestral skill; eclectic
       in character, the music suggests styles ranging from
       Wolf-Ferrari to Kurt Weill." (See: W3a)

WB3.   Smith, Cecil. "*Jumping Frog* Shares Bill with Bach and
       Blitzstein." *Musical America* 70:11+ (June 1950)
            Review of the June 7, 1950 New York City
       premiere performance. "All three of the new productions
       were a trifle high-schoolish in tone, for Mr. Flusser tends
       to treat every amusing situation as low comedy,
       resorting to horseplay and slapstick when a more
       discreet technique would have served his purpose
       better." (See: W3c)

WB4.   "Jumpin' Opera." *Time* 55:51 (June 19, 1950)
            Review of the June 7, 1950 performance. "It was
       just about the livest and jumpin'est opera yet turned out
       by a young composer in the U.S." (See: W3c)

WB5.   "I.U. Offers Operatic World Premieres." *Music News*
       42:19 (July 1950)
            Brief review of the premieres of *The Jumping Frog
       of Calaveras County* and Bernard Rogers's *The Veil*
       performed by Indiana University's Opera Department.
       (See: W3a)

WB6.   Allen, Ross. "New Operas Bow at Indiana University."
        Musical Courier 142:8 (July 1950)
                Review of the May 18, 1950 premieres of *The
        Jumping Frog of Calaveras County* and Bernard Rogers's
        The Veil. "The musical idiom is somewhat suggestive of
        the cowboy song, the barroom piano or the show
        number." Ross compares Foss's new opera to similar
        works of Bernstein, Copland, and Weill. (See: W3a)

WB7.   Harris, Henry. "New Publications in Review: Opera."
        Musical Courier 144:29 (September 1951)
                Review of the Carl Fischer vocal score. "A story
        of distinctly American flavor is here set to music with a
        fresh appealing American tang. The texture of the music
        is light, without thick orchestration, and solos alternate
        frequently with ensembles."

WB8.   Bain, Wilfred C. "Music Reviews: Lukas Foss." *Notes*
        9:487-488 (June 1952)
                Review of the Carl Fischer piano-vocal score.
        "Jean Karsavinas' libretto...has the folky idiom of speech
        of the frontier, and...Foss' music is amazingly
        American....The music is graphic and occasionally
        thematic devices are used as labels."

WB9.   Laine, Juliette. "Letter from LA." *Opera News* 17:16-17
        (October 27, 1952)
                Review of the March 28, 1952 Los Angeles
        premiere performance. "The music is more difficult,
        vocally, than its humor would suggest, and its heavy
        orchestration too often permits the brasses to obliterate
        the voices." (See: W3d)

WB10. "Reviews of Music: Lukas Foss." *Music Review* 14:249
        (August 1953)
                Review of the Carl Fischer vocal score publication.
        "The orchestral writing sounds brittle on the piano...and
        the score gives no indication of instrumentation to help
        the player....There is much parlando,...whose effect
        depends almost wholly on American intonation."

WB11. Jolly, Cynthia. "Three Round Match in Venice." *Opera
        News* 18:16 (October 19, 1953)
                Review of the European premiere performance in
        Venice. "It came over direct and refreshing, with really
        pungent harmony and an astonishing variety in a
        homogeneous framework." (See: W3e)

WB12. Sabin, Robert. "Sixth Regional Composers' Forum
        Conducted by Alabama University." *Musical America*
        75:33 (May 1955)
                Review of the April 23, 1955 performance. (See:
        W3f; See also: WB71)

WB13.   Kestin, Diane. "Western Folklore in Modern American Opera." *Western Folklore* 16:2 (January 1957)
   Discussion of the utilization of folklore in American opera with a paragraph on Foss's use of Mark Twain and folksong melodies in the score.

WB14.   Zoff, Otto. "Auf dem Wege zur Amerikanischen Oper." *Melos* 24:138-139 (May 1957)
   This chiefly biographical sketch of Foss includes some details of *The Jumping Frog of Calaveras County's* storyline. "[It] is full of charm and wit....[Foss's] problem is that he's never quite at home....You can't spend ten years of your life in a European country and not be influenced."

WB15.   Bollert, Werner. "Von der Opera Buffa zum Musical." *Musica* 14:506 (August 1960)
   Review of the opera. "Although the composer placed this 'milieu-influenced' folkwork primarily in song, the whole drama seems somewhat silly and the humor of the work seems rigid. The young performers themselves give the impression of not going all out for this work." (translation)

WB16.   Bezner, Kevin. "Opera-à-la Carte: Foss *The Jumping Frog of Calaveras County*." *High Fidelity/Musical America* 34:MA23 (August 1984)
   Review of the February 25 and 26, 1984 performances by the Opera-à-la-Carte company of Jacksonville, Florida. "*The Jumping Frog of Calaveras County*...is as American as blue jeans and sneakers." (See: W3h)

W4.   **Griffelkin** (1953-55; Mainz: B. Schott's Söhne, 1955, c1958; Vocal Score: New York: Carl Fischer, 1990.)

Cast: Devil's Grandmother, alto; Griffelkin, soprano/mezzo soprano; Statue, soprano; Letterbox, tenor; First Lion, baritone; Second Lion, bass; A Boy, child soprano/mezzo soprano; A Girl, mezzo soprano; Their Mother, soprano; Policeman, baritone; Shopkeeper, mezzo soprano; Three Housewives, 2 sopranos, 1 mezzo soprano; Oldest Devil, bass; Eight Young Devils, soprani; Chorus (Children, More Devils, Toys). Orchestra (2 flutes, 2 oboes, 2 clarinets, 2 bassoons, 2 horns, 2 trumpets, trombone, tuba, timpani, percussion, piano, strings).
Contents: Act I. Hell's Nursery -- Act II. A Public Square -- Act III. In a Garden or Street.
Commissioned by: NBC-TV (National Broadcasting Company).
Dedication: to the composer's mother, Hilde Schindler Foss.
Duration: 2 hours (93 minutes of music).
Opera in three acts. English text by Alastair Reid; German text by Michael Thomas Mann. Based on the story "The Little Devil's Birthday" which was told to Foss as a child by his mother.

The eight year-old Foss convinced his mother to write a libretto based on the story and began to compose music for it. He abandoned the project by age nine, since it seemed childish, but began anew years later which resulted in the present opera.

FIRST PERFORMANCE

W4a.   November 6, 1955. NBC Television Opera Theatre. Mary Kreste, Devil's Grandmother; Adelaide Bishop, Griffelkin; Mignon Dunn, Statue; Andrew McKinley, Letterbox; Paul Ukena, Uncle Skelter and Lion; Lester Watson, Lion; Oliver Andes, A Boy; Rose Geringer, A Girl; Alice Richmond, Their Mother; Lee Cass, Policeman; Robert Holland, Shopkeeper; Frances Paige, Joan Moynagh, Jean Handzlik, Three Housewives; Samuel Chotzinoff, producer; Peter Herman Adler, music and artistic director; Kirk Browning, director; Rouben Ter-Arutunian, sets and costumes; Robert Joffrey, choreography. Abridged format. (See: WB18, WB19, WB20, WB21, WB22, WB23, WB24, WB25, WB26, WB27)

OTHER PERFORMANCES

W4b.   August 6, 1956. Theatre Concert Hall, Berkshire Music Center, Tanglewood, Lenox, Massachusetts. Regina Sarfaty, Devil's Grandmother; Mildred Allen, Griffelkin; Malcolm Bernstein; Elaine Quint; Boris Goldovsky, stage director; Robert O'Hearn, stage designer. First performance of the complete opera. (See: WB28, WB29, WB30)

W4c.   March 1973. Karlsruhe, Germany. Badische Staatstheater Karlsruhe; Rose-Marie Freni, Griffelkin. European premiere. (See: WB31, WB32, WB33, WB34)

W4d.   February 27-March 17, 1985. Skylight Theater, Milwaukee, Wisconsin. Leslie Fitzwater, Griffelkin; Carol Greif, Statue; Nicholas Saverine, Letterbox; Carl Glaum, John Keyes, Lions; Paul Hauer, A Boy; Mary Paul, A Girl; Judith Erickson, Their Mother; John Kuether, Policeman; Francesca Zambello, director; Michael Barrett, musical director; Peter Horne, stage design; Kathleen Blake, costumes. (See: WB35, WB36, WB37, WB38)

BIBLIOGRAPHY

WB17.   "N.B.C.-TV to Give Two New Operas." *New York Times* June 29, 1954:34.
Announcement of the commissioning of new operas from Foss and Stanley Hollingsworth by NBC-TV.

WB18. Elias, Albert J. "Keeping Pace with Radio & TV Music." *Etude* 73:18 (October 1955)
An outline of NBC-TV's season of operas of which this was the opening production on November 6, 1955. (See: W4a)

WB19. Reynolds, Naomi. "From the Reviewing Stand: New Programs in Radio and Television." *Music Clubs Magazine* 35:20-21 (November 1955)
Announcement of the premiere performance of *Griffelkin* on NBC-TV's Sunday opera performances. It tells of the story line, the background, and the librettist. (See: W4a)

WB20. Sargeant, Winthrop. "Musical Events." *New Yorker* 31:143-144 (November 12, 1955)
Review of the premiere performance on NBC-TV. "This little fairy-tale plot...[was] smothered by Mr. Foss's incredibly busy music and by a production that never stood still long enough to permit a moment of relaxing charm." (See: W4a)

WB21. Sabin, Robert. "Foss's *Griffelkin* Has Premiere as TV Opera on NBC." *Musical America* 75:30 (November 15, 1955)
Review of the November 6, 1955 premiere performance. The review includes an extensive listing of names of cast and crew. "*Griffelkin* deserves to be heard again soon. It brought a gust of fresh air into our theater." (See: W4a)

WB22. Kolodin, Irving. "*Griffelkin* on TV, Anda, Strovinsky [*sic*]." *Saturday Review* 38:41 (November 19, 1955)
Review of the November 6, 1955 premiere performance on NBC-TV. "He can write for the orchestra as well as for voices, and his harmonic feeling is both savorous and distinctive....[However] it is, for one thing, much too long for its amusing but tenuous story." (See: W4a)

WB23. Levinger, Henry W. "Lukas Foss Opera Premiered on NBC-TV." *Musical Courier* 152:38 (December 1, 1955)
Review of the November 6, 1955 premiere performance on NBC-TV. Even though color had been introduced to television, *Griffelkin* was broadcast in black-and-white. Although he enjoyed the production, Levinger felt that the musical phrases were too choppy and the comic situations didn't always project across the screen. "The cast was excellent....All of them seemed to have drunk the magic liquid, for the show was very much alive." (See: W4a)

WB24. "Opera Off the Beat." *Opera News* 20:32 (December 19, 1955)

Review of the November 6, 1955 premiere performance on NBC-TV. "The texture of the score...is so elaborate as to dazzle rather than beguile an audience...The skill and care with which it was all done could not atone for such superfluous busyness." (See: W4a)

WB25.   "Among Commissions Awards." *Pan Pipes* 48:21 (January 1956)
Review of the November 6, 1955 NBC-TV premiere performance. "Foss' NBC commissioned opera, *Griffelkin*, with libretto by Alastair Reid, had a brilliant world premiere...by the NBC Opera-Theatre, opening the yearly NBC opera series." (See: W4a)

WB26.   Reisfeld, Bert. "Sorgenkind Fernsehoper: I. In Amerika." *Musica* 10:94-95 (January 1956)
Review of the NBC-TV production of *Griffelkin*. "The artistic distance from this opera to the central opera tradition can only be measured in light years. The technical TV aspect of the work is interesting...but does not suppress Foss's real talent." (translation) (See: W4a)

WB27.   Elias, Albert J. "Let's Talk About Spectaculars!" *Etude* 74:58 (February 1956)
Review of the NBC Opera Theatre production. "While it had considerable strength and rhythmic pulse...only the orchestral interlude to the final scene on Earth...had melodic appeal....Little about the music made you want to hear more of it." (See: W4a)

WB28.   Waldrop, Gid. "Berkshire Festival." *Musical Courier* 154:9 (September 1956)
Review of the premiere performance of the unabridged three-act version of *Griffelkin* at the Berkshire Music Center. "*Griffelkin* is a delightful work, and shows the composer to be very stage minded....[However] it was neither a finished nor a professional performance." (See: W4b)

WB29.   "World of Music." *Etude* 74:4 (October 1956)
Notice of the August 6 and 7, 1956 first stage performance as the principal production of the Berkshire Music Center's Opera Department. (See: W4b)

WB30.   Safford, Lauren Tappen. "Tanglewood Imps." *Opera News* 21:15 (November 19, 1956)
Review of the August 6, 1956 theater premiere. Safford praised the singing, acting, dancing, and scenery. "Given a strong libretto [Foss] might make outstanding contributions to the modern opera repertory. As it stands, *Griffelkin* is too slim for the opera house and too difficult for opera workshops." (See: W4b)

WB31.   Trumpff, G.A. "Karlsruhe: Märchenoper mit
Jugendlichen: *Griffelkin* von Lukas Foss." *Neue
Zeitschrift für Musik* 134:160-161 (March 1973)
Review of the February 2, 1973 Karlsruhe
performance. "For all the appropriate sounds Foss has
created...swirling like old ladies' gossip yet with the
orderly awareness of the police, this child's play with
parental wisdom gives an effective production."
(translation) (See: W4c)

WB32.   Halász, Gábor. "Teufelchen unter den Menschen:
Karlsruhe besorgt die europaeische Erstauffuehrung von
Lukas Foss' Jugendoper." *Opern Welt* no. 3:42 (March
1973)
Review of the February 2, 1973 first European
performance. "This musical work combines many
different elements--rhythms from Stravinsky, thematic
content from Hindemith, lyric melodies from Richard
Strauss, the spiritual presence of Britten. Foss succeeds
in creatively writing the heterogenious elements and
stamping a single style on the work. His work is
thoughtful and humorous." (translation) (See: W4c)

WB33.   Koch, Gerhard R. "Teufelsmaerchen: Lukas Foss'
Jugendoper *Griffelkin* in Karlsruhe." *Hifi Stereophonie*
12:382 (April 1973)
Review of the February 2, 1973 performance in
Karlsruhe. "Foss's music is well done....The whole work
operates on both an innocent and a more serious level
simultaneously. Be that as it may, the children appear to
enjoy it." (translation) (See: W4c)

WB34.   Honolka, Kurt. "Karlsruhe." *Opera (Eng.)* 24:450 (May
1973)
Review of the February 5, 1973 performance in
Karlsruhe, Germany. It was produced by Hans Peter
Knell and conducted by Frithjof Haas. The reviewer felt
that the work was "a hopeless old-style Christmas story
in no way appealing to the young people" and that the
orchestral music was too dry. (See: W4c)

WB35.   Johnson, Lawrence B. "*Griffelkin* Rises: Skylight
Version of Foss' Opera is an American Premiere."
Milwaukee Sentinel Let's Go February 22, 1985.
Promotional piece for the February 27, 1985
production. Background information on the story line is
given as well as an interview with Foss regarding the
production. Foss viewed the orchestral reduction with
mixed emotions stating "'I'm very hopeful that the
synthesizer can represent all the colors of my Mozart-size
orchestra...but it may be a bit like looking at a painting in
black and white.'" (See: W4d)

WB36.   Chute, James. "Child in Foss Grows Into Impish Opera."
Milwaukee Journal February 24, 1985:2.
Promotional piece for the February 27, 1985
production. In this interview with Foss, he reflects that
he has learned that in order to launch an opera properly,
it must be promoted. Foss also remarked that he would
like to see *Griffelkin* become the American Christmas
opera in place of Humperdinck's *Hansel and Gretel*. The
remainder of the article centers around Foss's
compositional style and philosophies of composition.
(See: W4d)

WB37.   Chute, James. "*Griffelkin* Stumps Skylight Directors."
Milwaukee Journal February 28, 1985.
Review of the February 27, 1985 production with
a score adaptation for piano and synthesizer by Michael
Barrett. This production of Griffelkin offered many
compromises including the use of piano and synthesizer
(as is frequently done at the Skylight Theater) and the
use of children, for soprano roles, whose voices were
reinforced by offstage adults. (See: W4d)

WB38.   Johnson, Lawrence B. "Foss' Fairy Tale Opera Delights
Audience." *Milwaukee Sentinel* February 28, 1985.
Review of the February 27, 1985 production.
"Everything about the show adds up to great fun, a
profound moral message delivered with a light touch." In
contrast to Chute's review (See: WB37), Johnson notes,
"[The] imaginative staging smartly exploits...[the]
economical sets...[and the] reduction for piano and
synthesizer serves well." (See: W4d)

W5.   **Introductions and Goodbyes** (1959; New York: Carl Fischer,
1961. Pub. pl. no. N3391. Pub. no. O 4193. Full score and
orchestral material available on rental.)

Cast: Mr. McCleary (the host), baritone; Nine Guests (four
women, five men); chamber chorus/vocal quartet (SATB);
orchestra (flute, clarinet, bassoon, horn, trumpet, percussion
(xylophone, tambourine, cymbals, triangle, doorbell), piano,
harp ad lib., strings). The nine guests are silent and are
played by actors or dancers; the chamber chorus/vocal
quartet (SATB) is invisible and should be seated in the
orchestra pit.
Commissioned by: Gian Carlo Menotti for the Festival dei Due
Mondi (1960 Festival of Two Worlds), Spoleto, Italy.
Dedication: Charles DeLancey, Richard Dufallo, and Lukas Foss.
Duration: 9 minutes.
Opera in one scene. The libretto by Gian Carlo Menotti consists
of a series of names in introductions and goodbyes. The
scene is a cocktail party.

FIRST PERFORMANCE

W5a. May 7, 1960. Carnegie Hall, New York City. John
Reardon, baritone; New York Philharmonic; Leonard
Bernstein, conductor. Concert premiere. (See: WB39,
WB40)

OTHER PERFORMANCES

W5b. June 1960. Spoleto, Italy. Premiere of the staged
production.

W5c. May 21, 1961. Ojai Festival, Ojai, California. Howard
Chitjian, baritone. Partly staged production. (See:
WB41)

W5d. June 3, 1963. St. Pancras Town Hall. Park Lane Group.
British premiere. (See: WB42)

W5e. February 2, 1979. Encompass Theatre, New York City.
Ron Boudreux, baritone; Nancy Rhodes, director. (See:
WB43)

BIBLIOGRAPHY

WB39. Sabin, Robert. "Bernstein Conducts New Foss Opera."
Musical America 80:39-40 (June 1960)
       Review of the May 7, 1960 preview performance.
"The musical idiom is piquant and transparent and not
too hard for an average audience to appreciate." (See:
W5a)

WB40. Rice, Curtis E. "New Foss Opera Bows in 'Music for the
Theatre.'" *Musical Courier* 161:23 (June 1960)
       Review of the May 7, 1960 premiere performance.
"Mr. Foss' new work is a nine minute trifle, witty and
soundly constructed." (See: W5a)

WB41. Goldberg, Albert. "Versatile New Director." *Musical
America* 81:38-39 (July 1961)
       Review of the May 21, 1961 performance.
"Howard Chitjian did stylishly with the single singing
role." (See: W5c)

WB42. Barnes, Clive. "Yankee Trio." *Music and Musicians* 11:4
(July 1963)
       Review of the June 3, 1963 British premiere
performance. "Perhaps seen as part of a revue it could
have been tolerably amusing, but personally I think I
could have done with the goodbye without the
introduction." (See: W5d)

WB43.   Hiemenz, Jack. "Opera Everywhere: Encompass Th.: Six One-Acters." *High Fidelity/Musical America* 29:MA32-33 (May 1979)
 Review of the February 2, 1979 performance. In this performance each couple consisted "of one live performer escorting a well-attired mannequin." (See: W5e)

BALLETS

W6.   **The Heart Remembers** (1944; manuscript)

For piano.
Written for Doris Humphrey.
Duration: 25 minutes.

FIRST PERFORMANCE

W6a.   1944. New York City. Humphrey-Weidman Group. (See: WB44)

BIBLIOGRAPHY

WB44.   Barlow, S.L.M. "With the Dancers." *Modern Music* 21:263-264 (May/June 1944)
 Review of dance performances by Doris Humphrey, Charles Weidman, and their company in 1944. Included in the performances was Foss's *The Heart Remembers*, which the reviewer did not see. (See: W6a)

W7.   **Within These Walls** (1944; manuscript)

For piano.
Written for Virginia Johnson.
Duration: 20 minutes.

W8.   **Gift of the Magi** (1944; New York: Hargail, 1945.)

For orchestra.
Commissioned by Ballet Theatre of New York and Simon Semenoff as a gift from Simon Semenoff to his wife.
Duration: 20 minutes.
Based on the O. Henry story of the same name.

FIRST PERFORMANCE

W8a.   October 15, 1945. Metropolitan Opera House, New York City. Ballet Theatre (Nora Kaye, John Kriza, dancers); Simon Semenoff, choreography; Raoul Pène DuBois, scene and costume design; Madame Karinska, costumes; Eugene Dunkel Studios, scenery.   (See: WB45, WB47, WB48)

OTHER PERFORMANCES

W8b.   1946. Boston, Massachusetts. Ballet Theatre. Boston premiere.

W8c.   February 1948. San Francisco, California. Civic Ballet of San Francisco. (See: WB49)

W8d.   Winter 1956. Monte Carlo. Festival Ballet (Melinda Plank, John Gilpin, dancers). (See: WB50)

W8e.   Summer 1956. London, England. Festival Ballet (Melinda Plank, John Gilpin, dancers). (See: WB50)

BIBLIOGRAPHY

WB45.   Chujoy, Anatole. "Ballet Season in Review." *Dance News* 7:5-6 (November 1945)
Review of the October 15, 1945 premiere performance. "In spite of some excellent dancing...*Gift of the Magi* is not a very good ballet....As it stands, the miming of the story and dancing of the ballet go their own ways and there is little connection between them....Mr. DuBois' Christmas-card set dominates the stage, Lukas Foss' music is of symphonic proportions, incongruous with the modest little piece." (See: W8a)

WB46.   "Creating and Producing a Ballet: Semenoff's *Gift of the Magi*." *Dance Magazine* 19:8-9 (December 1945)
A description of the process Semenoff went through to bring his idea to life by hiring the right people to compose, dance and design his ballet.

WB47.   Fine, Irving. "Symphonic Works and Fauré Anniversary." *Modern Music* 23:57 (Winter 1946)
Review of the premiere performance by Ballet Theatre. "The inventiveness and tuneful appeal of Foss's music were obscured by the hit-or-miss quality of the orchestration." (See: W8a)

WB48.   Lederman, Minna. "With the Dancers." *Modern Music* 23:71-72 (Winter 1946)
Review of the premiere performance. The music is described as "over-ambitious, over-insistent. The mild O. Henry sentiment seemed to die away in clanging dissonances." (See: W8a)

WB49.   "San Francisco." *Dance Magazine* 22:52 (March 1948)
Brief mention of the February 1948 performance. It was "done with greater style [than it had been done in New York] by Ballet Theatre." (See: W8c)

WB50.   "Semenoff to Do *Gift* for London." *Dance News* 27:3 (November 1955)

Announcement that London's Festival Ballet would stage *Gift of the Magi* during the Winter season of 1955-56 in Monte Carlo (See: W8d) and in the Spring season of 1956 in London (See: W8e).

WB51.   "Contrast in Festival's Guests." *Dance and Dancers* 7:25 (January 1956)
Brief announcement of a performance by Festival Ballet, featuring newcomer Melinda Plank, a student of Simon Semenoff.

CHORAL MUSIC

W9.   **Cantata Dramatica** (1940; manuscript; withdrawn.)

For tenor, chorus, and orchestra.

W10.   **We Sing (Cantata for Children)** (1941; manuscript)

For children's chorus, and piano.
Duration: 8 minutes.

W11.   **The Prairie** (1943; New York: G. Schirmer, 1944 (vocal score). Pub. pl. no. 40798. Pub. no. Ed. 1793. Orchestral material available on rental.)

For soli (SATB), chorus (SATB), and orchestra (flute, oboe, English horn, clarinet, bass clarinet, bassoon, trumpets, horn, trombone, timpani, percussion, piano, strings).
Contents: I. I Was Born on the Prairie -- II. Dust of Men -- III. They Are Mine -- IV. When the Red and the White Men Met -- V. In the Dark of a Thousand Years -- VIa. Cool Prayers -- VIb. O Prairie Girl -- VIc. Songs Hidden in Eggs -- VII. To-morrow.
Prizes: 1944 New York Music Critics Circle Citation as best new American work.
Duration: 48 minutes.
A dramatic, secular cantata based on the poem "Cornhuskers" by Carl Sandburg which was published by Henry Holt and Co.
Movement VIa, *Cool Prayers*, was published separately by New York: G. Schirmer, 1944. (G. Schirmer's Secular Choral Music) Pub. pl. no. 41414. Pub. no. Octavo no. 9605.
The first performance of this work was preceded by *The Prairie. Symphonic Suite* (see: W40).

FIRST PERFORMANCE

W11a.   May 14, 1944. Town Hall, New York City. Patricia Neway, soprano; Alice Howland, alto; Lucius Metz, tenor; Elwyn Carter, baritone; Collegiate Chorale; Members of the N.B.C. and C.B.S. Concert Orchestras; Robert Shaw, conductor. (See: WB52)

OTHER PERFORMANCES

W11b. January 1945. Carnegie Hall, New York City.
Westminster Choir; New York Philharmonic-Symphony
Orchestra; Artur Rodzinski, conductor. (See: WB53,
WB54)

W11c. March 13, 1961. Royce Hall Auditorium, University of
California, Los Angeles, California. Enid Clement,
soprano; Teresa Racz, alto; UCLA Symphony; Lukas
Foss, conductor. Performance of three excerpts from
the work. Sandburg recited the poetry before the
performance. (See: WB57)

BIBLIOGRAPHY

WB52. Thomson, Virgil. "Music." *New York Herald Tribune*
May 16, 1944:14 (Late city ed.)
        Review of the May 14, 1944 first performance.
"The performance...was in every way excellent and
clear. The work itself showed musicianship, imagination,
and direct expressive powers of no mean order."
Thomson tried to categorize Foss's style, comparing him
with Haydn, Hindemith, and Weill. "Mr. Foss's language
is elegant, scholastic, dainty....It is dry and clean and
pleasant, and it is adjusted for precise depiction rather
than for emotional excitement." (See: W11a)

WB53. "Champagne & Cornbread." *Time* 45:75 (January 29,
1945)
        Review of the January 1945 performance. "Lukas
Foss's music is far from Sandburg's prairie: it is modern,
glittering, sophisticated, plainly rooted in Europe....Critics
gently pronounced Composer Foss a promising young
man." (See: W11b)

WB54. Fuller, Donald. "Stravinsky's Visit; New Music in 1945."
Modern Music 22:178 (March/April 1945)
        Review of a 1945 performance. "*The
Prairie*...though far too long and weighted down by the
fruitless choice of a Carl Sandburg text, is impressive for
its controlled handling of such a full medium." (See:
W11b)

WB55. Berger, Arthur. "Scores and Records." *Modern Music*
22:200 (March/April 1945)
        Review of the piano-vocal score published by G.
Schirmer. "Much of the writing is clean, and when
examined in detail does not crumble away....He shows a
soft lyric inspiration and a personal style of which we
may expect him...to develop fruitfully."

WB56. Fine, Irving. "Young America: Bernstein and Foss."
Modern Music 22:242-243 (May/June 1945)

> The similarities and differences between Foss's writing and his influence by Copland are outlined in this brief analysis of *The Prairie*. "*The Prairie* was an extremely ambitious undertaking...[and is] one of the most impressive contributions to American choral literature...." Foss's writing involves counterpoint and a rich harmony which is not as pure as Copland's.

WB57.   Greene, Patterson. "Sandburg Keeps Audience Rapt." *Los Angeles Examiner* March 15, 1961:II,6.
> Review of the March 13, 1961 performance which included poetry readings by Carl Sandburg, Copland's *Lincoln Portrait*, and various works by Ruggles, Ives and Mennin. "The Foss music...accords with the varying moods of the poem and also...enhances them." (See: W11c)

WB58.   Foss, Lukas. "*The Prairie, A Parable of Death*, and *Psalms*." In: *The Composer's Point of View: Essays on Twentieth Century Choral Music By Those Who Wrote It*, ed. Robert Stephan Hines. Norman, OK: University of Oklahoma Press, 1963:3-13.
> (See: B48)

WB59.   Mellers, Wilfrid. "Today and Tomorrow: Lukas Foss and the Younger Generation." In *Music in a New Found Land*. New York: A. A. Knopf, 1965:220-235.
> (See: B71)

WB60.   Pisciotta, Louis Vincent. "Texture in the Choral Works of Lukas Foss." Chap. in "Texture in the Choral Works of Selected Contemporary American Composers." Ph.D. diss., Indiana University, 1967:200-233. *Dissertation Abstracts* 28:4658A (May 1968) UMI# 68-7253.
> (See: B91)

WB61.   Browne, Bruce Sparrow. "The Choral Music of Lucas Foss." Part I of D.M.A. diss., University of Washington, 1976:26-58. *Dissertation Abstracts* 37:1287A (September 1976) UMI# 76-20709.
> This dissertation includes an analysis of this early choral work by Foss. (See: B153)

W12.   Tell This Blood (1945; manuscript; withdrawn.)

For a cappella chorus.
Duration: 4 minutes.

W13.   Adon Olom: A Prayer (1947; *Menorah Journal* 36:26-32 (no. 1, 1948); New York: G. Schirmer, 1951.)

For cantor or tenor, chorus (SATB), and organ.
Duration: 7 minutes.
Title translated: The Lord of all.

BIBLIOGRAPHY

WB62. Foss, Lukas. "*Adon Olum*: Psalm for Mixed Chorus, Cantor and Organ." *Menorah Journal* 36:26-32 (no. 1, 1948)
> Publication of the score.

W14. **Behold! I Build an House** (1950; Bryn Mawr, Pa.: Mercury Music Corp., 1950. (Contemporary Choral Series) Pub. no. 352-00384.)

For chorus (SATB) and organ.
Dedication: "Composed for the Dedication exercises of the Boston University, Daniel L. Marsh Chapel, March 14, 1950."
Prizes: 1957 American Academy and National Institute of Arts and Letters.
Duration: 12 minutes.
Manuscript is located at Boston University. Inscribed: "Presented to Daniel L. Marsh, president of Boston University on March 14th, 1950 composed for the dedication exercises of the Boston University Daniel L. Marsh Chapel by Lukas Foss."
A Biblical cantata; text from the Book of Chronicles.
This work was orchestrated in 1986 for the Oshkosh Symphony by Foss.

FIRST PERFORMANCE

W14a. March 14, 1950. Daniel L. Marsh Chapel, Boston University, Boston, Massachusetts.

BIBLIOGRAPHY

WB63. "Music Reviews: Sacred Choral Music." *Notes* 8:402-403 (March 1951)
> Review of the Mercury Music publication. "It is composed in a very free style with considerable imagination, and would be appropriate in extolling the sanctity of any other church and for the praise of God in general."

WB64. Browne, Bruce Sparrow. "The Choral Music of Lucas Foss." Part I of D.M.A. diss., University of Washington, 1976:59-69. *Dissertation Abstracts* 37:1287A (September 1976) UMI# 76-20709.
> (See: B153)

WB65. Pisciotta, Louis Vincent. "Texture in the Choral Works of Lukas Foss." Chap. in "Texture in the Choral Works of Selected Contemporary American Composers." Ph.D. diss., Indiana University, 1967:200-233. *Dissertation Abstracts* 28:4658A (May 1968) UMI# 68-7253.
> (See: B91)

W15.   **A Parable of Death (Ein Märchen vom Tod)** (1952; Vocal
score: New York: Carl Fischer, 1953. Pub. pl. no. N1933. Pub.
no. O3835. Full scores (orchestral and chamber versions) and
parts available on rental.)

> For narrator, tenor, chorus (SATB divisi), and orchestra (2 flutes
> (2nd doubles piccolo), 2 oboes, 2 clarinets, 2 bassoons, 2
> horns, 2 trumpets, trombone, timpani, percussion (snare
> drum, bass drum, cymbal, triangle, tam tam, glockenspiel),
> piano, strings)/chamber group (string quintet, organ, piano,
> and percussion).
> Contents: I. Prologue -- II. Lovers ("There once were two
> people...") -- III. Who Built This House -- IV. Listen! -- V. Tears
> Rising to Drown Me -- VI. We Know Him Not -- VII. "By
> Springtime There Appeared in the Garden."
> Commissioned by: Louisville Philharmonic Society for Vera
> Zorina.
> Composed while at the American Academy in Rome.
> Dedication: none.
> Duration: 32 minutes.
> Narrative text taken from *Märchen vom Lieben Gott* and the sung
> words from poems by Rainer Maria Rilke (1875-1926); the
> metrical English version is by Anthony Hecht.

FIRST PERFORMANCE

W15a.   March 11, 1953. Columbia Auditorium, Louisville,
Kentucky. Farrold Stephens, tenor; Vera Zorina,
narrator; Choir of the School of Church Music, Southern
Baptist Theological Seminary; Louisville Orchestra;
Robert Whitney, conductor. (See: WB66)

OTHER PERFORMANCES

W15b.   April 12, 1953. Town Hall, New York City. Walter
Carringer, tenor; Vera Zorina, narrator; Robert Shaw
Chorale, Robert Shaw, conductor. New York premiere.
(See: WB68)

W15c.   May 23, 1953. Ojai, California. Ojai Festival Orchestra;
Lukas Foss, conductor. West Coast premiere. (See:
WB69)

W15d.   April 23, 1955. University of Alabama. Arline Hanke,
narrator; Frederick Loadwick, tenor; University of
Alabama Chorus and Orchestra; Roland Johnson,
director; Lukas Foss, conductor. (See: WB75; See also:
W3f)

BIBLIOGRAPHY

WB66.   Kuppenheim, Hans F. "Foss' *Parable of Death* Scores in
Louisville." *Musical Courier* 147:19 (April 1, 1953)

Review of the March 11, 1953 premiere performance. "Foss has written music of enormous density and powerful concentration...it commands the attention of the listener throughout." (See: W15a)

WB67. Foss, Lukas. "First Comes the Word." *New York Times* April 12, 1953:II,7.
Foss discusses how he bases his setting of poetry to music by using Bach as an example. The music must not take a back seat to nor be overbearing to the story.

WB68. Kolodin, Irving. "Robert Shaw & Choral Novelties--Return of Mitropoulos." *Saturday Review* 36:31 (April 25, 1953)
Review of the April 12, 1953 New York premiere performance. "There is intermittently, beauty of a sort in Foss's writing, but much of it seemed to me striving for an atmosphere which he never attained." (See: W15b)

WB69. Goldberg, Albert. "Premieres Mark Seventh Ojai Festival." *Musical America* 73:30 (July 1953)
Review of the May 23, 1953 West Coast premiere performance. Mr. Goldberg refers to this as "the most striking success among new works" presented at the festival. (See: W15c)

WB70. Morton, Lawrence. "Current Chronicle: United States: Los Angeles." *Musical Quarterly* 39:595-600 (October 1953)
Analysis and review of *A Parable of Death* with a story synopsis. "The *Parable* is a short oratorio fashioned after Bach's *Passions*....Foss seems to write his best music when he has a text to follow."

WB71. Wilson, J. Kenneth. "New Music: Orchestral." *Musical Courier* 149:41 (May 15, 1954)
Review of the Carl Fischer publication. "The composer has molded a form bearing characteristics of both a cantata and a melodrama."

WB72. Finney, Ross Lee. "Music Reviews: Vocal Music." *Notes* 11:609 (September 1954)
Review of the Carl Fischer publication. "A narrator, speaking against an orchestral background that is interesting but never overdone, unfolds the deeply moving parable....Lukas Foss has achieved a significant musical statement."

WB73. Flanagan, William. "New Music: Lukas Foss's *A Parable of Death*." *Musical America* 74:24 (November 15, 1954)
Review of the Carl Fischer publication. "Its aims are similar to those of the great classical choral works of Bach, Haydn, and Beethoven; the work is designed to leave its audience limp."

WB74.   Keys, Ivor. "Review." *Music and Letters* 36:100-101
(January 1955)
Review of the Carl Fischer vocal score. The
reviewer remarks how well the text could be sung in
either German or English easily, that the harmonies are
strongly tonal, and the tenor soloist part is written in a
baroque melismatic style.

WB75.   Sabin, Robert. "Sixth Regional Composers' Forum
Conducted by Alabama University." *Musical America*
75:33 (May 1955)
Review of the April 23, 1955 performance. *A
Parable of Death* is described as "a deeply felt and
eloquent work, one of the best that Mr. Foss has given
us. It was performed with amazing skill and inspiration."
(See: W15d; See also: WB12)

WB76.   Foss, Lukas. "*The Prairie, A Parable of Death*, and
Psalms." In: *The Composer's Point of View: Essays on
Twentieth Century Choral Music By Those Who Wrote It*,
ed. Robert Stephan Hines. Norman, OK: University of
Oklahoma Press, 1963:3-13.
(See: B48)

WB77.   Mellers, Wilfrid. "Today and Tomorrow: Lukas Foss and
the Younger Generation." In *Music in a New Found
Land*. New York: A. A. Knopf, 1965:220-235.
(See: B71)

WB78.   Pisciotta, Louis Vincent. "Texture in the Choral Works of
Lukas Foss." Chap. in "Texture in the Choral Works of
Selected Contemporary American Composers." Ph.D.
diss., Indiana University, 1967:200-233. *Dissertation
Abstracts* 28:4658A (May 1968) UMI# 68-7253.
(See: B91)

WB79.   McCray, James E. "Choral Conductors Forum: Lukas
Foss: *A Parable of Death*: Comments on Structure and
Performance." *American Choral Review* 18:12-13 (July
1976)
Review of the music from a vocal conductor's
perspective offering advice on problems which may
occur in performance.

WB80.   Browne, Bruce Sparrow. "The Choral Music of Lucas
Foss." Part I of D.M.A. diss., University of Washington,
1976:70-94. *Dissertation Abstracts* 37:1287A
(September 1976) UMI# 76-20709.
(See: B153)

W16.   Psalms (1955-56; Version for chorus and 2 pianos: New York:
Carl Fischer, 1957, 1967. Pub. pl. no. N 2747-45. Pub. no. O

4034. Full score and orchestral accompaniment available on rental.)

For chorus (SATB) and orchestra (organ/piccolo, 2 clarinets, bassoon; 2 horns, trumpet, trombone, timpani, 4 percussion (xylophone, timpani, deep gong, chimes, tenor drum, bass drum, snare drum, cymbal, woodblocks, clave, triangle, glockenspiel), 1 or 2 harps, 2 pianos, strings (large number of strings only with large chorus))/2 pianos.
Contents: Part I (Andante) -- Part II (Allegro-Vivace) -- Part III (Largo).
Commissioned by: Stockbridge Bowl Association of Stockbridge, Massachusetts.
Dedication: none.
Prizes: American Academy and National Institute of Arts and Letters, 1957.
Duration: 13 minutes.
Texts from: Part I: Psalm 121:1, 2; Psalm 95:4; Part II: Psalm 98:1, 4, 6; Part III: Psalm 23:1, 2, 3.

FIRST PERFORMANCE

W16a. May 9, 1957. Carnegie Hall, New York City. Schola Cantorum; Hugh Ross, director; New York Philharmonic-Symphony; Dmitri Mitropoulos, conductor. (See: WB81, WB82, WB83)

OTHER PERFORMANCES

W16b. June 1987. Aldeburgh Festival, England. European premiere as part of the 40th Aldeburgh Festival. (See: WB111)

BIBLIOGRAPHY

WB81. Kolodin, Irving. "Concert with a Theme, Variations Without." *Saturday Review* 40:25 (May 25, 1957)
Review of the May 9, 1957 premiere performance. "A good new work by Foss is no uncommon thing--in fact, it is more difficult to think of the ones he has recently produced which haven't...rewarded the attention." (See: W16a)

WB82. Sabin, Robert. "Orchestras in New York: Mitropoulos Conducts Premieres of Two Works." *Musical America* 77:18 (June 1957)
Review of the May 9, 1957 premiere performance. "*Psalms* will have to wait for a better performance to be judged fairly, for this premiere was a noisy, hurried, helter-skelter affair." (See: W16a)

WB83. "N.Y. Philharmonic-Symphony, Mitropoulos, conductor." *Musical Courier* 155:33 (June 1957)

Review of the May 9, 1957 premiere performance. "The work is ebullient and almost slick in its lavish use of contrapuntal devises, assymetrical rhythms, jazz idioms and fiery orchestral colors." (See: W16a)

WB84.   Lowens, Irving. "Music Reviews: Choral Music." *Notes* 16:151 (December 1958)
Review of the Carl Fischer publication for mixed voices and two pianos. Here, *Psalms* is referred to as "healthily adolescent." The reviewer, however, does not feel the piece "would wear well on frequent hearing."

WB85.   Foss, Lukas. "*The Prairie, A Parable of Death,* and *Psalms.*" In: *The Composer's Point of View: Essays on Twentieth Century Choral Music By Those Who Wrote It.* Norman, OK: University of Oklahoma Press, 1963:3-13. (See: B48)

WB86.   Pisciotta, Louis Vincent. "Texture in the Choral Works of Lukas Foss." Chap. in "Texture in the Choral Works of Selected Contemporary American Composers." Ph.D. diss., Indiana University, 1967:200-233. *Dissertation Abstracts* 28:4658A (May 1968) UMI# 68-7253. (See: B91)

WB87.   Libbey, Theodore W. Liner notes to Pro Arte PAD 169, 1984. (See: D14)
Foss refers to the central part of the piece "Make a Joyful Noise Unto the Lord" as sounding like "a joyful Biblical band." Also noted is a brief history of the use of Psalms in music. The liner notes incorrectly attribute some of the melodic material as coming from "Foss's unsuccessful musical" *The Skin of Our Teeth.* That musical was written by Bernstein.

W17.   **Fragments of Archilochos** (1965; New York: Carl Fischer; Mainz: B. Schott's Söhne, 1966. Pub. pl. no. N4914. Pub. no. O4652. Performance material available on rental.)

For countertenor, male speaker, female speaker, 4 small choirs, 8-12 singers each (I. soprano, mezzo; II. mezzo, alto; III. tenor, baritone; IV. baritone, bass), optional large chorus (4 groups of 8-60 singers each divided the same way as the small chorus), mandolin, guitar, and 3 percussionists (I. muffled small gongs or cowbells, small drums (bongos, timbali), woodblocks, temple blocks, snare drum, anvil or large pipe, bass drum; II. chimes (chromatic scale), 2 timpani (high, low), vibraphone; III. antique cymbal, 3 cymbals (high, medium, low), wood chimes, glass chimes (or sea shells)).
Commissioned by: The State University College at Potsdam, New York in honor of Helen M. Hosmer.
Dedication: none.
Duration: 10 minutes.

There are 325 different combinatorial possibilities for every phrase. The mandolin and guitar parts are edited by Stanley Silverman. The text is from *The Fragments of Archilochos*, translated into English from the Greek by Guy Davenport, c1964 by the Regents of the University of California.

FIRST PERFORMANCE

W17a.   May 1965. State University of New York, College at Potsdam. Crane University Chorus (State University of New York, College at Potsdam); Lukas Foss, conductor.

OTHER PERFORMANCES

W17b.   February 3, 1967. Philharmonic Hall, New York City. Richard Levitt, countertenor; Collegiate Chorale; Abraham Kaplan, conductor. First New York performance. (See: WB88, WB89, WB90, WB91)

BIBLIOGRAPHY

WB88.   Ericson, Raymond. "Kaplan's Chorus at Philharmonic." *New York Times* February 4, 1967:16.
Review of the February 3, 1967 performance. "Mr. Foss's work seems like a period piece of our own time...[with] a heterogeneous mixture of sounds....The performance...seemed tentative and lost in the big auditorium." (See: W17a)

WB89.   Rich, Alan. "Choral Performances." *American Choral Review* 9:26-28 (Spring 1967)
Review of the February 3, 1967 New York premiere performance. The performance was less than satisfactory and Foss had wanted to conduct it himself. Perhaps for this reason, it here receives comments such as "terribly old hat" and "[Foss's] heart isn't really in it at all." (See: W17a)

WB90.   Anderson, Owen. "New Works: New York." *Music Journal* 25:97 (March 1967)
Review of the February 3, 1967 New York premiere performance. "As the text was almost completely unintelligible (and one suspects it would be with any performing group), whatever intriguing possibilities might develop in the juxtaposition of phrases was completely lost." (See: W17a)

WB91.   Jacobson, Bernard. "Collegiate Chorale." *High Fidelity/Musical America* 17:MA12 (April 1967)
Review of the February 3, 1967 New York premiere performance. "His partially aleatoric but, to judge from one hearing, carefully planned work makes use of varied effects including speaking voices with megaphones, solo voices in the chorus, and a colorful

ensemble including guitar, mandolin, and sundry
percussion." (See: W17a)

WB92.   *Lukas Foss on the New Lukas Foss.* New York: Carl
Fischer, 1969:9.
(See: B112)

WB93.   Bailey, Donald Lee. "A Study of Stylistic and
Compositional Elements of *Anthem* (Stravinsky),
Fragments of Archilochos (Foss), and *Creation Prologue*
(Ussachevsky)". D.A. diss., University of Northern
Colorado, 1976. *Dissertation Abstracts* 37:1859A-
1860A (October 1976) UMI# 76-23159.
In his dissertation, Bailey has analyzed three
significant post-1960 choral works to better understand
the modern techniques involved with preparing the
scores for performance. Foss's work (*Fragments of
Archilochos*) was determined to have aleatoric
performance aspects as well as determinate
compositional form.

W18.   Three Airs for Frank O'Hara's Angel (Trois Airs Pour l'Ange de Frank O'Hara) (1972; Paris: Éditions Salabert; New York: G. Schirmer, 1972. Pub. pl. no. E.A.S. 17.049.)

For male speaker, soprano, women's chorus (divided in 2:
minimum 4 voices each; each singer uses a pitch pipe or
harmonica), mandolin/guitar, and/or harp/harpsichord, and
tape -or- soprano, flute, piano, and percussion (vibraphone,
gong, cymbal, flexaton, superball mallet, bass bow).
Commissioned by: Composer's Showcase.
Duration: 10 minutes.
Settings of "Frank O'Hara"s Angel" by Violet Lang, "Three Airs"
by Frank O'Hara, and "Four Little Elegies, no. 48" by Frank
O'Hara.

FIRST PERFORMANCE

W18a.   April 26, 1972. Whitney Museum, New York City.
Susan Belling, soprano; Arnold Weinstein, reader. (See:
WB94, WB95, WB96)

OTHER PERFORMANCES

W18b.   December 3, 1972. Albright-Knox Art Gallery, Buffalo,
New York. Sylvia Dimiziani, soprano; Fredonia Chamber
Singers (State University of New York College at
Fredonia); William Graf, director; Dennis Kahle,
percussion; Lukas Foss, piano; Oswald Rantucci,
mandolin; Guy Klucevsek, accordion; tape. (See: D18)

W18c.   January 1, 1973. Amsterdam. Five Centuries Ensemble.
First performance in Amsterdam. (See: WB97)

W18d.   April 18, 1982. Slee Chamber Hall, State University of New York at Buffalo. Lois Stipp, soprano; Michael DeLuca, speaker; University Choir Women; Harriet Simons, conductor. (See: WB98, WB99; See also: W56h, W76n, W109b)

W18e.   October 7, 1982. Composers' Forum, Symphony Space, New York City. Rosalind Rees, soprano; Women of the Gregg Smith Singers; Gregg Smith, conductor. (See: WB100; See also: W56i, W88f, W109e)

W18f.   December 7, 1982. Boston University Concert Hall. Boston University School of Music. Marjorie McDermott, soprano; Collegium in Contemporary Music; Lukas Foss, piano. (See: D20; See also: W49c, W76o, W89b)

BIBLIOGRAPHY

WB94.   Hughes, Allen. "Composers Honor Frank O'Hara With Vocal Works." *New York Times* April 28, 1972:34.
Review of the April 26, 1972 premiere performance which included works by seven composers including Foss to commemorate Frank O'Hara. "[The Foss work was] a little cantata-like work that was imaginative and rather effective." (See: W18a)

WB95.   DeRhen, Andrew. "Composer's Showcase: Foss, et al." *High Fidelity/Musical America* 22:MA13 (August 1972)
Review of the April 26, 1972 premiere performance. "Lukas Foss lived up to his reputation as a cheerful iconoclast with his...mini-cantata whose accompaniment included a mandolin." (See: W18a)

WB96.   Niemann, Suzanne. "Whitney Museum." *Music Journal* 30:74 (September 1972)
Mentions the April 26, 1972 premiere performance as part of the Composer's Showcase. (See: W18a)

WB97.   "First Performances." *The World of Music* 15:67 (no. 2, 1973)
Listing of the first performance of *Three Songs* [*sic*] *for Frank O'Hara's Angel* January 1, 1973 in Amsterdam by the Five Centuries Ensemble. (See: W18c)

WB98.   Putnam, Thomas. "UB Features Foss Creations." *Buffalo Courier Express* April 19, 1982:B6.
Review of the April 18, 1982 60th birthday concert at the State University of New York at Buffalo. "The women [of the] University Choir sang Foss's pulsing lines neatly, and with an assumed child-like tone that seemed appropriate." (See: W18d; See also: WB279, WB370, WB447)

WB99. Trotter, Herman. "Influence of Foss Recalled in Program Saluting Composer." *Buffalo Evening News* April 19, 1982:B9.
Review of the April 18, 1982 performance as part of a program in honor of Foss's 60th year. "[The work consists of] a vital and intriguing mix of rhythmic chant interrupted by chirping words over an instrumental ostinato...and a kind of competition between the soprano and an initially intrusive, then central narration." (See: W18d; See also: WB280, WB371, WB448)

WB100. Holland, Bernard. "Concert: Lukas Foss Works Played at Composers' Forum." *New York Times* October 10, 1982:85.
Review of the October 7, 1982 performance. "The daintiest moments in the evening came in *Three Airs for Frank O'Hara*...Mr. Smith's chorus sounded uneasy in the textual passages but created pleasant sound effects elsewhere." (See: W18e; See also: WB281, WB399, WB449)

W19. Lamdeni (Teach Me) (1973; New York: G. Schirmer; Paris: Editions Salabert, 1975. Instrumental parts available on rental.)

For chorus and 6 instruments of plucked and beaten sounds (any mixture) all amplified if possible with loudspeakers on stage (I & II: mandolin, glockenspiel, or xylophone (2 of either or combination); III & IV: vibraphone or any plucked instrument (2 of either or combination); V & VI: guitar or marimba (2 of each or combination)).
Contents: I. Baruch Hagever (male choir) -- II. Wa-eda Mah (women's choir) -- III. Mi al Har Horev (mixed choir).
Dedication: "Composed for Testimonium 1974, Jerusalem and dedicated to Recha Freier."
Duration: 10 minutes.
Based on 12th century synagogue chants. Written in neumatic notation by Obadiah Hager. Words in romanized Hebrew. Edited and arranged by Dr. Israel Adler (Acum, Israel).

FIRST PERFORMANCE

W19a. 1974. Testimonium 1974, Jerusalem.

OTHER PERFORMANCES

W19b. March 22, 1975. Albright-Knox Art Gallery, Buffalo, New York. State University of New York at Buffalo Choir; Dennis Kahle, Donald Knaack, Jan Williams, Margaret Knaack, percussion; Joseph Kubera, harpsichord; Harriet Simons, conductor. (See: D21)

W20. American Cantata (1976; revised 1977; piano-vocal score: New York: Boosey & Hawkes; Amberson Enterprises, 1981,

c1977 (photocopy of holograph; first publication for sale). Pub.
pl. no. BH.BK.810. Performance materials available on rental.)

For 2 soloists (soprano, tenor), a male and a female voice
speaking through battery powered megaphones, a voice from
a loudspeaker, boy's voice (live or taped), double chorus
(SSAATTBB), large or small orchestra (flute, oboe, clarinet,
bassoon (opt. saxophone), 2 trumpets, 2 trombones, timpani,
percussion, harp, 2 electric guitars (2nd doubles on electric
bass guitar), classical guitar, 2 five-string banjos, piano
(celesta), electric organ, accordion, harmonica, strings (1
violin doubling on mandolin). May be performed by full
orchestra or a minimum of 20, including solo strings.
Contents: I. Prologue (The Promise of America) -- II. Earth,
Water, Air -- III. Love -- IV. Money (Scherzo) -- V. Trial and
Error.
Commissioned by: American Choral Directors' Association with
support from the National Endowment for the Arts.
Composed on an NEA C/L Program Fellowship while in Jerusalem.
Duration: 37 minutes.
Words assembled by Arieh Sachs and Lukas Foss from Haiku,
black sorrow songs, contemporary jibberish statements, and
words by Whitman, Thoreau, Moody, Croffut, Wolfe, Franklin,
and Jefferson. Foss refers to this as a "pivotal" work leading
to his third compositional period. (Bassin, 31. See: B215)

FIRST PERFORMANCE

W20a.   July 24, 1976. Interlochen, Michigan. American Choral
Directors' Association Bicentennial Chorus; World Youth
Orchestra; Lukas Foss, conductor. (See: WB102)

OTHER PERFORMANCES

W20b.   December 12, 1976. Festival Theatre, Krannert Center,
University of Illinois at Champaign-Urbana. Larry
Parsons, tenor; Patricia Ludvigson, soprano; Joan
Lehrman, Charles Petering, narrators; Frank Knowles,
Michael Richardson, comedians; David Lewman, voice of
a youth; Oratorio Society; University Chorale; Members
of the University Symphony Orchestra; Lukas Foss,
conductor. (See: WB103)

W20c.   December 1, 1977. Avery Fisher Hall, Lincoln Center,
New York City. Joseph Evans, tenor; Linda Herman,
Robert Convery, speakers; Patricia Ludvigson, brief vocal
solo; Westminster Choir; New York Philharmonic;
Leonard Bernstein, conductor. New York premiere; first
performance of the revised version. (See: WB104,
WB105, WB106, WB107)

W20d.   May 1, 1981. Brooklyn Academy of Music, Brooklyn,
New York. Linn Maxwell, soprano; Joseph Evans, tenor;
Brooklyn Philharmonia Chorus; New York University

Choral Arts Society; Brooklyn Philharmonia; Lukas Foss, conductor.

BIBLIOGRAPHY

WB101. Foss, Lukas. *"American Cantata."* *Choral Journal* 16:14-17 (April 1976)
In this article Foss comments on the composing of this piece and how the text of the work was assembled from historical statements, poems, magazine gibberish to form a tragic drama. The article also includes the text of the work.

WB102. Webb, Guy B. *"American Cantata* and the Bicentennial Chorus."* *Choral Journal* 17:22 (October 1976)
Review of the July 24, 1976 premiere performance. The review is written by a member of the chorus. The group, which consisted of full quartet representation from almost every state, rehearsed the work for a week. "The concept of a truly national chorus in connection with an in-depth study of one aspect of choral music--American choral music--was exciting and very rewarding." (See: W20a)

WB103. Reed, Arnold. *"American Cantata* Examines the Promise of U.S." *News-Gazette (Champaign, Ill.)* December 13, 1976:A3.
Review of the second performance of *American Cantata*. A power failure forced the moving of 300 performers, their equipment, risers, and chairs from the Great Hall to the Festival Theatre at the Krannert Center. Despite the strange and large, open performance space, "the resulting balance between chorus and orchestra was excellent." Of the work itself, "There could hardly be a better year to ask ourselves [if we have truly adhered to the basic tenants set forth of 'life, liberty, and the pursuit of happiness.']...One would be hard pressed to find a musical work which forces us to do so in such a compelling manner." (See: W20b)

WB104. Schonberg, Harold C. "Music: Bernstein Leads Foss Cantata." *New York Times* December 2, 1977:C18. Reprinted in *American Choral Review* (See: WB108)
Review of the December 1, 1977 New York premiere performance of the revised version. "Foss is the complete eclectic. His *American Cantata* is smart, slick, and very, very thin." (See: W20c)

WB105. "Concert Reviews: New York Philharmonic." *Variety* December 7, 1977:72.
Review of the December 1, 1977 performance. "The work, as conducted by Leonard Bernstein, was a solid chunk of Americana." (See: W20c)

WB106. Breuer, Robert. "Neues aus dem New Yorker Musikleben." *Oesterreichische Musikzeitschrift* 33:49 (January 1978)
 Brief description of the revised version of *American Cantata*. (See: W20c)

WB107. Kerner, Leighton. "Three Cheers for Two Americans." *Village Voice* January 2, 1978:64.
 Review of the December 1977 New York premiere and the premiere of the extensively revised version. "*American Cantata's* verbal materials...project a pessimistic view of where we've been and where we are. It's silent about where we're going, as if it couldn't bear to look." (See: W20c)

WB108. Schonberg, Harold C. "Choral Performances: New York." *American Choral Review* 20:17-18 (July 1978) Reprinted from the *New York Times*.
 (See: WB104)

WB109. Bassin, Joseph Philip. "An Overview of the Third Period Compositional Output of Lukas Foss, 1976-1983." Ed.D., Columbia University Teachers College, 1987:31-42. *Dissertation Abstracts* 48:1573A-1574A (January 1988) UMI# 87-21079.
 (See: B216)

W21. **Then the Rocks on the Mountain Begin to Shout** (1978; manuscript)

For a cappella chorus (SSATB).
Originally composed for brass quintet (see: *Brass Quintet*, W86). It was later arranged for orchestra (see: *Quintets for Orchestra*, W59).
Duration: 17 minutes.
The text is comprised of vowel sounds. The title was derived from Charles Ives's *From the Steeples and the Mountains*.

FIRST PERFORMANCE

W21a. November 9, 1985. St. Peter's Church, New York City. Gregg Smith Singers; Gregg Smith, conductor.

BIBLIOGRAPHY

WB110. Bassin, Joseph Philip. "An Overview of the Third Period Compositional Output of Lukas Foss, 1976-1983." Ed.D., Columbia University Teachers College, 1987:120-131. *Dissertation Abstracts* 48:1573A-1574A (January 1988) UMI# 87-21079.
 (See: B216)

W22.   De Profundis (1984; New York: Carl Fischer.)

For a cappella chorus (large or small).
Commissioned by: Gregg Smith Singers and Dale Warland
     Singers.
Duration: 8 minutes.
Text in Latin and English; both sung simultaneously.

FIRST PERFORMANCE

W22a.   1983. St. Paul, Minnesota. Dale Warland Singers; Dale
          Warland, conductor.

OTHER PERFORMANCES

W22b.   March 5, 1985. Jewish Museum, New York City. Gregg
          Smith Singers; Gregg Smith, conductor.

W22c.   June 1987. Aldeburgh Festival, England. European
          premiere as part of the 40th Aldeburgh Festival. BBC
          Singers; John Poole, conductor. (See: WB111)

BIBLIOGRAPHY

WB111. Kerner, Leighton. "Nary a Dud." *Village Voice* August
         18, 1987:80.
              Review of the 40th Aldeburgh Festival where Foss
         was the composer-in-residence. Performed were the
         European premieres of *De Profundis* and *Renaissance
         Concerto* (See: W63c) as well as *Echoi* (See: W74j),
         Thirteen Ways of Looking at a Blackbird (See: W33e),
         Time Cycle (See: W31h), and *Psalms* (See: W16b). *De
         Profundis* was part of a choral concert by the BBC
         Singers, conducted by John Poole. The work is
         described as a "concentration of different emotional
         connotations...[allowing Foss to achieve] such musico-
         dramatic weight...that's essential to great art." (See:
         W22c)

W23.   With Music Strong (1988; New York: Carl Fischer.)

For chorus and orchestra.
Commissioned by: Milwaukee Symphony Orchestra Women's
     League in honor of Margaret Hawkins, choral director and the
     50th anniversary of the Milwaukee Symphony Orchestra.
Duration: 28 minutes.
Introduction based on *Quintets for Orchestra* (See: W59). Text
     structured by the composer from many poems by Walt
     Whitman.

FIRST PERFORMANCE

W23a.   April 15, 1989. Uihlein Hall, Milwaukee, Wisconsin.
Milwaukee Symphony Chorus and Orchestra; Lukas
Foss, conductor. (See: WB112)

BIBLIOGRAPHY

WB112. Raabe, Nancy Miller. "New Work Shows Foss' Inventive
Brilliance." *Milwaukee Sentinel* April 17, 1989.
Review of the April 15, 1989 premiere
performance. The work is described as "bright,
imaginative [and] full of conceptual challenges...The
Milwaukee Symphony Chorus' performance...was
nothing short of virtuosic, its 170 voices merging as an
impulse from one mind and one heart." (See: W23a)

MUSIC FOR SOLO VOICE

W24.   **Wanderers Gemütsruhe (Song for a Wanderer)** (1938; New
York: Southern Music Publishing Co., 1951. Pub. pl. no. 67-4.)

For medium voice and piano.
Duration: 3 minutes.
Text from Johann Wolfgang von Goethe's "Westöstlicher Divan";
   English lyric by Williard R. Trask. This piece was included in
   Three Songs on Texts by Goethe. (See: W25)

BIBLIOGRAPHY

WB113. Sabin, Robert. "American Songs Reveal Wide Variety of
Styles." *Musical America* 71:30 (July 1951)
Review of the Southern Music Publishing Company
publication. "*Wanderers Gemütsruhe*...is a setting of
Goethe's metaphysical poem about the nature of vileness
and evil and the most sensible human attitude towards
them....Foss has provided a whirlwind accompaniment
that hurries the words along too fast...and that
completely overshadows the vocal part."

WB114. Flanagan, William. "Music Reviews: Solo Songs."
Notes 8:753 (September 1951)
Review of the voice and piano publication by
Southern Music Company. Mr. Flanagan describes the
piece as "a Hindemith-like setting of Goethe's German
text."

WB115. Quillian, James W. "The New and the Good."
Repertoire 1:157 (January 1952)
Review of the Southern Music publication for
medium voice and piano. "This poem has been
singularly neglected even by German composers....It
does not seem to lend itself to nor call for being made

into a song." Mr. Quillian also remarks that this "bombastic" work should only be sung in German.

W25.   Three Songs on Texts by Goethe (Drei Goethe Lieder)
(1938; manuscript.)

For medium voice and piano.
One of the songs was published separately as *Wanderers Gemütsruhe*. (See: W24)
Duration: 7 minutes.

W26.   Where the Bee Sucks: Ariel's Song from The Tempest
(1940; New York: G. Schirmer, 1951; New York: Carl Fischer, 1979, c1951. Pub. pl. no. V2486.)

For high/medium voice and piano.
Dedication: none.
Duration: 3 minutes.
Text from Shakespeare's *The Tempest*. Written as incidental music to a children's production at the King-Coit School in Manhattan. (See also: *Incidental Music for Shakespeare's Tempest*, W1)

BIBLIOGRAPHY

WB116. Sabin, Robert. "American Songs Reveal Wide Variety of Styles." *Musical America* 71:30 (July 1951)
Review of the G. Schirmer publication. "*Where the Bee Sucks*...is a straightforward setting of the Shakespearean lyric with a charming accompaniment. The vocal part takes some curious liberties with the verse rhythms and accents, but the music has the proper insouciance."

W27.   Melodrama and Dramatic Song for Michelangelo (1940; manuscript.)

For voice and orchestra.
Duration: 15 minutes.
Text by C. F. Meyer.

W28.   Song of Anguish (1945; New York: Carl Fischer, 1953. (Carl Fischer study score, no. 8) Pub. pl. no. N1945. Parts available on rental.)

For baritone/bass and orchestra (piccolo, 2 flutes, 2 oboes, 2 clarinets, bass clarinet, 2 bassoons, contra bassoon, 4 horns, 3 trumpets, 3 trombones, tuba, harp, piano/celesta, 4 percussion (1. 4 timpani; 2. bass drum, vibraphone; 3. suspended cymbal, triangle, tam-tam; 4. side drum, tom tom, chimes, xylophone), strings) or piano.
Commissioned by: Kulas Foundation in Cleveland.
Dedication: none.
Duration: 20 minutes.

First Biblical solo-cantata; text from the Book of Isaiah.

FIRST PERFORMANCE

W28a. March 10, 1950. Symphony Hall, Boston,
Massachusetts. Marko Rothmüller, baritone; Boston
Symphony; Lukas Foss, conductor. The first
performance was to have been performed by the
Cleveland Orchestra but had to be cancelled because of
the singer's illness. (See: WB118)

OTHER PERFORMANCES

W28b. Summer 1948. Jacob's Pillow. Pauline Kohner, dancer;
Doris Humphrey, choreography. Version for baritone,
dancer, and piano. The work was choreographed under
the title "Voice in the Wilderness." (See: WB117)

BIBLIOGRAPHY

WB117. Lloyd, Margaret. *The Borzoi Book of Modern Dance*.
New York: A. A. Knopf, 1949; reprint, New York: Dance
Horizons, 1974.
        Included in this book is a description of the dance
version of *Song of Anguish*. (See: W28b)

WB118. Burk, John N. "*Song of Anguish*." *Boston Symphony
Concert Bulletin* no. 18:982-991 (March 10, 1950)
        Program notes for the March 10, 1950
performance. It includes the text from the cantata, a
brief biogaphical sketch, and a works list. (See: W28a)

WB119. Burkat, Leonard. "Current Chronicle: United States:
Boston." *Musical Quarterly* 36:441-443 (July 1950)
        Review and comparison of *Song of Anguish* and
Song of Songs. It includes musical examples. "[The
soloist] is never separated from the orchestra but rests
intimately surrounded by it. The voice is another line
within the texture created by the orchestra."

WB120. Wilson, J. Kenneth. "New Music: Orchestral Works."
Musical Courier 149:38 (April 1, 1954)
        Review of the Carl Fischer publication. "A full
orchestral palette is employed by the composer, though
at no time does the orchestration sound thick."

WB121. Finney, Ross Lee. "Music Reviews: Vocal Music."
Notes 11:609 (September 1954)
        Review of the Carl Fischer publication. "The
orchestral setting is substantial and subtle and the vocal
utterance deeply moving from the first statement to the
dreadful conclusion...Lukas Foss has achieved a
significant musical statement."

W29.   **Song of Songs** (1946; VOCAL SCORE (Foss's reduction): New
York: Carl Fischer, 1950. Pub. no. O3661. Score and parts
available on rental. FULL SCORE: New York: Carl Fischer, 1960.
(Carl Fischer Study Score Series; no. 14) Pub. pl. no. N3330.)

For soprano/mezzo soprano and orchestra (piccolo, 2 flutes, 2
oboes, English horn, 2 clarinets, bass clarinet, 2 bassoons,
contrabassoon, 4 horns (3 & 4 optional), 3 trumpets, 2
trombones, timpani, 2 percussionists (suspended cymbal,
snare drum, triangle, bass drum, glockenspiel, tom tom), harp,
strings).
Contents: I. Awake, O North Wind -- II. Come My Beloved -- III.
By Night on My Bed -- IV. Set Me As a Seal.
Commissioned by: The League of Composers for Ellabelle Davis.
Prizes: Naumburg Recording Prize, 1957.
Dedication: none.
Duration: 27 minutes.
Second Biblical solo-cantata; text from the Song of Solomon.
Movements II and IV may be sung separately in recital.

FIRST PERFORMANCE

W29a.   March 7, 1947. Symphony Hall, Boston, Massachusetts.
Ellabelle Davis, soprano; Boston Symphony Orchestra;
Serge Koussevitzky, conductor. (See: WB122)

OTHER PERFORMANCES

W29b.   March 14, 1947. New York City. Ellabelle Davis,
soprano; Boston Symphony Orchestra; Serge
Koussevitzky, conductor. New York premiere. (See:
WB122)

W29c.   August 19, 1947. Hatch Memorial Shell, Charles River
Esplande, Boston, Massachusetts. José Limón,
choreography, dancer; Miriam Pandor, dancer. First
performance in dance format; third choreographed work
of José Limón. (See: WB124)

W29d.   Summer 1950. Tanglewood, Massachusetts. Ellabelle
Davis, soprano; Boston Symphony Orchestra; Leonard
Bernstein, conductor. (See: WB126)

W29e.   December 11, 1951. Chicago, Illinois. Adele Addison,
soprano; Chicago Symphony Orchestra; Rafael Kubelik,
conductor. (See: WB132)

W29f.   March 18, 1955. Los Angeles, California. Henny
Ekstrom, contralto; Los Angeles Philharmonic; Lukas
Foss, conductor. West Coast premiere. (See: WB133)

W29g.   January 8, 1956. New York City. Ellabelle Davis,
soprano; New York Philharmonic-Symphony; Dmitri
Mitropoulis, conductor. (See: WB134)

W29h. January 26, 1958. Carnegie Hall, New York City.
Jennie Tourel, mezzo soprano; New York Philharmonic;
Leonard Bernstein, conductor. (See: WB135)

W29i. February 13, 1962. Festival Hall, London, England.
Noreen Berry, soprano; London Symphony Orchestra;
Aaron Copland, conductor. (See: WB136)

W29j. September 13, 1986. Avery Fisher Hall, Lincoln Center,
New York City. Sheri Greenawald, soprano; Israel
Philharmonic Orchestra; Leonard Bernstein, conductor.

BIBLIOGRAPHY

WB122. *"Song of Solomon*--and Foss." *Newsweek* 29:90 (March
17, 1947)
Review of the first performances as performed by
the Boston Symphony for eight performances in nine
days. It summarizes various reviews from major
newspapers including *The Post*, *The Herald*, and *The
Globe*. Ellabelle Davis was praised for her performances
and Foss was praised more for his musical composition
than for his text setting. (See: W29a, W29b)

WB123. Bauer, Marion and Claire R. Reis. "Twenty-Five Years
with the League of Composers." *Musical Quarterly*
34:10 (January 1948)
Brief history behind the League of Composers
Composers' Fund and the Commission Plan which would
fund composers and guarantee that new compositions
would be performed. *Song of Songs* was one of these
commissioned works.

WB124. Lloyd, Margaret. *The Borzoi Book of Modern Dance.*
New York: A. A. Knopf, 1949; reprint, New York: Dance
Horizons, 1974.
This book contains a description of the first
performance as a dance. (See: W29c)

WB125. Burkat, Leonard. "Current Chronicle: United States:
Boston." *Musical Quarterly* 36:441-443 (July 1950)
(See: WB119)

WB126. Smith, Cecil. "High Quality of Tanglewood Maintained
by Koussevitzky." *Musical America* 70:5 (September
1950)
Review of the Summer 1950 performance. "Miss
Davis sang with ease and great beauty of tone, and with
selfless absorption in the music and the text." (See:
W29d)

WB127. "New Publications in Review: For Voice." *Musical
Courier* 142:28 (October 1, 1950)

Review of the Carl Fischer edition. "The textual treatment is sympathetic and there is a great deal of ingenuity to the harmonic underpinning."

WB128. Smith, Cecil. "New Music: Vocal Music." *Musical America* 70:31-32 (November 15, 1950)
Review of the piano reduction score published by Carl Fischer. "Although a great deal is lost by the substitution of a piano for the orchestra, the musical ideas are still dynamic when divested of their instrumental color."

WB129. Flanagan, William. "Music Reviews: Lukas Foss." *Notes* 8:124 (December 1950)
Review of the Carl Fischer piano-vocal score. "The piano reduction, though no more limited than most, produces a more-than-usual longing for the sensitive and evocative scoring of the original."

WB130. Cowell, Henry. "American Composition Committee Reviews." *Music Clubs Magazine* 30:19 (February 1951)
Review of the Carl Fischer publication for high voice and piano. "It seems rather simple and easy to understand, although especially interesting."

WB131. Thorolfson, Frank. "New Music: Solo." *Music News* 43:21 (February 1951)
Review of the Carl Fischer publication, "The cantata is exceedingly well integrated, eloquent, and grateful to sing."

WB132. Borowski, Felix. "The *Song of Songs*: Second Biblical Solo Cantata for Soprano and Orchestra by Lukas Foss." *Chicago Symphony Program Notes* 61:262-264 (December 11, 1951)
Program notes to the December 11, 1951 concert. It includes the text to the work. (See: W29e)

WB133. Goldberg, Albert. "Works by Prokofieff, Warren, Foss, Tansman Introduced on West Coast." *Musical America* 75:27 (April 1955)
Review of the March 18, 1955 West Coast premiere performance. "This proved to be a work of strong emotional appeal, deftly orchestrated, and difficult but grateful to sing." (See: W29f)

WB134. Sabin, Robert. "Ellabelle Davis Sings Foss Cantata." *Musical America* 76:21 (January 15, 1956)
Review of the January 8, 1956 performance. Miss Davis's singing of Foss's *Song of Songs* is described as "profoundly exciting" and "able to produce and sustain the seemingly endless tones" of the work. (See: W29g)

WB135. Simek, Julius Franz. "Shapero & Foss Works Led by Bernstein." *Musical America* 78:32 (March 1958)
    Review of the January 26, 1958 performance. "Miss Tourel gave the solo part...the sovereign fullness of her vocalism, and impeccable phrasing combined with the musical insight of a great artist." (See: W29h)

WB136. Taylor, Mark. "Aaron Copland...." *Music & Musicians* 10:41 (March 1962)
    Review of the February 13, 1962 performance of American music. Noreen Berry substituted on short notice for Josephine Veasey as soprano soloist. The piece is referred to as "pale echoes of Hindemith [with a] wandering vocal line." The "indistinct projection [of the soloist] failed to...draw any attention to the work." (See: W29i)

WB137. "Two Foss Works Are Nominated for Arts Award." *Buffalo Evening News* December 2, 1963:30.
    Notice of the nomination of *Time Cycle* (See: W31) and *Song of Songs* by the National Academy of Recording Arts and Sciences as "best classical compositions of a recent season by a contemporary composer."

WB138. Nelson, Clifford Keith. "An Analysis of *Song of Songs* by Lukas Foss." M.M. thesis, The University of Arizona, 1983. *Masters Abstracts* 22:282 (September 1984) UMI# MA13-22303.
    Nelson examines Foss's rhythmic style, use of dynamics, texture, and key schemes, and the way he combines the vocal line with the orchestra.

W30. **For Cornelia** (1955; manuscript)

For voice and piano.
Duration: 3 minutes.
Based on the Yeats poem "For Anne Gregory." The work could not be published because of copyright clearance problems.

W31. **Time Cycle** (1959-60; ORCHESTRAL SCORE: New York: Carl Fischer, 1962. (Carl Fischer study score series, no. 19) Pub. pl. no. N3654. Orchestral material available on rental.) (See also: W32)

For soprano and orchestra (2 flutes (2nd doubles piccolo), 2 clarinets (2nd doubles bass clarinet), 2 horns, 2 trumpets, trombone, 3 percussion (4 timpani, vibraphone, xylophone, glockenspiel, chimes, Eb antique cymbal, high and medium high woodblocks, temple blocks, high and medium high suspended cymbals, gong, tambourine, snare drum, bass drum, triangle), harp, celesta/piano, strings).

Contents: 1. We're Late (W.H. Auden) -- 2. When the Bells Justle (A. E. Housman) -- 3. Sechzehnter Januar (Franz Kafka) -- 4. O Mensch, Gib Acht (Friedrich Nietzsche).
Commissioned by: Adele Addison with funds from the Ford Foundation's Humanities and Arts Program.
Prizes: New York Music Critics Circle Award, Orchestral category, 1961.
Dedication: "For Adele Addison."
Duration: 22 minutes; 30 minutes with improvisations.
Holograph in ink (?) located at State University of New York at Buffalo. Publisher's label pasted on: New York: Carl Fischer, 1960. 19 p.
Based on poems or prose excerpts from "We're Late," *The Collected poetry of W.H. Auden*, Random House, 1945; "When the Bells Justle," *My Brother, A.E. Housman* by Laurence Housman, Charles Scribner's Sons, 1938; "Sechzehnte Januar," by Franz Kafka, published by Schocken Books, 1949; and "O Mensch, Gib Acht" from *Thus spake Zarathustra* by Friedrich Nietzsche. The texts to 1 and 2 are in English; the texts to 3 and 4 are in German with English translations supplied by Foss. There was hope of eventually adding texts by Dante and Baudelaire to be sung in the original Italian and French. Between each song, the Improvisation Chamber Ensemble would perform original improvisations not necessarily related to the previous song.

FIRST PERFORMANCE

W31a.   October 20, 1960. Carnegie Hall, New York City. Adele Addison, soprano; Improvisation Chamber Ensemble (Lukas Foss, piano; Richard Dufallo, clarinet; Howard Colf, violoncello; Charles DeLancey, percussion); New York Philharmonic; Leonard Bernstein, conductor. (See: WB139, WB140, WB141, WB142, WB143)

OTHER PERFORMANCES

W31b.   June 1961. Adele Addison, soprano; Los Angeles Festival Orchestra. West Coast premiere. (See: WB146)

W31c.   November 3, 1961. Boston, Massachusetts. Adele Addison, soprano; Improvisation Chamber Ensemble (Lukas Foss, piano; Richard Dufallo, clarinet; Howard Colf, violoncello; Charles DeLancey, percussion); Boston Symphony Orchestra; Lukas Foss, conductor. (See: WB147, WB148)

W31d.   November 21, 1962. Los Angeles, California. Improvisation Chamber Ensemble (Lukas Foss, piano; Richard Dufallo, clarinet; Howard Colf, violoncello; Charles DeLancey, percussion); Los Angeles Philharmonic Orchestra. (See: WB149)

W31e. September 1962. Berlin Philharmonic; Lukas Foss,
        conductor. (See: WB150)

W31f. May 1967? Frankfurter Ballett; Todd Bolander,
       choreography. Ballet adaptation. (See: WB154)

W31g. October 1970. City Center, New York. Susan Belling,
       soprano; Joffrey Ballet; Todd Bolander, choreography;
       Seymour Lipkin, conductor; Jennifer Tipton, stage
       lighting. First New York performance as a ballet. (See:
       WB156, WB157)

W31h. June 1987. Aldeburgh Festival, England. (See:
       WB111)

BIBLIOGRAPHY

WB139. Fleming, Shirley. "Philharmonic Presents Foss' *Time
       Cycle.*" *Musical Courier* 162:31 (November 1960)
       Review of the October 20, 1960 performance.
       "Praise for the vivid handling of the vocal part...to Miss
       Addison....How [the Improvisation Chamber Ensemble]
       wove its almost hypnotic patterns of tone and
       color...was a success--and an exciting one." (See:
       W31a)

WB140. Kolodin, Irving. "Welcome *Nabucco*--Richter--Egk--Foss."
       Saturday Review 43:44 (November 5, 1960)
       Review of the October 20, 1960 premiere
       performance. "[The texts] are provided with a balance
       wheel of rhythm and a mainspring of melodic line which
       have tension yet extreme flexibility....Thanks to
       Bernstein's penetration and Miss Addison's virtuosity,
       the composer...had a once-in-a-lifetime experience:
       perfection." (See: W31a)

WB141. Trimble, Lester. "Music." *The Nation* 191:354
       (November 5, 1960)
       Review of the October 20, 1960 premiere
       performance. "Despite the complexity of Foss's over-all
       conception, every note and measure of the piece
       sounded as if it were carefully integrated with the
       whole....The Lukas Foss Improvisation Chamber
       Ensemble...responded... with exactly the same qualities
       of emotionally charged technical perfection [as did the
       Orchestra and Adele Addison]." (See: W31a)

WB142. Sabin, Robert. "Foss *Time Cycle* has World Premiere."
       Musical America 80:34-35 (December 1960)
       Review of the October 20, 1960 premiere
       performance. "A new work of profound beauty,
       impressive technical mastery and unmistakable
       inspiration made this concert one of the most stirring
       that the Philharmonic has given in recent years....Miss

Addison...allowed no trace of its terrifying difficulty to appear in her performance [as] she met them all with heavenly serenity." (See: W31a)

WB143. Breuer, Robert. "Lukas Foss Improvisiert." *Melos* 28:8-9 (January 1961)
Review of the October 20, 1960 premiere performance. "Formed as a musical collage, one is reminded of Stockhausen and Penderecki." (translation) (See: W31a)

WB144. "Carter, Foss and Poulenc Works Get Music Critics' Circle Awards." *New York Times* April 19, 1961:34.
Time Cycle is described in this article which announces the winners of the 1961 New York Music Critics' Circle Awards.

WB145. "Foss, Poulenc, Carter Gain NY Critic's Awards." *Musical Courier* 163:6 (May 1961)
Foss's *Time Cycle*, along with Francis Poulenc's *Gloria* and Elliott Carter's *String Quartet no. 2*, were selected by the Music Critics' Circle of New York as the best new works in the orchestral, choral, and chamber music divisions respectively for works produced between January 1960 and April 1961.

WB146. Robin, Harry. "Music of Our Time." *Musical America* 81:10 (July 1961)
Review of the West Coast premiere performance. "Sung with conviction and glowing voice by Adele Addison. The interludes...seem impertinent, and much too controlled...the conducting by Mr. Foss tenuous, perhaps inadequate for a definitive performance of this startling, disturbing work." (See: W31b)

WB147. Foss, Lukas. "*Time Cycle*, Four Songs for Soprano and Orchestra." *Boston Symphony Concert Bulletin* 81:304-312 (November 3, 1961)
Concert notes for the November 3, 1961 performance. It includes the text to the songs, analyses of the texts and music, and some performance history. "In summing up the difference between composition and improvisation, the composer says: 'In composition all becomes 'fate.' Improvisation remains 'chance,' 'hazard,' *corrected* by the will.'" (See: W31c)

WB148. Dumm, Robert. "Boston." *Musical Courier* 164:61 (January 1962)
Review of the November 3, 1961 Boston performance. "Since Bostonians never boo, the Friday audience racked up its disgust in the number of walkouts it prompted, while the Saturday-nighters floated a foaming applause." (See: W31c)

WB149. Turner, Robert. "*Time Cycle*, for Soprano and
Orchestra." *Los Angeles Philharmonic Orchestra
Symphony Magazine* November 21, 1962:39+
Program notes for the November 21, 1962
performance. "The presence of extremely difficult vocal
intervals does not mean that the work is 'unvocal.'...The
only structural element common to all the movements is
a unifying chord." Included are the texts to the four
poems and analyses of the movements. (See: W31d)

WB150. Stuckenschmidt, H.H. "Rückblick auf Siebzehn Tage
Berliner Festwochen." *Melos* 29:393+ (December
1962)
Review of a performance by the Berlin
Philharmonic. "Foss seeks to musically connect the past
with the present....Foss has a real sense of tone and
color [in his music]." (translation) (See: W31e)

WB151. Salzman, Eric. "Report from NY: The New Virtuosity."
Perspectives of New Music 1:183-185 (no. 2, 1963)
A brief analysis of *Time Cycle* and the
Improvisation Chamber Ensemble in the context of
organization and variable compositions/performances of
"works-in-progress."

WB152. "Two Foss Works Are Nominated for Arts Award."
Buffalo Evening News December 2, 1963:30.
(See: WB137)

WB153. Mellers, Wilfrid. "Today and Tomorrow: Lukas Foss and
the Younger Generation." In *Music in a New Found Land*.
New York: A. A. Knopf, 1965:220-235.
(See: B71)

WB154. Jungheinrich, Hans-Klaus. "Getanzte Zeitstrukturen in
Frankfurt." *Melos* 34:213 (June 1967)
Review of the ballet adaptation of *Time Cycle*
performed by the Frankfurter Ballett. "The experimental
nature of the work is better revealed here (during the
ballet scenes) than during the musical ensemble parts.
The ballet version of *Time Cycle* is worth seeing."
(translation) (See: W31f)

WB155. *Lukas Foss on the New Lukas Foss.* New York: Carl
Fischer, 1969:6.
(See: B112)

WB156. Pion, S. "N.Y. City Center." *Music Journal* 29:69
(January 1971)
Review of the October 1970 Joffrey Ballet
performance. "Bolander's craftsmanship is
unimpeachable, but the dancers seem to be things used
by him, zombies mindedlessly making the motions."
(See: W31g)

WB157. Maskey, Jacqueline. "The Dance: Joffrey." *High Fidelity/Musical America* 21:MA19+ (March 1971)
    Review of the October 1970 ballet performance. "The Joffrey dancers...did their considerable best...The lighting...was some of the very best I have ever seen on the City Center stage." (See: W31g)

WB158. Gallaher, Christopher Summers. "Density in Twentieth-Century Music." Ph.D. diss., Indiana University, 1975. *Dissertation Abstracts* 36:1889A-1890A (October 1975) UMI# 75-23425.
    Foss's *Time Cycle* is included in this analysis of vertical and horizontal density in music of the mid-twentieth century. "This study explored the possible relationships between the passage of time and events in new music and the subsequent creation of structural goals based on these relationships."

W32.   Time Cycle (1960; New York: Carl Fischer, 1964. Pub. pl. no. N3987. Pub. no. O4282.)

For soprano and chamber group (clarinet, violoncello, piano and celesta, percussion (timpano, vibraphone, xylophone, chimes, Eb antique cymbal, high and medium high woodblocks, temple blocks, suspended cymbal, gong, tambourine, bongos, snare drum, bass drum, triangle).
No improvisations are included in this version. (For contents and other details see: W31)

FIRST PERFORMANCE

W32a.   July 10, 1961, Berkshire Music Festival, Tanglewood, Lenox, Massachusetts. Fromm Foundation Players; Lukas Foss, piano/celesta/conductor. Performed as part of a Fromm Foundation Concert.

OTHER PERFORMANCES

W32b.   October 16, 1961. Plummer Park's Fiesta Hall, Los Angeles, California. Grace-Lynne Martin, soprano; Improvisation Chamber Ensemble (Lukas Foss, piano; Richard Dufallo, clarinet; Howard Colf, violoncello; Charles DeLancey, percussion). (See: WB159)

W32c.   March 11, 1962. The New School, New York City. Adele Addison, soprano; Improvisation Chamber Ensemble (Lukas Foss, piano; Richard Dufallo, clarinet; Howard Colf, violoncello; Charles DeLancey, percussion). New York premiere of the chamber version; presented by the Fromm Music Foundation. (See: WB160, WB161, B40; See also: W73a, W74b)

W32d. July 13, 1962. Festival Theatre, Stratford Festival,
Stratford, Ontario. Grace-Lynne Martin, soprano;
Improvisation Chamber Ensemble (Lukas Foss, piano;
Richard Dufallo, clarinet; Howard Colf, violoncello;
Charles DeLancey, percussion); Members of the National
Festival Orchestra; Lukas Foss, conductor. The work
was performed a second time on the same program with
choreography: Angela Leigh, Earl Kraul, Jacqueline
Ivings, David Shields, Lilian Jarvis, dancers; Grant Strate,
choreographer. Canadian premiere. (See: WB162,
WB163, WB164, WB165)

W32e. May 9, 1965. Albright-Knox Art Gallery, Buffalo, New
York. Sylvia Dimiziani, soprano; Sherman Friedland,
clarinet; Jay Humeston, violoncello; Frederic Myrow,
piano; Jan Williams, percussion; Richard Dufallo,
conductor. (See: D30)

W32f. October 7, 1981. Louise Lincoln Kerr Cultural Center,
Arizona State University, Tempe, Arizona. New Music
Ensemble; Glenn Hackbarth, director; Lukas Foss,
conductor. (See: D31; See also: W79e, W85e)

W32g. April 25, 1983. Music Annex, Indiana University,
Bloomington, Indiana. Virginia Palmer, soprano and
lecturer; Marlene Macomber, clarinet; Timothy
Mutschlecner, violoncello; William Crowle, piano;
Rebecca Kite, percussion. (See: D33).

W32h. March 4, 1987. Merkin Concert Hall, New York City.
Carmen Pelton, soprano; Music Today; Gerard Schwarz,
conductor. (See: WB166)

BIBLIOGRAPHY

WB159. Goldberg, Albert. "Gathering Momentum." *Musical
America* 81:14-15 (December 1961)
Review of the October 16, 1961 performance.
"The latest revision [i.e., version]...dispensing with the
ensemble improvisations...seemed to be a definite
improvement." (See: W32b)

WB160. Salzman, Eric. "Music: A Foss Afternoon." *New York
Times* March 12, 1962:36.
Review of the March 11, 1962 premiere
performance. "Enhanced by the beautiful singing of Miss
Addison, [*Time Cycle*] made a genuine dramatic
impression...enhanced and made more elegant in the
chamber version." (See W32c; See also: WB325,
WB327)

WB161. Helm, Everett. "Foss on Foss." *Musical America* 82:37
(May 1962)

Review of the March 11, 1962 New York premiere performance of the chamber version. "*Time Cycle,* magnificently sung by Adele Addison, is as impressive in this arrangement...as in the orchestral version." (See: W32c; See also: WB326, WB328)

WB162. Kraglund, John. "Foss, Schoenberg Take Honors at Stratford." *Toronto Globe and Mail* July 13, 1962.
Review of the July 13, 1962 performance. "[*Time Cycle* is] attractive and easy to listen to, although the general mood is dark and the vocal line a trifle strained...and the new, improvised interludes proved particularly fascinating....Then came Mr. Strate's choreographed version of *Time Cycle*, without the interludes and at that point most of my respect for everyone evaporated." (See: W32d)

WB163. Kidd, George. "A Musical Shocker." *Telegram (Toronto)* July 14, 1962:42.
Review of the July 13, 1962 performance. "[Grace-Lynne Martin] surmounted [the vocal] hazards brilliantly in her both performances of the work....Like the music, the dancing...was way out. It was certainly not conventional in its style, but it had a dramatic touch that was imaginative and warm with its blending with the music." (See: W32d)

WB164. "Experiment in Time." *Time* 80:47 (July 27, 1962)
Review of the July 13, 1962 performance. The texts to the four songs are presented. Foss's intention to add texts in French and Italian to the cycle is mentioned. The music for the work is described as "spare" and the piece "manages to be both intricate and delicate." (See: W32d)

WB165. Schabas, Ezra. "Toronto: Gould and Company at Stratford." *Musical Courier* 164:38 (September 1962)
Review of the chamber version performed in Stratford, Ontario as part of the Festival concert entitled the Schoenberg Heritage. "The net result was an amorphous combination of brilliantly executed musical sounds but with little more to commend it." After the presentation, the work was again performed with choreography. (See: W32d)

WB166. Henahan, Donal. "Concert: Music Today." *New York Times* March 6, 1987:C29.
Review of the March 4, 1987 concert by Music Today (directed by Gerard Schwarz) in Merkin Concert Hall, New York City. Carmen Pelton sang the vocal part. "The most interesting piece [on the program]...was the oldest...It served to remind one of the score's quality and durability." (See: W32h)

W33. **Thirteen Ways of Looking at a Blackbird** (1978; New York: Pembroke Music, 1980. Pub. pl. no. PCB114.)

For soprano/mezzo-soprano, flute, piano, percussion (inside piano on strings: tape-covered triangle beaters, large and small cowbells, large and small Japanese bowls, superball mallet, flexaton, Jew's harp), 2 tape recorders for tape delay in no. XIII.
Commissioned by: Radio Station WFMT, Chicago.
Prizes: American Composers Alliance Recording Award for recording CRI SD 442. (See: D34)
Dedication: none.
Duration: 16 minutes.
Text by Wallace Stevens from the poem of the same name.

FIRST PERFORMANCE

W33a. December 1978. WFMT Radio, Chicago, Illinois. Sylvia Dimiziani, soprano; Eberhard Blum, flute; Yvar Mikhashoff, piano; Jan Williams, percussion. Taped on December 3, 1978 for the broadcast (See: W33b)

OTHER PERFORMANCES

W33b. December 3, 1978. Baird Recital Hall, State University of New York at Buffalo, Buffalo, New York. Sylvia Dimiziani, soprano; Eberhard Blum, flute; Yvar Mikhashoff, piano; Jan Williams, percussion. Concert premiere; preview performance. Earlier in the day, the piece was taped for the official Chicago commission premiere performance. (See: W33a, WB167, WB168)

W33c. February 11, 1980. Buffalo Seminary Chapel, Buffalo, New York. Rachel Lewis, soprano; Laurence Trott, piccolo; Yvar Mikhashoff, piano; Jan Williams, percussion.

W33d. November 1, 1983. Cooper Union, New York City. Bowery Ensemble. (See: B189; See also: W76p, W85f, W103c, W109f)

W33e. June 1987. Aldeburgh Festival, England. European premiere as part of the 40th Aldeburgh Festival. (See: WB111)

BIBLIOGRAPHY

WB167. Putnam, Thomas. "Sweet Feelings, Elusive Colorings, Mark *Blackbird*." *Buffalo Courier Express* December 4, 1978:23.
Review of the December 3, 1978 "preview" performance. "Foss has set the poetry with often exotic melodies that let words sing, with tonal effects that mirror the poet's sense and nonsense, and with a variety

of musical language that respects the multiple ways of the poet's observations." (See: W33b)

WB168. Dwyer, John. "*Blackbird* Ends Foss' Weekend on High Note." *Buffalo Evening News* December 4, 1978:34.
Review of the December 3, 1978 performance. "It is genuinely a setting for poetry, and with near-conventional and near-tonal means it achieves mystery and surprise. It also has a nerve-sensitive awareness of texture. It was an admirable performance." (See: W33b)

WB169. Bassin, Joseph Philip. "An Overview of the Third Period Compositional Output of Lukas Foss, 1976-1983." Ed.D., Columbia University Teachers College, 1987:51-60. *Dissertation Abstracts* 48:1573A-1574A (January 1988) UMI# 87-21079.
(See: B216)

W34.   Measure for Measure (1980; Paris: Éditions Salabert; New York: G. Schirmer.)

For tenor and chamber orchestra.
Duration: 10 minutes.
Foss chose words about music from Shakespeare's: *The Tempest, Merchant of Venice, Twelfth Night, Hamlet, Julius Caesar, A Midsummer Night's Dream*. Orchestral accompaniment based on Foss's *Salomon Rossi Suite*. (See: W58)

BIBLIOGRAPHY

WB170. Bassin, Joseph Philip. "An Overview of the Third Period Compositional Output of Lukas Foss, 1976-1983." Ed.D., Columbia University Teachers College, 1987:108-112. *Dissertation Abstracts* 48:1573A-1574A (January 1988) UMI# 87-21079.
(See: B216)

ORCHESTRAL MUSIC

W35.   Two Symphonic Pieces (1939-40; manuscript; lost.)

For orchestra.

W36.   Two Pieces for Orchestra (Zwei Stucke für Orchester)
(1941; manuscript)

For orchestra.
Contents: 1. Dance Sketch -- 2. Allegro Concertante.
Duration: 9 minutes.

W36a.   January or February, 1943. New York Little Symphony.

BIBLIOGRAPHY

WB171. Berger, Arthur. "Once Again, the One-Man Show, 1943:
        Mid-Winter, January-February." *Modern Music* 20:178
        (March/April 1943)
            Brief comparison of this work written by a young
        Foss with comparable works by David Diamond, Morton
        Gould, and André Mathieu.

W37.   Concerto No. 1 for Clarinet (1941; New York: G. Schirmer,
         1942.)

For clarinet and orchestra.
Duration: 23 minutes.
Revised as *Concerto No. 1 for Piano* (See: W38). Movement II,
    Elegy, was published separately (See: W45).

W38.   Concerto No. 1 for Piano (1943; New York: G. Schirmer,
         1944.)

For piano and orchestra.
Revision of *Concerto No. 1 for Clarinet* (See: W37).
Duration: 24 minutes.

W38a.   1944. Broadcast by C.B.S. Radio. C.B.S. Philharmonic.
        (See: WB172)

W38b.   1944. Lukas Foss, piano; Boston Symphony Orchestra;
        Serge Koussevitzky, conductor.

BIBLIOGRAPHY

WB172. Mills, Charles. "Over the Air." *Modern Music* 22:138
        (January/February 1945)
            Review of the premiere performance broadcast
        over C.B.S. Radio. "A youthful wit and dry lyricism
        pervade this well-made score, which is attractive,
        capricious and amusing throughout." (See: W38a)

W39.   Symphony No. 1 in G (1944; New York: G. Schirmer, 1945.)

For orchestra.
Duration: 28 minutes.

FIRST PERFORMANCE

W39a.   February 4, 1945. Pittsburgh, Pennsylvania. Pittsburgh
        Symphony; Fritz Reiner, conductor. (See: WB173)

OTHER PERFORMANCES

W39b.   Spring 1946. New York City. New York City
        Symphony; Lukas Foss, conductor. New York premiere.
        (See: WB175)

BIBLIOGRAPHY

WB173. Dorian, Frederick. "Premieres and Novelties for
       Pittsburgh." *Modern Music* 22:125-126
       (January/February 1945)
            During the 1944/45 concert season, the Pittsburgh
       Symphony performed many premiere works. Mentioned
       among them is Foss's *Symphony No. 1* performed for the
       first time in Pittsburgh. (See: W39a)

WB174. Fine, Irving. "Young America: Bernstein and Foss."
       Modern Music 22:243 (May/June 1945)
            Symphony in G is mentioned briefly as a work in
       which Foss began to develop his own style, one which is
       tonal, less dissonant, and conservative. "In
       achievement, the symphony deserves to rank at least as
       high as *The Prairie.*"

WB175. Fuller, Donald. "Airborne over New York: Spring 1946."
       Modern Music 23:117 (Spring 1946)
            Review of the Spring 1946 New York premiere
       performance. "One finds little Hindemith and few
       stringent formal Coplandisms....Foss appears more likely
       to bring forth his complete individuality after a struggle
       with his original obsessions, rather than by disregarding
       them for a free manner." (See: W39b)

W40.   The Prairie. Symphonic Suite (1943; New York: G. Schirmer, 1944.)

For orchestra.
Duration: 16 minutes.
Orchestral suite based on themes from the cantata of the same
    name. (See: W11)

FIRST PERFORMANCE

W40a.   October 15, 1943. Boston, Massachusetts. Boston
        Symphony Orchestra; Serge Koussevitzky, conductor.
        (See: WB176, WB177)

BIBLIOGRAPHY

WB176. "Foss Work Played in Boston." *New York Times* October 16, 1943:11
Notice of the October 15, 1943 first performance. "Lukas Foss...became the youngest American composer ever to have a composition performed by the Boston Symphony Orchestra. The composer appeared on the stage after the world premiere...to receive a friendly hug and a fatherly pat on the head from Conductor Serge Koussevitzky." (See: W40a)

WB177. Smith, Moses. "Boston Goes All Out for Premieres." *Modern Music* 21:102-104 (January/February 1944)
Brief review of the orchestral work as performed on the Boston Symphony's 1943/44 season. "The themes are good, the workmanship talented, if a little immature. A genuine lyrical talent was at work." (See: W40a)

W41. **Ode** (1944; revised 1958; New York: G. Schirmer, 1945; Revised version: New York: Carl Fischer, 1960. Pub. pl. no. N3331. (Carl Fischer study score series, no. 15) Orchestral material available on rental.)

For orchestra (piccolo, 2 flutes, 2 oboes, English horn, 2 clarinets, bass clarinet, 2 bassoons, contrabassoon, 4 horns, 3 trumpets, 3 trombones, tuba, timpani, percussion, 1 or 2 harps, piano, strings).
Duration: 10 minutes.
Inspired by the poem "For Whom the Bell Tolls" by John Donne.
Full title: "Ode To Those Who Will Not Return."

FIRST PERFORMANCE

W41a. March 15, 1945. Carnegie Hall, New York City. New York Philharmonic-Symphony; George Szell, conductor. (See: WB178, WB179, WB180)

OTHER PERFORMANCES

W41b. October 17, 1958. Philadelphia Orchestra; Eugene Ormandy, conductor. Revised version.

BIBLIOGRAPHY

WB178. Downes, Olin. "Foss Music Played at Carnegie Hall." *New York Times* March 16, 1945:20.
Review of the March 15, 1945 premiere performance. "[The] general idea [of *Ode*] is 'crisis, war, and, ultimately, faith.'" Foss's musical style and ideas are noted as not developed to reflect his intentions accurately. "The score is episodic;...[its motives do] not develop significantly." (See: W41a)

WB179. Fuller, Donald. "Russian and American Season, 1945."
Modern Music 22:255 (May/June 1945)
Review of the March 15, 1945 premiere
performance of the original version. "It has a rare feeling
for sonorities....The sustained, elevated tone of this *Ode*
expresses a more original musical thinking...than he has
yet offered." (See: W41a)

WB180. Fine, Irving. "Young America: Bernstein and Foss."
Modern Music 22:243 (May/June 1945)
In describing recent works of 1945, *Ode* was
thought to be "the weakest, though to hear Foss play it
on the piano [was] an exciting experience." Fine
believed that the work was too romantic in nature and
orchestrated weakly. (See: W41a)

W42.   Pantomime (Gift of the Magi Suite) (1945; New York:
Hargail, 1945.)

For orchestra.
An orchestral suite written after the ballet *Gift of the Magi* (See:
W7).
Duration: 20 minutes.

W43.   Concerto for Oboe (1948; revised 1958; oboe and piano
version: New York: Southern Music Publishing Co., 1952. Pub.
pl. no. 112-35. Pub. no. 60223-324. Orchestral material,
c1978, available on rental.)

For oboe and orchestra or chamber group (flute, clarinet,
bassoon, horn, trumpet, trombone, strings/string quintet).
Contents: I. Moderato-Allegro -- II. Andante (On a Sicilian Folk
Song) -- III. Finale (Moderato).
Commissioned by: Whitney Tustin.
Dedication: none.
Duration: 18 minutes.

FIRST PERFORMANCE

W43a.   1950. Boston, Massachusetts. Ralph Gomberg, oboe;
Boston Symphony Orchestra; Charles Munch, conductor.

BIBLIOGRAPHY

WB181. Sabin, Robert. "Two New Compositions for Oboe and
Orchestra." *Musical America* 72:26 (November 15,
1952)
Review of the Southern Music Publishing Company
publication. "Foss has not been kind to the oboist in this
concerto, but most of the difficulties are musically
justified and the rewards are solid."

WB182. "New Music: Oboe and Orchestra." *Musical Courier* 146:31 (November 15, 1952)
Review of the Southern Music Publishing Company publication. "[The work] offers considerable rhythmic freedom and vivacity of style."

WB183. Persichetti, Vincent. "Music Reviews." *Notes* 10:139 (December 1952)
Review of the Southern Music publication. "The concerto is not at the top of the list of contemporary concertos, but it has attractive soloistic qualities and a certain charm that should give it a temporary popularity in oboe circles."

W44. **Recordare** (1948; New York: Southern Music Pub. Co.; New York: Carl Fischer.)

For orchestra.
Dedication: Mahatma Gandhi.
Duration: 13 minutes.
This composition was begun on the day that Gandhi died.

FIRST PERFORMANCE

W44a. December 31, 1948. Boston Symphony Orchestra; Lukas Foss, conductor. Also premiered on this program was Howard Hanson's *Piano Concerto*. (See: WB184)

BIBLIOGRAPHY

WB184. Wolffers, Jules. "Boston Has U.S. Festival: Koussevitzky Offers Two Premieres of New Scores by Hanson and Foss." *Musical Courier* 139:8 (January 15, 1949)
Review of the December 31, 1948 premiere performance. Written by Foss in honor of Gandhi, it shows "nobility and reflectiveness." Wolffers also notes "there is a tentative atmosphere through the piece which may mark the first gropings towards a new style." (See: W44a)

WB185. Burkat, Leonard. "Current Chronicle: United States: Boston." *Musical Quarterly* 35:287-289 (April 1949)
This review of *Recordare* is also a review of Foss as composer. He is mentioned to be full of enthusiasm and capable of writing music that is at times erotic. The single theme of this slow-fast-slow twelve-minute work is unable to be developed and causes the work to be disjunct.

W45. **Elegy** (1949; New York: G. Schirmer.)

For clarinet and orchestra.
Commissioned by: Artie Shaw.

Movement II of *Concerto No. 1 for Clarinet*. (See: W37)
Duration: 9 minutes.

W46. **Concerto No. 2 for Piano and Orchestra** (1949-51; new
arrangement 1952; 2 piano score of the revised version: New
York: Carl Fischer, 1953. Pub. pl. no. N1937. Pub. no. O3838.
Full score and parts available on rental.)

For piano and orchestra (piccolo, 2 flutes, 2 oboes, 2 clarinets,
bass clarinet/tenor saxophone, 2 bassoons, contrabassoon, 4
horns, 3 trumpets, trombone, tuba, timpani, percussion,
piano, strings).
Contents: I. Allego Sostenuto -- II. Adagietto -- III. Allegro
Vivace.
Prizes: 1951 Mark M. Horblit Award (Boston Symphony); 1954
New York Music Critics' Circle Award (best new instrumental
work).
Dedication: "Dedicated to the memory of Serge Koussevitsky."
Composed in Rome, Italy (while there on a scholarship at the
American Academy).
Duration: 34 minutes.
The revision contains a completely rewritten first movement and
changes, cuts, extensions, and new endings in the second
and third movements.

FIRST PERFORMANCE

W46a.   October 7, 1951. Venice, Italy. Lukas Foss, piano;
Orchestre Venice.

OTHER PERFORMANCES

W46b.   November 2, 1951. Boston, Massachusetts. Lukas
Foss, piano; Boston Symphony Orchestra; Richard
Burgin, conductor. American premiere. (See: WB186,
WB187)

W46c.   November 17, 1951. Carnegie Hall, New York City.
Lukas Foss, piano; Boston Symphony Orchestra; Charles
Munch, conductor. New York premiere. (See: WB188,
WB189)

W46d.   June 16, 1953. 7th annual Los Angeles Music Festival,
Los Angeles, California. Lukas Foss, piano; Los Angeles
Philharmonic; Franz Waxman, conductor. Revised
version premiere; consisting of a completely rewritten
first movement, with changes, cuts, extensions, and new
endings to the second and third movements. (See:
WB191)

W46e.   November 6, 1953. Cincinnati, Ohio. Lukas Foss,
piano; Cincinnati Symphony. (See: WB192)

W46f. March 24, 1955. Chicago, Illinois. Lukas Foss, piano; Chicago Symphony; Fritz Reiner, conductor. (See: WB193)

W46g. February 1956? Lukas Foss, piano; Südwestfunk Studio Orchestra; Franz Waxman, conductor. (See: WB194)

W46h. March 25, 1960. Tchaikovsky Conservatory, Moscow. Lukas Foss, piano; Soviet State Symphony Orchestra; Aaron Copland, conductor. (See: WB195, WB196)

BIBLIOGRAPHY

WB186. "*Concerto No. 2 for Piano.*" *Boston Symphony Concert Bulletin* no. 4:168+ (November 2, 1951)
Concert notes for the first American performance, November 2, 1951. Foss writes, "The *Concerto* differs from most modern concertos...in the sense that it is not merely a concertizing piece, but rather a symphony in which the leading part is assigned to the soloist." (See: W46b)

WB187. Wolffers, Jules. "Boston Introduces Foss Piano Concerto." *Musical Courier* 144:20 (December 1, 1951)
Review of the November 2, 1951 American premiere performance. Charles Munch was to have conducted this performance but was taken ill the day before the performance. "While piano and orchestra are skillfully joined, the solo instrument predominates. The keyboard part is difficult, requiring musicianship and technical skill in equal proportions." (See: W46b)

WB188. Smith, Cecil. "Foss Piano Concerto Given New York Premiere." *Musical America* 71:20, 23 (December 1, 1951)
Review of the November 17, 1951 New York premiere performance. Mr. Munch was ill with a fever throughout this performance, however, "the performance of the concerto was superlative in every detail, and [Munch's] conducting of it constituted one of his best achievements since he took over the orchestra and one of his most successful services to music." Foss is praised for his new concerto style and excellent performance. (See: W46c)

WB189. Kolodin, Irving. "Foss and Others: In Brief." *Saturday Review* 34:42 (December 1, 1951)
Review of the November 17, 1951 performance. "To judge from the lack of glibness or conviction in this piece, neither his mind nor his heart were in it." (See: W46c)

WB190. "Horblit Award Given." *The Southwestern Musician* 18:23 (May 1952)

Announcement of the awarding of the 1951 Mark M. Horblit Award to Lukas Foss for *Concerto No. 2 for Piano*. It mentions that he was living in Rome while on a Prix de Rome scholarship.

WB191. Goldberg, Albert. "Revised Version of Foss Piano Concerto Heard in Los Angeles Music Festival." *Musical America* 73:30 (July 1953)

Review of the June 16, 1953 premiere performance of the revised version. "After the sweep of the first movement, the slow second movement sounds pale and disappointing....Mr. Foss [played] a solo part that rivals, if not outranks, most of the literature hitherto produced in this form." (See: W46d)

WB192. "*Concerto No. 2, for Piano and Orchestra*." *Cincinnati Symphony Program Notes* 73:146-152 (November 6, 1953)

Program notes for the November 6, 1953 revised version performance. It includes remarks from the critic of the *Los Angeles Times* regarding the June 1953 premiere: "It may leave you exhausted at the end, it may make you wonder who besides Mr. Foss will dare tackle it." The article also includes a brief biographical sketch of Foss and a structural description of the piece. (See: W46e)

WB193. "Chicago Symphony." *Violins and Violinists* 16:106 (March/June 1955)

Listing of the first Chicago Symphony performance March 24, 1955 with Lukas Foss, pianist and Fritz Reiner, conductor. (See: W46f)

WB194. "Konzertantes Heldenleben aus Amerika." *Melos* 23:81 (March 1956)

Review of the Südwestfunk Studio Orchestra performance. It discusses Foss's influence by Hindemith, Bach, Mozart, and Stravinsky. "The work is brilliant and powerful." (translation) (See: W46g)

WB195. "Copland and Foss in Soviet Concert." *New York Times* March 26, 1960:14.

Review of the March 25, 1960 performance. Performed were Copland's *Third Symphony*, Foss's *Concerto No. 2 for Piano*, and Shostakovich's *Ninth Symphony*. "Mr. Foss received an ovation after the performance of his difficult work....The audience called him back...and began the rhythmic applause... [demanding] an encore." (See: W46h)

WB196. Grigoriev, Leonid and Platek, Yser. "Two American Composers in Moscow." *Music Journal* 18:60-61 (June/July 1960)

Review of a performance at the Grand Hall of the
Moscow Conservatory in 1960 by Foss, pianist, the
State Symphony Orchestra, and Aaron Copland,
conductor. On the program were Copland's *Third
Symphony*, Foss's *Concerto No. 2 for Piano*, and
Shostakovich's *Ninth Symphony*. "That Foss was an
excellent pianist we could see for ourselves, for he
played his own...composition requiring a high level of
technique." (See: W46h)

W47. **Symphony of Chorales** (1955-58; New York: Carl Fischer,
rental only. Photocopy of holograph available on rental, marked
"unrevised.")

For orchestra (3 flutes (3rd doubles piccolo), oboe, English horn,
    2 clarinets, bass clarinet and/or tenor saxophone, 2 bassoons,
    contrabassoon, 4 horns, 3 trumpets, 3 trombones, tuba,
    timpani, 3 percussion, harp, optional mandolin (3rd
    movement), piano, strings).
Contents: I. Toccata (Chorale 90) -- II. Chorale 77, 78 -- III.
    Chorale 139 -- IV. Chorale 133.
Commissioned by: The Koussevitzky Music Foundation.
Dedication: "Composed for Dr. Albert Schweitzer at the request
    of the 'Friends of Albert Schweitzer' foundation, Boston,
    Mass."
Duration: 31 minutes.
Based on chorale tunes of J.S. Bach: Chorale 90, *Hilf Gott, lass
    mirs gelingen*; Chorale 77, 78, *Herr ich habe misgehandiest*;
    Chorale 139, *Nun ruhen alle Walder* (Now Slumber Does
    Descend O'er Man, Beast, Town and Land); and Chorale 133,
    Nun danket alle Gott.

FIRST PERFORMANCE

W47a.   October 24, 1958. Pittsburgh Symphony Orchestra;
         William Steinberg, conductor.

OTHER PERFORMANCES

W47b.   October 31, 1958. Symphony Hall, Boston,
         Massachusetts. Boston Symphony Orchestra; Lukas
         Foss, conductor. Boston premiere. (See: WB197, D41)

W47c.   April 9, 1959. Carnegie Hall, New York City. New York
         Philharmonic; Leonard Bernstein, conductor. New York
         premiere. Repeated April 12, 1959. (See: WB198,
         WB199, WB200, WB201, B21)

W47d.   January 18, 1963. Cincinnati, Ohio. Cincinnati
         Symphony Orchestra; Lukas Foss, conductor.
         Performance of *Chorale Prelude No. 3* only. (See:
         WB203)

BIBLIOGRAPHY

WB197. Durgin, Cyrus. "New England Opera Begins Ambitious
Boston Engagement." *Musical America* 78:40
(December 1, 1958)
Review of the October 31, 1958 Boston premiere
performance. "Mr. Foss displayed notable authority in
conducting his own music, which, though on the longish
side, and episodic, is large-scale, cleverly written, and
scored with a genuinely expert touch." (See: W47b)

WB198. "Foss Is Commentator." *New York Times* April 10,
1959:22.
Foss "discussed [*Symphony of Chorales*] and its
relationship with the Bach chorales on which it is built"
prior to its performance by the New York Philharmonic at
the April 9, 1959 concert. (See: W47c)

WB199. "Lukas Foss." *Variety* April 22, 1959:82.
Review of the April 12, 1959 performance. On
the program, Foss conducted his *Symphony of Chorales*
as well as performing on harpsichord while he conducted
Handel's *Harpsichord Concerto in F Major*, and piano
while conducting Mozart's *Piano Concerto in C Major*.
The reviewer gave Foss high marks for his conducting
and performing, but felt that he was "as yet--least
accomplished as a composer." (See: W47c)

WB200. Kolodin, Irving. "Floyd of 'Wuthering Heights'--Ward,
Foss." *Saturday Review* 42:24 (April 25, 1959)
Review of the April 9, 1959 performance. "Foss
seems determined to prove that he, too, can write
'modern music,' with results that are hardly musical and
not really modern." (See: W47c)

WB201. Sabin, Robert. "Lukas Foss Guest with Philharmonic."
Musical America 79:22-23 (May 1959)
Review of the April 9, 1959 New York premiere
performance. On this concert, Foss also conducted the
Handel F major harpsichord concerto and Mozart's K.
467 piano concerto from the keyboards. "The
Symphony of Chorales is one of the most emotionally
stirring and intellectually satisfying works of recent
decades." (See: W47c)

WB202. Copland, Aaron. "America's Young Men of Music."
Music and Musicians 9:11 (December 1960)
Foss is briefly mentioned along with Harold
Shapero, Irving Fine, Arthur Berger, and Leonard
Bernstein as coming from the "Boston School."
"*Symphony of Chorales* should certainly be heard....It
has a very original sound."

WB203. Sagmaster, Joseph. *"Chorale Prelude No. 3* from *Chorale Symphony* for Orchestra by Lukas Foss." *Cincinnati Symphony Orchestra Programs* January 18, 1963:457-466.
> Program notes for the January 18, 1963 performance. It also announces Foss's appearance as the first lecturer of the Corbett lecture series of composers at the University of Cincinnati College-Conservatory of Music on January 21, 1963. (See: W47d)

W48. Concerto for Improvising Instruments and Orchestra
(1960; manuscript)

For 5 improvising solo instruments (flute, clarinet, violoncello, percussion, and piano) and orchestra.
Contents: I. Chorale (Variations) -- II. Intermezzo (without orchestra) -- III. Finale (Fugue) -- IV.
Duration: 18 minutes.
The accompaniments for the movements are composed and performed by the members of the Improvisation Chamber Ensemble.

FIRST PERFORMANCE

W48a. October 7, 1960. Philadelphia, Pennsylvania. Improvisation Chamber Ensemble (Lukas Foss, piano; Robert Drasnin, flute; Richard Dufallo, clarinet; Howard Colf, violoncello; Charles DeLancey, percussion); Philadelphia Orchestra; Eugene Ormandy, conductor. (See: WB204, WB205, WB206, WB207)

OTHER PERFORMANCES

W48b. October 11, 1960. Carnegie Hall, New York City. Improvisation Chamber Ensemble (Lukas Foss, piano; Robert Drasnin, flute; Richard Dufallo, clarinet; Howard Colf, violoncello; Charles DeLancey, percussion); Philadelphia Orchestra; Eugene Ormandy, conductor. New York premiere. (See: WB208, WB209)

BIBLIOGRAPHY

WB204. "Classical Hipsters." *Time* 76:80 (October 24, 1960)
> This review of the October 7, 1960 premiere performance. It also includes a description of the compositional procedure Foss and the Improvisation Chamber Ensemble went through to produce the composition. The musicians refer to it as "the difference between playing slapjack and playing bridge." The author of the article compares the composition to "the small-toned, pointillistic compositions of Anton von Webern." (See: W48a)

WB205. Kolodin, Irving. "Debut of Guilini--Michel Bloch--Foss."
Saturday Review 43:29 (October 29, 1960)
Review of the October 7, 1960 premiere
performance. "In his *Concerto for Improvising Solo
Instruments and Orchestra* Lukas Foss may have hit upon
something which some other composers have sought in
vain--unreviewable music." (See: W48a)

WB206. de Schauensee, Max. "Barber Premiere." *Musical
America* 80:23 (November 1960)
Review of the October 7, 1960 premiere
performance. Referred to as a "symphonic jam session,"
Mr. de Schauensee remarks, "This made fascinating
listening and proved also a source of wonder that all
hands kept together with no detectable slipup." (See:
W48a)

WB207. Singer, Samuel L. "Philadelphia Dedicates New
$150,000 Organ." *Musical Courier* 162:20 (November
1960)
Review of the October 7, 1960 premiere
performance. Foss felt ensemble improvisation would be
taught in universities in a few years. As for the work at
hand, Singer says, "It fascinated the members of the
Orchestra. It both fascinated and frustrated many
listeners, too....The idea...is better on paper than in
performance." (See: W48a)

WB208. Cohn, Arthur. "Philadelphia Orchestra Premieres Foss
Novelty." *Musical Courier* 162:17 (November 1960)
Review of the October 11, 1960 performance. "It
was best when it touched the zone nearest true
improvisation...otherwise it left one listener rather bored.
It did stimulate the audience, even though a few left and
a boo or two was heard." (See: W48b)

WB209. Sabin, Robert. "Ormandy Celebrates Quarter Century."
Musical America 80:49 (November 1960)
Review of the October 11, 1960 performance. "I
must admit that Mr. Foss' ensemble improvisation
experiments do not seem to me to have been very
fruitful....I cannot help feeling that this particular type of
music-making is more fun for the participants than for
the listeners....It is to Mr. Ormandy's credit that he kept
everything smoothly together." (See: W48b)

W49.   Elytres (1964; Mainz: B. Schott's Söhne; New York: Carl Fischer,
1965. Performance materials available on rental.)

For chamber orchestra; may be played by 11 minimum, 22
maximum (solo flute, 2 solo violins and ensemble (3 distant
violins or groups of 1-4 each, pitchless percussion (1-3
players: medium cymbal, deep cymbal, sizzle cymbal,
suspended antique or finger cymbal, large pipe or anvil,

sandpaper, glass chimes, chimes in G# and B, almenglocken, and gong), harp, vibraphone, piano keys, piano strings).
Commissioned by: The Southern California Symphony Association.
Dedication: none.
Duration: 10 minutes.
A copy edited in pencil by Foss is located at the Music Library, State University of New York at Buffalo.
Score directions for the combinatorial possibilities for performance are in English and German.

FIRST PERFORMANCE

W49a. December 8, 1964. Los Angeles Philharmonic Orchestra; Zubin Mehta, conductor.

OTHER PERFORMANCES

W49b. April 18, 1966. Philharmonic Hall, New York City. New York Philharmonic Orchestra, Lukas Foss, conductor. (See: WB210; See also: D42)

W49c. December 7, 1982. Boston University School of Music, Boston University Concert Hall. Collegium in Contemporary Music; Lukas Foss, conductor. (See: D45; See also: W18f, W76o, W89b)

BIBLIOGRAPHY

WB210. Davis, Peter G. "NY Philharmonic: Foss and Kirchner." *High Fidelity/Musical America* 16:MA19 (July 1966)
Review of the April 18, 1966 performance. "Since all four participating instrumental groups have been assigned music of an impersonal nature--all soft and diddly, played in high registers--the chances that *Elytres* will ever sound more interesting than it did on this occasion strike me as being pretty slim." (See: W49b)

WB211. *Lukas Foss on the New Lukas Foss*. New York: Carl Fischer, 1969:8-9.
(See: B112)

WB212. Waugh, Jane L. "Chance, Choice and Lukas Foss." In *First American Music Conference, University of Keele*, 1977:37-50.
A paper from the Proceedings of the First American Music Conference, April 18-21, 1975, presented by the music department of Keele University and its Centre for American Music and the United States Information Service. Ms. Waugh discusses Foss's aleatoric music including *Time Cycle* (See: W31), *Paradigm* (See: W76), and includes an extensive discussion of *Elytres*. Performance schemes and possibilities for performance are outlined.

W50.   **For 24 Winds (Discrepancia; or, Stillscape)** (1966; Mainz: B. Schott's Söhne; New York: Carl Fischer, 1968. Pub. pl. no. N5064. Parts available on rental.)

For wind orchestra divided into 7 groups (I. 2 flutes, alto flute/3 flutes; II. 2 oboes, English horn; III. Eb clarinet, clarinet, bass clarinet/2 clarinets, bass clarinet; IV. 2 bassoons, contrabassoon; V. horn, alto saxophone, tenor saxophone, baritone saxophone/4 horns; VI. 3 trumpets/cornets, horn; VII. 3 trombones, tuba).
Dedication: none.
Duration: ca. 12 minutes.
"Any instrument can be replaced by any other wind instrument but always in the indicated register."
The original commissioned work was entitled *Stillscape*. A new explosive ending was added to the work and renamed *For 24 Winds*.

FIRST PERFORMANCE

W50a.   May 11, 1966. Caracas, Venezuela at the Inter-American Festival of Music, sponsored by the Institute of Culture and Fine Arts. The first performance was under the title *Discrepancia*.

OTHER PERFORMANCES

W50b.   July 17, 1966. Ravinia Festival, Chicago, Illinois. United States premiere.

W50c.   October 11, 1966. Berlin Festival. European premiere.

BIBLIOGRAPHY

WB213. *Lukas Foss on the New Lukas Foss.* New York: Carl Fischer, 1969:10.
(See: B112)

W51.   **Cello Concert** (1967; New York: Carl Fischer; Mainz: B. Schott's Söhne, 1968. Pub. pl. no. N5673. Solo violoncello part sold separately; orchestral material available on rental.)

For violoncello and orchestra (2 horns, trumpet, 2 trombones, harp, vibraphone, percussion, piano, piano strings, organ, strings, tape replay).
Contents: I. Prologue -- II. Lento -- III. Doppio piu Presto -- IV. Sarabande by Bach.
Commissioned by Mstislav Rostropovich for the Berlin Festival.
Dedicated to: Mstislav Rostropovich.
Duration: 28 minutes.
Sarabande based on J.S. Bach's *Sarabande in C minor* from the 5th violoncello suite. Violoncello part edited with bowings and fingerings by Rostropovich.

FIRST PERFORMANCE

W51a. March 5, 1967. Carnegie Hall, New York City. Mstislav Rostropovich, violoncello; London Symphony Orchestra; Lukas Foss, conductor. (See: WB214, WB215, WB216, WB217)

OTHER PERFORMANCES

W51b. 1966-67. Kleinhans Music Hall, Buffalo, New York. Mstislav Rostropovich, violoncello; Buffalo Philharmonic Orchestra; Lukas Foss, conductor. (See: D46)

W51c. April 1, 1973. Kleinhans Music Hall, Buffalo, New York. Douglas Davis, violoncello; Buffalo Philharmonic Orchestra; Michael Tilson Thomas, conductor.

BIBLIOGRAPHY

WB214. Hughes, Allen. "Foss Work Played by Rostropovich." *New York Times* March 6, 1967:41.
Review of the March 5, 1967 premiere performance. "The work is so far out that no other virtuoso would touch it. Mr. Rostropovich...not only touched it, he asked Mr. Foss to compose it and took the trouble to memorize it for performance." (See: W51a)

WB215. "Pffhonk!" *Time* 89:70 (March 17, 1967)
Review of the May 5, 1967 premiere performance. "The applause at the end was louder than the boos, but much of that could have been a tribute to Rostropovich's bravery rather than Foss's." (See: W51a)

WB216. "New Works: New York, Mstislav Rostropovich." *Music Journal* 25:63-64 (May 1967)
Review of the March 5, 1967 premiere performance. "On initial hearing the orchestral part seemed generally more interesting than the cellist's even when the Bach *Sarabande in C Minor* was used as raw material." The other concerts of the Rostropovich marathon are also reviewed. (See: W51a)

WB217. Fleming, Shirley. "The Rostropovich Whirlwind." *High Fidelity/Musical America* 17:MA9 (May 1967)
Detailed review of a series of eight concerts in 18 days by Rostropovich and the London Symphony Orchestra led by Gennadi Rozhdestvensky at Carnegie Hall from February 23-March 12, 1967. (See: W51a)

WB218. *Lukas Foss on the New Lukas Foss*. New York: Carl Fischer, 1969:10-11.
(See: B112)

WB219. Dale, S.S. "Contemporary Cello Concerti LXV: Foss and Klughardt." *Strad* 89:149+ (June 1978)
Provides an in-depth analysis of this aleatory composition. Of the final movement, which is based on Bach's *Sarabande* from the fifth violoncello suite, Dale states, "He is not afraid of distorting the material which I fear might cause many players and listeners to reject the work."

W52.   Baroque Variations (1967; Mainz: B. Schott's Söhne; New York: Carl Fischer, 1968. Pub. pl. no. N 5217. Pub. no. O4760.)

For orchestra (3 flutes/piccolo, recorder, 2 oboes/English horn, 3 clarinets/soprano saxophone/Eb clarinet, bassoon, soprano saxophone, 3 horns, 3 trumpets, trombone, tuba, 4 percussion (vibraphone, high and low cymbals, chimes, timpani, xylophone, bass drum, triangle, gongs, whip, drum, pipe, temple block, cowbell, claves, bottle in bag to break with hammer, tam-tam, woodchimes, anvil, woodblock), electric piano, electric guitar with foot pedal, electric organ, harpsichord, celesta,strings (minimum 6, maximum 12; bass, 3 only)).
Contents: I. On a Handel Larghetto -- II. On a Scarlatti Sonata -- III. On a Bach Prelude (Phorion).
Commissioned by: The Lincoln Center Foundation, New York City for the Lincoln Center Festival, 1967. *Phorion* commissioned by the Association of Women's Committees of Symphony Orchestras.
Dedication: none.
Duration: 25 minutes (Phorion: 10 minutes).
I. Based on Handel's *Concerto Grosso #12*; II. Based on Scarlatti's *Sonata #23*; III. Based on J.S. Bach's *Prelude* from *Partita in E major for Solo Violin*. "Phorion" is Greek for "stolen goods."

FIRST PERFORMANCE

W52a.   July 7, 1967. Ravinia. Chicago Symphony; Seiji Ozawa, conductor. First performance of the entire work.

OTHER PERFORMANCES

W52b.   April 27, 1967. Philharmonic Hall, New York City. New York Philharmonic; Leonard Bernstein, conductor. Premiere of movement III, *Phorion* only. Repeated May 1, 1967. (See: WB220, WB221)

W52c.   May 12, 1967. Musica Viva; Lukas Foss, conductor. First European performance of movement III, *Phorion*.

W52d.   March 10, 1968. Kleinhans Music Hall, Buffalo, New York. Buffalo Philharmonic Orchestra; Lukas Foss, conductor. (See: WB222, WB223; See also: D47)

W52e. September 11, 1968. Carnegie Hall, New York City. Buffalo Philharmonic Orchestra; Lukas Foss, conductor. First New York performance of the entire work. (See: WB225, WB226, WB228)

W52f. 1969. Darmstadt, Germany. Radio-Sinfonie-Orchester des Hessischen Rundfunks; Lukas Foss, conductor. (See: WB230)

W52g. 1969, between September 21 and October 9. Berlin Music Festival, Berlin, Germany. Berlin Philharmonic Orchestra; Lukas Foss, conductor. (See: WB231, WB232, WB233)

W52h. 1970. Royan, France. French Radio Orchestra; Lukas Foss, conductor. (See: WB234)

W52i. 1971. Buenos Aires, Argentina. Lukas Foss, conductor. (See: WB236)

W52j. April 25, 1975. Bühnen, Frankfurt, Germany. Kammer-Tanz-Abend der Städt. First ballet performance. (See: WB239)

W52k. 1975. Manchester, England. Hallé Orchestra; Lukas Foss, conductor. First British performance. (See: WB240)

W52l. 1985. Hannover, Germany. Rundfunkorchester Hannover; Othmar Mága, conductor. (See: WB245, WB246)

W52m. May 14, 1988. New York State Theater, New York City. New York City Ballet (Helene Alexopoulos, Lindsay Fischer, Margaret Tracey, Leslie Roy, Shawn Stevens, dancers); Ib Andersen, choreography; Barbara Matera, costume supervision; Mark Stanley, lighting; New York City Ballet Orchestra; Gordon Boelzner, conductor. Uses movements I and II only. First performance of this choreographed version. (See: WB247)

BIBLIOGRAPHY

WB220. Hughes, Allen. "Music: *Phorion* by Foss." *New York Times* April 28, 1967:32.
Review of the April 27, 1967 premiere performance. It gives information regarding the commissioning of the work, which included the guaranteed performance by ten major orchestras. "It consists in a way, of Mr. Foss's remake of the *Prelude* from Bach's *Partita in E for Solo Violin*. And what a remake!...The musical result...repelled many listeners...but if they had heard it as the score for, say, a

Fellini film...they would probably have accepted it
without question." (See: W52b)

WB221. Jacobson, Bernard. "N.Y. Philharmonic: Bernstein."
High Fidelity/Musical America 17:MA12 (July 1967)
Review of the May 1, 1967 performance. "Fifteen
entertaining minutes before the intermission were spent
on...*Phorion*...an ingenious plundering of the *Prelude*
from Bach's solo violin *Partita* in E major. The
treatment...is varied, often witty, and sometimes weirdly
beautiful." (See: W52b)

WB222. Foss, Lukas and Downes, Edward. "*Baroque Variations*
(1967)." *Buffalo Philharmonic* March 10, 1968:27-29.
In these program notes for the March 10, 1968
performance, Foss explains "the compositions are not so
much 'variations' on three familiar pieces of baroque
music as they are 'dreams' about these pieces." He
uses inaudibility techniques to keep the original work
present at all times, but in various degrees of obscurity.
(See: W52d)

WB223. Plotkin, Frederick. "Festival of the Arts Today, No. 2."
High Fidelity/Musical America 18:MA24-25 (June 1968)
Review of the festival held in Buffalo, New York,
March 2-17, 1968, including a fine arts display, dance
performances by Merce Cunningham and Company (John
Cage, musical director), and concerts by the Buffalo
Philharmonic Orchestra and the State University of New
York at Buffalo's Center for Creative and Performing
Arts. Foss's works *Non-Improvisation* (See: W75d) and
Baroque Variations were performed. "A standing ovation
greeted...*Baroque Variations*." The festival also saw the
premieres of works by Penderecki, Xenakis, and
Pousseur. (See: W52d; See also: WB353)

WB224. Jacobson, Bernard. Liner notes to Nonesuch H-71202,
1968. (See: D47)
Compares and contrast Foss's and Cage's ideas on
aleatoric composition. *Baroque Variations* is defined as a
piece where carefully notated work stands along side the
aleatoric work. It includes Foss's comments on the
work, referring to it as dreams about three familiar
Baroque works.

WB225. Schonberg, Harold C. "Foss Brings His Own *Baroque
Variations*." *New York Times* September 12, 1968:57.
Review of the September 11, 1968 performance.
"The Foss work caused the biggest commotion of the
evening, arousing mingled boos and cheers with the
cheers predominating....There were even a few hysterical
giggles from a lady up in the balcony." (See: W52e)

WB226. Dwyer, John. "Buffalo Philharmonic Emerges From N.Y. Test With Laurels." *Buffalo Evening News* September 12, 1968:72.
Review of the September 11, 1968 performance as part of the week long International Music Congress concert for music critics, scholars, and musicians from 25 countries. The Buffalo Philharmonic Orchestra, under Foss's direction, performed Isang Yun's *Re'ak*, Charles Ives' *Calcium Light Night* (arranged by Cowell), Foss's *Baroque Variations*, Krystof Penderecki's *Capriccio for Violin* (with Paul Zukofsky, violinist), and Milton Babbitt's *Correspondence*. The performance brought the Buffalo Philharmonic Orchestra to world attention and recognition for their excellent performance. (See: W52e)

WB227. Schonberg, Harold C. "M & A Reviews: The Press." *Music & Artists* 1:44 (October 1968) Excerpted from the *New York Times* September 12, 1968:57.
(See: WB225)

WB228. Brozen, Michael. "Debuts & Reappearances: Buffalo Philharmonic." *High Fidelity/Musical America* 18:MA14 (December 1968)
Review of the September 11, 1968 New York premiere performance. "The piece has certain eclectic charm, but it does go on." (See: W52e)

WB229. *Lukas Foss on the New Lukas Foss.* New York: Carl Fischer, 1969:11-12.
(See: B112)

WB230. Lewinski, Wolf-Eberhard von. "Kranichsteiner Talfahrt, 1969." *Melos* 36:429-430 (October 1969)
Review of a 1969 Darmstadt performance. "With *Baroque Variations*, Lukas Foss has made a name for himself....At times it is charming, at times reflective. But in spite of the Hammond organ, it is witty overall." (translation) (See: W52f)

WB231. Stuckenschmidt, H.H. "Blachers Jüdische Komödie und Moderne Konzerte bei den Berliner Festwochen." *Melos* 36:474-475 (November 1969)
Review of a Fall 1969 performance during which Ives's *Orchestral Set No. 2*, Hans Werner Henze's *Ariosi*, and Foss's *Baroque Variations* were performed. "*Baroque Variations* shows futuristic images of the world, but motifs from Handel, Scarlatti, and J. S. Bach also appear....Foss directed the 'unshocked' symphony members with his usual bravura." (translation) (See: W52g)

WB232. Bachmann, Claus-Henning. "Berliner Festwochen 1969." *Oesterreichische Musikzeitschrift* 24:644-645 (November 1969)

Review of the 1969 Berlin performance. "Lukas Foss, an American from Berlin, has a definate relationship with tradition. He brought along to the Philharmonic his *Baroque Variations*, which is neither a synthesis of the present and the past (as with Stravinsky) nor a conscious removal from tradition, but rather a break from what has been and an accumulation of fragments into a composed memory, a dream of the rest." (translation) (See: W52g)

WB233. Stibilj, Milan. "Berlinske svecane nedelje 1969." *Zvuk* n. 101:50-51 (1970)

Review of a concert by the Berlin Philharmonic Orchestra, Lukas Foss, conductor, at the Berlin Music Festival, September 21-October 9, 1969. Foss conducted Ives's *Orchestral Set No. 2* and his own *Baroque Variations*. Of the latter, it was appreciated by the audience, although the author questioned the lasting artistic value of this avant-garde music. (Article in Yugoslavian.) (See: W52g)

WB234. Gill, Dominic. "Festivals: Royan." *Musical Times* 111:631-632 (June 1970)

Review of a new-music festival held in Royan, France during which the French Radio Orchestra under Foss's direction performed his *Baroque Variations*. "The tension broke, seizing the audience in its frenzy. The music ended in uproar, the audience standing, cheering, screaming, applauding, shouting abuse....As one young lady raced down the aisle to hurl her chair into the orchestra, one did pause to wonder if perhaps she wasn't taking the improvisatory elements in her score a little too seriously." (See: W52h)

WB235. Foss, Lukas. "Foss Talks About 'Stolen Goods' and the Mystique of the New." *Music and Artists* 3:34-35 (September/October 1970)

In his use of Bach's *Partita in E major for solo violin*, Foss defends that he is not destroying Bach, but rather using it as source material. He describes the different techniques he used in composing and performing this work.

WB236. Montes, J. "Buenos Aires hat Moderne Konzerte in Huelle und Fuelle." *Melos* 38:157-158 (April 1971)

Review of a 1971 concert in Buenos Aires where Foss conducted *Baroque Variations* as well as other compositions. "*Baroque Variations* is a work with remarkable power....It is an amusing piece also, composed with a good ear for instrumental effects,

although somewhat too long." (translation) (See:
W52i)

WB237. Myers, Marceau Chevalier. "A Study and Interpretive
Analysis of Selected Aleatory Compositions for Orchestra
by American Composers." Ed.D. diss., Columbia
University, 1972:60-77. *Dissertation Abstracts* 33:904A
(September 1972) UMI# 72-23709.
  Phorion is analysed and its performance
procedures are discussed in this dissertation. "A major
portion of the study is devoted to the development of
interpretive analyses of four selected aleatory orchestral
compositions by American composers....In *Phorion* Lukas
Foss has constructed an aleatory composition in which
the various possibilities for employing choice and chance
are limitless, and yet he is able to maintain some degree
of control over the composition's final outcome."

WB238. Gruhn, Wilfried. "Bearbeitung als Kompositorische
Reflexion in Neuer Musik: Lukas Foss: *Baroque
Variations* (1967)." *Musica* 28:525-528
(November/December 1974)
  In this discussion of arrangement as compositional
reflection in new music, Foss's *Baroque Variations
(Phorion)* is analysed. "Foss uses the *Partita* of Bach,
destroys its syntactical structure and injects his own
meaning. One no longer hears Bach...but hears Foss
instead....Bach's *Partita* is turned into a kaleidoscope of
sounds." (translation)

WB239. "Uraufführungen." *Musikhandel* 26:172 (no. 4, (1975)
  Listing of the first performance with ballet, April
25, 1975. (See: W52j)

WB240. Larner, Gerald. "Manchester." *Musical Times* 116:559
(June 1975)
  Review of the first British performance. "There are
three movements... offering long quotations perforated
with silences in which the orchestra continues to scrape
and blow, but without producing a sound." (See:
W52k)

WB241. Braun, William Ray. "Three Uses of Pre-existent Music in
the Twentieth Century." D.M.A. diss., University of
Missouri, Kansas City, 1974. *Dissertation Abstracts*
36:7033A (May 1976)
  The author has analyzed several works, including
Foss's *Baroque Variations*, to show how many 20th
century composers are using pre-existent music to
compose their works. "[Foss] turned to pre-existent
music not only in [his] search for material and inspiration,
but to fill a need for new compositional techniques,
styles, and even personal identity."

WB242. Dibelius, Ulrich. "Historisches Bewusstsein und Irrationalität." In *Die Neue Musik und die Tradition*. Mainz: B. Schott's Söhne, c1978:69-79. *RILM* #78-4225.

"The development of music since 1945 is described as a departure from the fundamental assumptions of composition;...recent music reflects more thoroughly the social situation, its purposes, and its possibilities." (translation) *Baroque Variations* is referred to in this paper.

WB243. Gruhn, Wilfried. "Lukas Foss *Phorion*; die Obsession eine Melodie von Johann Sebastian Bach in den *Baroque Variations*." *Musik und Bildung* 13:140-153 (March 1981)

This analytical article on *Phorion* centers around the "obsession of a melody" in the compositional style. Foss explained that "*Baroque Variations* are not so much variations on three familiar Baroque works as they are dreams about these works....The experience of the listener can be compared to a look into a kaleidoscope." (translation) The conclusion of the article includes material for lesson planning such as the reworking of older music, introduction to new music, form, variations, and the relation of new composer and old music.

WB244. Hambroeus, Bengt. "Drömmen om Havsvågan och Sextondelsnoterna; en Kommentar till Lukas Foss' *Phorion*." *Nutida Musik* 26:43-44 (no. 1, 1982/1983)

The author presents a discussion on the composition of *Baroque Variations*, with references to the borrowed materials and when and for whom it was composed. It contains an excerpt from the Carl Fischer score for *Phorion*. (Article in Swedish.)

WB245. Gojowy, Detlef. "Das Leibhaftige Knurren des Andalusischen Hundes: Die Tage der Neuen Musik Hannover 1985." *Neue Zeitschrift für Musik* 146:43 (March 1985)

Concert listing of a Bach-Handel-Scarlatti 1685/1985 concert by the Rundfunkorchester Hannover, Othmar Mága, conductor, which also included works by Stockhausen, Krol, and Leitermeyer. (See: W52l)

WB246. Schönburg, Wolf-Christoph von. "Berührung Mit den Anderen Künsten: Bei den 27. Tagen der Neuen Musik in Hannover." *Neue Musikzeitung* 34:2 (April/May 1985)

This concert was one of the high points of the new music festival in Hannover. The article describes how theater, ballet, and film elements were incorporated into the performances. (See: W52l)

WB247. Kisselgoff, Anna. "Ray Charles at a Peter Martins City Ballet Premiere." *New York Times* May 16, 1988:C14.

> Review of the May 14, 1988 ballet performance.
> "Mr. Andersen...has sophisticated ideas worth
> developing....The spare and provocative treatment Mr.
> Foss gives to Baroque music does not find its equivalent
> in the contrast Mr. Andersen sets up between a
> contemporary duet..." (See: W52m)

W53.　**Geod** (1969; New York: Carl Fischer; Mainz: B. Schott's Söhne,
1973, c1969. Pub. pl. no. N5610. Pub. no. O4894. Orchestral
material available on rental.)

For large orchestra in four groups (I. 8 violin 1, 8 violin 2, 8 violin
3, 8 violas, 8 violoncellos, 8 basses; II. flute, alto flute,
English horn, 2 clarinets, bass clarinet, 3 bassoons, electric
piano, electric harpsichord, harp; III. 2 trumpets, 4 horns, 3
trombones; IV. 11 instruments (preferably folk instruments of
the country of performance), (boy) soprano or small choir
(men and women/women only/children only); 4 percussion (1.
pedal timpani, Japanese bowl, Jews harp, xylophone, blocks;
2. 2 or 3 antique cymbals, 2 suspended cymbals, glass
chimes, triangle; 3. chimes, timbali/bongos, traps; 4. 2
different size gongs, 3 or 4 cowbells, tambourine)); with
optional voices or choir.
Written for Reicha Frier.
Dedication: none.
Duration: 28-45 minutes.
Parts are in score format. The work involves a principal
    conductor and four sub-conductors, one for each of the four
    groups into which the orchestra is divided.

FIRST PERFORMANCE

W53a.　1969. Jerusalem Symphony.

OTHER PERFORMANCES

W53b.　December 6, 1969. Radio House, Hamburg, Germany.
　　　Norddeutscher Rundfunk, NDR-Sinfonieorchester; Lukas
　　　Foss, Stewart Challender, Mathias Husmann, Christof
　　　Prick, Helmut Franz, conductors. Performed with
　　　German folk music. Repeated January 16, 1970. (See:
　　　WB248, WB249, WB250, WB251, WB252, WB254,
　　　WB255)

W53c.　March 17, 1970. Kleinhans Music Hall, Buffalo, New
　　　York. Buffalo Philharmonic Orchestra; The Road; The
　　　Grateful Dead; Lukas Foss, Melvin Strauss, Fred Ressel,
　　　Jesse Levine, William Lane, conductors. The
　　　performance also included Sonavision's (Michigan) laser-
　　　beam and prism light show. American premiere. (See:
　　　WB256, WB257, WB258, WB259; See also: W75e)

W53d.　January 22, 1971. Munich Musica Viva Festival,
　　　Munich, Germany. Symphonieorchester des Bayerischen

Rundfunks; Lukas Foss, conductor. (See: WB260, WB262, WB264)

W53e. March 11, 1972. Brooklyn Academy of Music, Brooklyn, New York. Brooklyn Philharmonia; Lukas Foss, conductor. (See: WB265, WB266; See also: W75g, W76i)

W53f. January 24, 1973. Köln. Bühnen der Stadt Köln. First performance as a ballet.

BIBLIOGRAPHY

WB248. Pollner, Von Ludwig. "Musik aus Buffalo: Alt für Neu." *Hamburger Morgenpost* December 8, 1969.
  Review of the December 6, 1969 performance. "The first performance of *Geod* proved Foss to be an amazing theoretician. As for his music, he says it best himself, 'A music without beginning or end, without development, without rhetoric.'...One thing is sure: one must respect Lukas Foss." (translation) (See: W53b)

WB249. "Macht und Ohnmacht der Phantasie." *Hamburger Abendblatt* December 8, 1969.
  Review of the December 6, 1969 performance. "After 23 minutes of questions and puzzles, the public left the first performance of *Geod Non-Improvisation II*....No doubt about it: this new work equalled a declaration of bankruptcy of musical imagination. Even the use of German folk music or tuba and Jew's harp offered no more than isolated dabs of color." (translation) (See: W53b)

WB250. Linke, Norbert. "Hohenfriedberger und Loreley." *Die Welt* December 8, 1969.
  Review of the December 6, 1969 performance. "The audience reacted in a perplexed manner to this 25-minute work, although they were warned in the program that 'the audience should not expect to be taught, shocked, or amused.'" (translation) (See: W53b)

WB251. Hofmann, Will. "Provokation im Neuen Werk: Fast Hundertprozentiges Buh für Lucas Foss." *Marburger Anzeigen und Nachrichten* December 9, 1969.
  Review of the December 6, 1969 performance. "One noticed immediately that the German folk songs had more value than the howling whine [of Foss's work]...A similar disappointment with almost everyone booing has never occurred in the history of this institution...The public was extremely annoyed." (translation) (See: W53b)

WB252. Wagner, Klaus. "Eine Unbeantwortete Frage: Werke von Charles Ives und Lukas Foss in Hamburg." *Frankfurter Allgemeine* December 17, 1969.
     Review of the December 6, 1969 performance. Also performed was Ives's *The Unanswered Question*. "The combination of Charles Ives and Lukas Foss' work made for an interesting and important evening....*Geod* combined elements of Prussian marches and folk songs...The music seemed like a mobile that circled in and around itself...and as if with a reference to Charles Ives and Thoreau, Foss acknowledged his ideal listener, 'He doesn't listen, he pays attention as if he's paying attention to nature.'...But there was no talk of such Rousseau-like a setting in the Hamburg concert. The audience was young and impatient....The question that Lukas Foss posed on whether national music is still possible or is already impossible was not answered, not decided. It remains open, like the form Foss chose; or, expressed by the title of one of Charles Ives' works, it remains 'The Unanswered Question.'" (See: W53b)

WB253. Wagner, Klaus. "Foss Dirigiert Foss im Hamburger 'Neuen Werk.'" *Melos* 37:53 (February 1970) (See: WB254)

WB254. Wagner, Klaus. "Foss Fuss: Helpless Laughter in Hamburg." *American Musical Digest* 1:23 (no. 6, 1970). Translated and abridged from *Melos*, February 1970 (See: WB253)
     Review of the January 16, 1970 premiere performance of *Geod* over North German Radio with Foss as conductor. "It was noteworthy that the young people were the ones who showed their impatience...Toward the end they gave rather drastic expression to it, with sounds of dogs barking and cats meowing, to the point where hardened members of the orchestra doubled up in laughter..." (See: W53b)

WB255. Foss, Lukas. "An Open Letter." *American Musical Digest* 1:23-25 (no. 6, 1970)
     An open letter to the members of the North German Radio Symphony Orchestra after their less than professional performance of *Geod*. Foss's critical review of the performance is given here in this English translation of the original letter first published in the *Frankfurter Allgemeine Zeitung*, February 10, 1970. (See: W53b)

WB256. Dwyer, John. "New World of Music for a Young Audience." *Buffalo Evening News* March 18, 1970:78.
     Review of the March 17, 1970 American premiere performance. "It's another Foss dream mosaic like *Phorion*, but with more explicit and direct nostalgia and childhood recall....Never mind culture's influence on the

teen-ager. Just think of it the other way around, and you'll see it was an important event." (See: W53c)

WB257. Brennan, James. "Orchestra's Rapport with Rock Bands Electrifies Audience." *Buffalo Evening News* March 18, 1970:78.
Review of the March 17, 1970 performance otherwise known as the "Philharmonic Rock Marathon." "One could feel the extraordinary rapport between the [Grateful] Dead's rock and the orchestral prose, and also between both of these and the highly responsive young audience." The short sets that the Dead and the Road performed are described, as well as the combined works on the program, *Geod* and *Non-Improvisation* (See: W75e). "The closing rock-Philharmonic challenge is the most exciting new concept of contemporary music....a rock audience finally listening to a symphony group on its own terms." (See: W53c; See also: WB354)

WB258. Putnam, Thomas. "Marathon." *American Musical Digest* 1:37 (no. 6, 1970) Excerpt from the *Buffalo Courier Express*, March 18, 1970.
Review of the March 17, 1970 performance. Referred to as "a strange imbalance of ecstasy and cool," the concert included sets by the individual rock bands and orchestra, works involving orchestra members with the rock bands, and a laser light show all to benefit the fiscally troubled Buffalo Philharmonic Orchestra. (See: W53c; See also: WB259)

WB259. Putnam, Thomas. "Foss Premiere." *High Fidelity/Musical America* 20:18 (June 1970)
Review of the March 17, 1970 American premiere performance. The performance employed five conductors (including Foss) and included a laser-beam light show. "*Geod* is a nostalgic, Ivesian collection of familiar tunes, played against a soft curtain of sustained tones." The concert concluded with a jam-session including The Road and the Grateful Dead with the Philharmonic which was "unprepared and unspontaneous." (See: W53c; See also: WB258)

WB260. Danler, Karl-Robert. "Hörbare und Unhörbare Musik: Lukas Foss in Münchens 'Musica Viva.'" *Neue Musikzeitung* 20:18 (February/March 1971)
Review of a performance at the second concert of the Munich Musica Viva Festival by the Symphonieorchester des Bayerischen Rundfunks, Lukas Foss, conductor. Foss describes *Geod's* "inaudible music" as "music without beginning and end....The listener is not allowed to be instructed, shocked, or amused for long. He should not pay attention, but should eavesdrop." (translation) (See: W53d; See also: WB263)

WB261. Pataki, Ladislaus. "Israeli Musik-Wochen." *Das Orchester* 19:150-151 (March 1971)
Review of a performance during Israeli Music Week in 1971(?) "In *Geod*, Lukas Foss laments the destruction of Jerusalem and the temple....He doesn't quite escape the danger of letting the initial striking impression sink too often into monotony." (translation)

WB262. "Muenchner Konzerte: 2. Konzerte der 'Musica Viva'." *Oper und Konzert* 9:22 (March 1971)
Review of the January 22, 1971 concert in Munich. "Both lively applause and amused boos greeted Foss's *Geod*....On a purely musical note, the performance was not quite amusing or pleasant enough to not become a little tiresome." (translation) (See: W53d)

WB263. Danler, Karl-Robert. "Unhörbare Musik--Hörbar Gemacht: Lukas Foss in Münchens." *Das Orchester* 19:144-145 (March 1971)
This is the same as Danler, Karl-Robert. "Hörbare und Unhörbare Musik: Lukas Foss in Münchens 'Musica Viva.'" (See: WB260)

WB264. Schmidt-Garre, Helmut. "Muenchen: Musica Viva--Immer Interessant." *Neue Zeitschrift für Musik* 132:257 (May 1971)
Review of the first performance of *Geod* on the second Musica Viva concert of the season in Munich. The work is referred to as "a trial exploration into the frontier of development." (translation) (See: W53d)

WB265. Davis, Peter G. "Philharmonia Puts Focus on Conductor In a Foss Marathon." *New York Times* March 13, 1972:41.
Review of the March 11, 1972 American music marathon. *Geod* was presented twice to display the aleatory aspects of the work. "The not unpleasant effect is rather like drowsing in a hammock on a summer night listening to echoes from the county fair on the other side of town." Also performed was *Paradigm* (See: W53e; See also: WB366).

WB266. Johnson, Tom. "A Hectic & Haphazard Success." *Village Voice* March 16, 1972.
Review of the American Music Marathon at the Brooklyn Academy of Music, March 11, 1972. Performed was a set of Foss's works including *Geod*, interrupted by *Non-Improvisation* (See: W75g), and *Paradigm* (See: W76i). "The total effect was almost macabre....How is it possible that an event which is so haphazard in purely musical terms, and so vague in theatrical terms, can be so successful in its own terms?

It is a very curious medium." (See: W53e; See also: WB357, WB367)

WB267. Harran, Don. "Report from Israel: Testimonium II, 1971." *Current Musicology* no. 15:38-40 (1973)
Review of the second in a series of concerts devoted to new compositions dealing with Jewish suffering throughout history. This concert dealt with the Middle Ages and was given in 1971. As for its Jewish theme, "in *Geod* the future of the world emerges into view, and there in the center stands Jerusalem!" Of the text, since German, American, and Indian raga versions exist, "*Geod* could just as well have been about any city."

WB268. Austin, William W. *Susanna, Jeanie, and The Old Folks at Home: The Songs of Stephen C. Foster From His Time To Ours*. New York: Macmillan, 1975: 317, 335-337.
This section explains the influence Stephen Foster had on contemporary composers, including Foss. In his selection of folk songs for use in *Geod*, Foss chose "Old Folks at Home" as source material.

W54.   **Orpheus** (1972; Paris; New York: Éditions Salabert; distributed by G. Schirmer, 1974. Pub. pl. no. E.A.S. 17113. Fully realized solo parts for violoncello, viola, or violin are available from the publisher.)

For violin/viola/violoncello and full/chamber orchestra (2 oboes, 2 harps, 2 chimes, piano-strings, strings), with tape delay (electronic echo).
Dedication: "for Gregor Piatigorsky."
Duration: ca. 21 minutes.
Composed in Villa Serbelloni, Bellagio, Italy.
A second version of this work was composed as *Orpheus and Euridice* (See: W62).

FIRST PERFORMANCE

W54a.   June 2, 1973. Ojai Festival, Ojai, California. Jesse Levine, viola; Ojai Festival Orchestra; Michael Tilson Thomas, conductor. (See: WB269)

OTHER PERFORMANCES

W54b.   January 29, 1979. Alice Tully Hall, Lincoln Center, New York City. Jesse Levine, viola; American Composers Orchestra; Lukas Foss, conductor. New York premiere. (See: WB270, WB271)

W54c.   January 29, 1988. Cooper Union, New York City. Jesse Levine, viola; Brooklyn Philharmonic Orchestra; Lukas Foss, conductor. (See: WB272, WB273)

BIBLIOGRAPHY

WB269. Monson, Karen. "Ojai: A Profusion of Premiers." *High Fidelity/Musical America* 23:MA21 (September 1973)
Review of the June 2, 1973 premiere performance. "*Orpheus* capitalizes on witty (not funny) aural fantasy." (See: W54a)

WB270. Schonberg, Harold C. "Music: A Night of Three Premieres." *New York Times* January 30, 1979:C8.
Review of the January 29, 1979 New York premiere performance. Along with the New York premiere of Foss's work, the New York premiere of Louise Talma's *The Tolling Bell* and the world premiere of Jeffrey Schwantner's *Aftertones of Infinity* were performed as well as Carl Ruggles's *Men and Mountains*. "*Orpheus* is one of those quasi-theater pieces that was considered hot stuff some 10 years ago....Here it is 1979, and already *Orpheus* is a weak period piece." (See: W54b)

WB271. Johnson, Tom. "*Orpheus* and the 'Solar Winds.'" *Village Voice* February 12, 1979: 79+
Review of the January 29, 1979 New York premiere performance. "As the music passes through its five or six distinctly different moods, specific musical techniques may occasionally remind one of the music of other composers, but Foss, the synthesizer, knits all of these sounds together into a seamless fabric that fits its subject like a glove. *Orpheus* is undoubtedly one of his finest works." (See: W54b)

WB272. Rockwell, John. "Music: Foss Series On Moderns." *New York Times* January 31, 1988:I,56.
Review of the January 29, 1988 concert entitled "Orpheus in the 20th Century" by the Brooklyn Philharmonic Orchestra. "The soulful sounds of the viola interacting with the string orchestra, which crowed and whooped and sighed along with him, was very telling." (See: W54c)

WB273. Porter, Andrew. "Another Orpheus Sings." *New Yorker* 64:106-107 (June 6, 1988)
Review of the January 29, 1988 Meet the Moderns concert. It included several twentieth century composers's renderings of the story of Orpheus as well as Foss's *Orpheus* with Jesse Levine as viola soloist. (See: W54c)

W55. **Fanfare** (1973; Paris: Éditions Salabert; New York: G. Schirmer.)

For orchestra.
Commissioned by: United States Information Agency for the 1st Istanbul Festival.

Duration: 10 minutes.

FIRST PERFORMANCE

W55a.   1973, between June 21 and July 15. Istanbul, Turkey.
Turkish Presidential Symphony of Ankara; no conductor.
(See: WB274)

BIBLIOGRAPHY

WB274. Bruno, Anne Turner. "Who Sent Lukas Foss as U. S.
Rep.?" *Variety* August 15, 1973:18.
Review of the highly successful first Istanbul
Festival, June 21-July 20, 1973. The work "was far
from joyous and earned no fans." The festival director
felt that the work was "not appropriate for a 50th
anniversary." (See: W55a)

W56.   Concerto for Solo Percussion and Orchestra (1974; Paris: Éditions Salabert, 1975.)

For solo percussion (Japanese bowl, marimba, 2 handbells on
xylophone, cymbal, wood blocks, temple blocks, claves,
cowbell, saw, bass drum, tom toms, anvil, log drum, bongos,
superball mallet, timpani sticks, Klaxon or bull horn, wood
chimes or small strung-up bells) and large orchestra
(flute/piccolo, oboe, clarinet/soprano saxophone, bassoon,
horn, 2 trumpets, 2 trombones, tuba, 3 percussion (I.
vibraphone, 3 timpani; II. chimes, bells; III. metal sheet,
cymbal, large tam tam, thin threaded rod), piano, electric
guitar, electric organ, strings)or small orchestra (same
woodwinds, brass, percussion, and keyboards, plus 5 violins,
2 violas, 2 violoncellos, and 1 bass [26 total]).
Commissioned by: the Ford Foundation for 1972 Ford award
winner Jan Williams.
Dedication: none.
Duration: 30 minutes.
Subtitled "All the Angels Have Big Feet" after Ezra Pound.

FIRST PERFORMANCE

W56a.   April 9, 1975. Fine Arts Building Auditorium, Rutgers
University, Camden, New Jersey. Jan Williams,
percussion; New Jersey Symphony Orchestra; Jesse
Levine, conductor. Repeated April 10, 1975, Glassboro
State College, Glassboro, New Jersey; April 13, 1975,
Orrie de Nooyer Auditorium, Hackensack, New Jersey.

OTHER PERFORMANCES

W56b.   June 23, 1975. Tel-Aviv. Jan Williams, percussion;
Israel Philharmonic Orchestra; Lukas Foss, conductor.

W56c.   October 6-7, 1975. Berlin. Jan Williams, percussion; resident orchestra; Lukas Foss, conductor. Recorded for Berlin Radio. (See: WB275)

W56d.   October 15, 1975. Paris. Jan Williams, percussion; Orchestre Nationale; Lukas Foss, conductor. European premiere. (See: WB275)

W56e.   February 22, 1976. Carnegie Hall, New York City. Jan Williams, percussion; American Symphony Orchestra; Kazuyoshi Akiyama, conductor. First New York performance. (See: WB275, WB276, WB277, WB278)

W56f.   May 7, 1976. Community Arts Auditorium, Detroit, Michigan. Jan Williams, percussion; Detroit Symphony Orchestra; Lukas Foss, conductor.

W56g.   September 3, 1976. Artpark, Lewiston, New York. Jan Williams, percussion; chamber orchestra; Lukas Foss, conductor; mechanical conductor by the Ashford Hollow Foundation. First chamber orchestra performance.

W56h.   April 18, 1982. Slee Chamber Hall, State University of New York at Buffalo. Jan Williams, percussion; Compass Players; James Kasprowicz, conductor. (See: WB279, WB280; See also: W18d, W76n, W109b)

W56i.   October 7, 1982. Composers' Forum, Symphony Space, New York City. Jan Williams, percussion; Jesse Levine, conductor. (See: WB281; See also: W18e, W88f, W109e)

BIBLIOGRAPHY

WB275. Putnam, Thomas. "Creative Troupe Off to Iceland." *Buffalo Courier Express* September 14, 1975:26.
           Outlines a 1975 tour by the State University of New York at Buffalo Creative Associates which also included *Ni Bruit Ni Vitesse* (See: W79). Williams continued in Europe after the Creative Associates tour to perform the *Concerto* in Berlin and Paris (See: W56c, W56d). The article also announces the New York premiere (See: W56e). "Foss would like to do away with the conductor. Mostly, the conductor is a metronome in this piece....In the chamber version [Foss] has the idea that a mechanical conductor can be constucted."

WB276. Hastings, Baird. "*Concerto for Solo Percussion and Orchestra*." *Carnegie Hall Program Notes* February 22, 1976:10.
           Program notes for the February 22, 1976 performance. Foss provides the following information on the work for the notes: "The percussionist/magician

affects the rest of the ensemble whatever he does. Wherever he turns or walks, a musical activity comes to pass....Though no two performances of the *Percussion Concerto* will be alike, the detail is tightly controlled by notation, traditional and new, and by footnotes and diagrams." (See: W56e)

WB277. Johnson, Harriett. "Lukas Foss' Big Boom." *New York Post* February 23, 1976:19.
Review of the February 22, 1976 New York premiere performance. "It is scored most ingeniously and emphatically for a variety of percussion...Rhythmically it ran like mad and Williams with it....Williams...proved by his autocratic command that beyond doubt he was the Primo Donno Assoluto of the day." (See: W56e)

WB278. Henahan, Donal. "Foss Creates Frolic for Percussionist." *New York Times* February 23, 1976:20.
Review of the February 22, 1976 New York premiere performance. "The concerto managed to stir up some theatrical interest...[however] much of this struck one as left over from esthetic ideas and performing experiments that seemed promising in the 1960's but have lost their punch...Mr. Williams, an extraordinary percussionist, made a great personal success of his part..." (See: W56e)

WB279. Putnam, Thomas. "UB Features Foss Creations." *Buffalo Courier Express* April 19, 1982:B6.
Review of the 60th birthday concert at the State University of New York at Buffalo, April 18, 1982. "The theatrical progress involved Williams in confrontations with the various instrumental sections....The orchestra...[serves] as the army that the soloist battles....The *Percussion Concerto* is successful because of Williams' commitment to it, it is performer music composed for an extraordinary performer." (See: W56h; See also: WB98, WB370, WB447)

WB280. Trotter, Herman. "Influence of Foss Recalled in Program Saluting Composer." *Buffalo Evening News* April 19, 1982:B9.
Review of the April 18, 1982 performance as part of a concert celebrating Foss's 60th year. "[Williams] gave a virtuoso performance...[with] formidable technique. The cannonading final moments brought cheers and shouts from the audience." (See: W56h; See also: WB99, WB371, WB448)

WB281. Holland, Bernard. "Concert: Lukas Foss Works Played at Composers' Forum." *New York Times* October 10, 1982:85.

Review of the October 7, 1982 performance. "Armed with mallets, Mr. Williams stalked through a 25-person orchestra eliciting sound from the players nearest him as he went, and whacking every percussion instrument in sight. The music offered a harrowing sonic violence and then threw in a Sousa march for comic relief." (See: W56i; See also: WB100, WB399, WB449)

W57. **Folksong for Orchestra** (1975-76; revised 1978; Paris; New York: Editions Salabert, 1976. Pub. pl. no. E.A.S.17250; revised version, New York: Éditions Salabert, 1978.)

For orchestra (woodwind I: flute/piccolo, oboe, clarinet, bassoon; woodwind II: flute, oboe, clarinet, bassoon; woodwind III: flute/piccolo, oboe, clarinet, bassoon; brass I: trumpet, 2 horns, trombone; brass II. trumpet, 2 horns, trombone; brass III: trumpet horn, trombone, tuba; xylophone, traps, piano, solo contrabass, harp, timpani, violins 1, 2, and 3, violas 1, 2, and 3, violoncellos 1, 2, and 3, basses 1, 2, and 3).
"Composed for the Baltimore Symphony Orchestra, Sergiu Comissiona, music director."
Dedication: none.
Duration: 13 minutes.
Photocopy of holograph with emendations in blue and red crayon, and pencil is located at the New York Public Library. On title page: "Old score with sketches for revision (in pencil)."
The directions for directing the combinatorial work are written in French and English. The main body of the work directs the performers to play either the notes in the boxes or the notes not in boxes. These are to alternate with silences by the performers.

FIRST PERFORMANCE

W57a. January 21, 1976. Lyric Theatre, Baltimore, Maryland. Baltimore Symphony Orchestra; Sergiu Comissiona, conductor. (See: WB282, WB283, WB284)

BIBLIOGRAPHY

WB282. Foss, Lukas. *"Folksong for Orchestra." Baltimore Symphony Orchestra Programs* p. 10 (January 21-22, 1976)
Program notes for the January 21, 1976 premiere performance. The notes were taken from Foss's description of the work on the original score manuscript. The work consists mainly of fragments of folksongs emerging and fading from the orchestra. (See: W57a)

WB283. "Premieres." *Music Journal* 34:28 (March 1976)
Notice of the January 21, 1976 premiere performance. "On the score of the piece Mr. Foss wrote: '*Folksong* is in essence a romantic, even nostalgic

> evocation of what I heard and loved when I came to
> America as a boy....'" (See: W57a)

WB284. Galkin, Elliott W. "Premieres: Foss, Moss, Weisgall."
High Fidelity/Musical America 26:MA21-22 (June 1976)
Review of the January 21, 1976 premiere
performance. "Foss recalls those folk tunes which he
learned during his youth...and exploits them brilliantly in
an evocation of spatial effects." (See: W57a)

W58. Salomon Rossi Suite (1974; Paris: Éditions Salabert; New
York: G. Schirmer, 1978, c1976. Pub. pl. no. E.A.S. 17.262.
Photocopy of holograph published. Parts available on rental.)

For orchestra (piccolo/soprano recorder, 2 oboes (2nd doubles
English horn), 2 bassoons, 2 trumpets, 2 trombones, harp, 3
timpani, strings (string quintet or string orchestra)).
Contents: I. Moderato Con Moto -- II. Allegro -- III. Andante -- IV.
Allegretto Sostenuto -- V. Lento -- VI. Allegro.
Composed on an NEA C/L Program Fellowship for the Jerusalem
Symphony Orchestra's 1974 tour.
Dedication: Jerusalem Symphony Orchestra.
Duration: 10 minutes.
Based on several sinfonia, a gagliarda and a sonata by Salomon
Rossi (cf. Newman, Joel & Rikko, Fritz. *A Thematic Index to
the Works of Salomon Rossi.* Hackensack, NJ: Joseph
Boonin, Inc., 1972): I. Sinfonia à4 (Newman & Rikko 276) --
II. Sinfonia 3 à3 (Newman & Rikko 293) -- III. Sinfonia à4
(Newman & Rikko 277) -- IV. Gagliarda à4 & à3 si placet detta
la Zambalina (Newman & Rikko 306) VI. Sinfonia à4
(Newman & Rikko 280). This piece was used as the basis for
Measure for Measure (See: W34).

FIRST PERFORMANCE

W58a. 1974. Jerusalem Symphony Orchestra.

OTHER PERFORMANCES

W58b. July 29, 1977. Indiana University School of Music.
Indiana University Festival Orchestra; Lukas Foss,
conductor. (See: D51)

W58c. February 5, 1983. Kleinhans Music Hall, Buffalo, New
York. Buffalo Philharmonic Orchestra; Lukas Foss,
conductor. (See: WB286)

BIBLIOGRAPHY

WB285. Foss, Lukas. "Program Notes: *Salomon Rossi Suite.*"
Paris: Éditions Salabert; New York: G. Schirmer, 1978,
c1976.
Program notes to the score. "The entire suite is a
20th century composer's loving homage to Rossi much

in the way Stravinsky's *Monumentum pro Gesualdo* is an homage to the Renaissance composer. Stravinsky, like Foss, had the respect to leave the notes alone, and to build with them a larger structure which can be played with modern instruments, without the loss of the old spirit."

WB286. Trotter, Herman. "Return of Lukas Foss Is Event to Remember For Those Who Do." *Buffalo Evening News* February 6, 1983:B3.
     Review of the February 5, 1983 performance. "The 1975 *Suite*...is [Foss's] reworking of themes by that recently rediscovered Renaissance composer for full modern orchestra...almost as though Foss were placing a magnifying glass over first one section of the orchestra then another....[It is a] highly attractive work." (See: W58c)

WB287. Bassin, Joseph Philip. "An Overview of the Third Period Compositional Output of Lukas Foss, 1976-1983." Ed.D., Columbia University Teachers College, 1987:108-112. *Dissertation Abstracts* 48:1573A-1574A (January 1988) UMI# 87-21079.
     (See: B216)

W59. **Quintets for Orchestra** (1979; New York: Pembroke, 1979. Pub. pl. no. PCB115.)

For orchestra divided into five groups (I. 2 flutes, 2 clarinets, bass clarinet; II. 2 oboes, English horn, 2 bassoons; III. trumpet, 2 horns, 2 trombones; 2 trumpets, horn, trombone, tuba; IV. organ; violin 1 and 2, viola, violoncello, bass; V. timpani/percussion, electric organ).
Dedication: none.
Duration: 17 minutes.
Originally composed for brass quintet (see: *Brass Quintet*, W86) and subsequently arranged for chorus (see: *Then the Rocks on the Mountain Begin to Shout*, W21).

FIRST PERFORMANCE

W59a. April 30, 1979. Severance Hall, Cleveland, Ohio. Cleveland Orchestra; Lukas Foss, conductor. (See: WB288)

OTHER PERFORMANCES

W59b. February 6, 1980. Indiana University School of Music, Bloomington, Indiana. Indiana University Symphony Orchestra; Thomas Baldner, conductor. (See: D53)

W59c. March 7, 1980. Tel Aviv Museum, Tel Aviv. Rundfunk Sinfonie Orchester; Lukas Foss, conductor. First performance outside the United States. (See: WB289)

W59d. January 29, 1981. Avery Fisher Hall, Lincoln Center, New York City. New York Philharmonic; Leonard Bernstein, conductor. New York premiere. (See: WB290, WB291)

BIBLIOGRAPHY

WB288. Hruby, Frank. "Debuts & Reappearances: Cleveland Orchestra: Lukas Foss Premiere." *High Fidelity/Musical America* 29:MA26-27 (September 1979)
Review of the April 30, 1979 premiere performance of the revised score. "As Foss now has it reconstructed... it is something that both the knowledgeable musician and the average concertgoer would have no objection to hearing again." (See: W59a)

WB289. Gradenwitz, Peter. "Neue Musik aus Vielen Ländern in Israel: Foss-Premiere." *Neue Zeitschrift für Musik* 141:251 (May/June 1980)
Review of the March 7, 1980 first performance outside the United States. The work is described as orchestral chamber music "because the orchestra is divided into five small groups. The article also mentions that this performance is part of a series sponsored by the Israeli Section of the IGNM of international composers at the Tel Aviv Museum. (See: W59c)

WB290. Henahan, Donal. "Music: Bernstein Leads 3 Works by Copland." *New York Times* January 30, 1981:C11.
Review of the January 29, 1981 New York premiere performance. "It seemed to be mostly padding, all stuffing and no pheasant....[It] left the conductor in what appeared to be emotional exhaustion." (See: W59d)

WB291. Kerner, Leighton. "Business Better than Usual." *Village Voice* March 18, 1981:70.
Review of the January 29, 1981 performance. "The music was not nearly so minimal as you might surmise. It...collided with a great, roaring eruption of dissonance that could be classed as nothing less than an Ivesean jackknife." (See: W59d)

WB292. Bassin, Joseph Philip. "An Overview of the Third Period Compositional Output of Lukas Foss, 1976-1983." Ed.D., Columbia University Teachers College, 1987:120-131. *Dissertation Abstracts* 48:1573A-1574A (January 1988) UMI# 87-21079.
(See: B216)

W60. **Night Music for John Lennon** (December 8, 1980-1981; New York: Pembroke, 1982. Pub. pl. no. PCB 121. Full score and orchestral parts available on rental.)

For brass quintet (2 trumpets, horn, trombone, trombone/tuba) and large or small orchestra (flute, oboe, clarinet, bassoon, horn, trumpet, trombone, piano, electric guitar, percussion (vibraphone, gong, cymbals, snare drum, anvil, musical saw), strings (minimum 5,4,4,3,1)).
Contents: Prelude -- Fugue -- Chorale.
Commissioned for the Canadian Brass by the Northwood Symphonette, Don Jaeger, conductor.
Dedication: "In memory of John Lennon's death, December 8, 1980."
Duration: 15 minutes.
This composition was begun on the night that John Lennon was shot and killed.

FIRST PERFORMANCE

W60a. April 1, 1981. Avery Fisher Hall, Lincoln Center, New York City. Canadian Brass (Frederick Mills, Ronald Romm, trumpets; Graeme Page, horn; Eugene Watts, trombone; Charles Daellenbach, tuba); Northwood Symphonette; Don Jaeger, conductor. (See: WB293)

OTHER PERFORMANCES

W60b. February 5, 1983. Kleinhans Music Hall, Buffalo, New York. Buffalo Philharmonic Orchestra; Lukas Foss, conductor. (See: WB294)

W60c. November 30, 1985. Philharmonic Hall, Liverpool, England. Alan Stringer, Desmond Worthington, trumpets; Alfred Dowling, horn; Eric Jennings, trombone; George Smith, tuba; Royal Liverpool Philharmonic Orchestra; Lukas Foss, conductor. United Kingdom premiere. (See: WB295, WB296, WB297, WB298, WB299, WB301)

W60d. March 13, 1989. Grand Rapids, Michigan. Grand Rapids Symphony; Lukas Foss, conductor.

BIBLIOGRAPHY

WB293. Hughes, Allen. "Northwood Symphonette, Conducted by Don Jaeger." *New York Times* April 5, 1981:50.
Review of the April 1, 1981 premiere performance. "Mr. Foss's music elicited an arresting performance....The Fugue sounded as though its various sections had been compressed into a tight mass and all the sections performed simultaneously....All in all, it is a composition that compels attention." (See: W60a)

WB294. Trotter, Herman. "Return of Lukas Foss Is Event to Remember For Those Who Do." *Buffalo Evening News* February 6, 1983:B3.
      Review of the February 5, 1983 performance. "Its haunting and tranquil prelude...[leads to the] tense and thrustingly ended tribute [to Lennon]. There are moments of chaos and cacophony, but it's one of Mr. Foss' most intriguing scores." (See: W60b)

WB295. Bawden, Rex. "Homage to a Pop Hero." *Liverpool Daily Post* November 29, 1985.
      Promotional piece for the November 30, 1985 United Kingdom premiere performance. Mention is made of the performance of the work previously by 17 United States orchestras and in Bogota, Mexico City, Ottawa, Jerusalem, and Monte Carlo. The work is described as a homage to John Lennon with a prelude and an elegy (fugue) that is "brutally cut short by a 'slammed' final bar." (See: W60c)

WB296. Leece, William. "Simple and Moving." *Liverpool Echo* December 2, 1985.
      Review of the November 30, 1985 United Kingdom premiere performance. The reviewer felt strongly enough of the work to suggest it become a standard part of the Royal Liverpool Orchestra repertory. (See: W60c)

WB297. Bawden, Rex. "Warmth for a Musical Homage." *Liverpool Daily Post* December 2, 1985.
      Review of the November 30, 1985 United Kingdom premiere performance. "Technically it has nothing to do with the former Beatle--emotionally, everything." (See: W60c)

WB298. Griffiths, Paul. "RLPO/Foss." *Times (London)* December 2, 1985.
      Review of the November 30, 1985 United Kingdom premiere performance. "The simple rhapsodising of the prelude, the sputtering machine movement of the fugue, the climaxes of haphazard counterpoint and the cosy chorale...[are all ended with] Foss's response to Lennon's shooting [which] is...[reproduced] as a slapped orchestral cut-off." (See: W60c)

WB299. Tierney, Neil. "Lukas Foss and RLPO." *Daily Telegraph* December 2, 1985.
      Review of the November 30, 1985 United Kingdom premiere performance. "Foss's night belongs to the frozen, grief-shrouded world of Picasso's 'Guernica' panels." (See: W60c)

WB300. Stucky, Steven. "New Music: Orchestral Music." *Notes* 42:390-392 (December 1985)
Review of the Pembroke publication. "The piece owes its popularity... to its modest orchestral requirements, its salable allusions to Lennon and to rock music, and its chic nostalgia for tonality....Its success is likely to prove ephemeral."

WB301. Burn, Andrew. "Liverpool." *The Musical Times* 127:224 (April 1986)
Review of the November 30, 1985 United Kingdom premiere by the Royal Liverpool Philharmonic Orchestra. "No Beatles tunes are quoted, but the nostalgia...is reminiscent of their music." (See: W60c)

WB302. Bassin, Joseph Philip. "An Overview of the Third Period Compositional Output of Lukas Foss, 1976-1983." Ed.D. diss., Columbia University Teachers College, 1987:141-172. *Dissertation Abstracts* 48:1573A-1574A (January 1988) UMI# 87-21079.
This dissertation includes a detailed analysis of this work. (See: B216)

W61. **Exeunt** (1980-82; New York: Pembroke, 1982. Pub. pl. no. PCB 124. Performance material available on rental.)

For orchestra (2 flutes (1 doubles piccolo), 2 oboes, 2 clarinets, 2 bassoons, 4 horns, 2 trumpets, 3 trombones, tuba, timpani, 3 percussion (chimes, vibraphone, xylophone, anvil, bass drum, cymbal, gong, snare drum), harp, piano, electric guitar, strings (minimum 8-6-6-6-4)).
Contents: Six continuous sections: Only the Wind's Home -- Bursts in the Violet Air -- Withered Stumps of Time -- Staring Forms and Broken Images -- Voices Singing Out of Empty Cisterns.
Commissioned by: N.E.A. Consortium.
Dedication: none.
Duration: 17 minutes.
An earlier version of this work entitled *Dissertation*, 1981 was commissioned by the Indiana University School of Music in conjunction with the Composer's Forum "Music of Our Time" for the Indiana University Festival Orchestra. Titles for the sections are from T.S. Eliot's *Wasteland*. "It's an atomic kind of doom piece." (Bassin 1987, 70; See: B216)

FIRST PERFORMANCE

W61a. July 2, 1981. Indiana University. Indiana University Festival Orchestra; Lukas Foss, conductor. Premiered under the title *Dissertation*. (See: D55)

OTHER PERFORMANCES

W61b.   March 22, 1983. Oakland, California. Oakland
Symphony; Paul Dunkel and Joseph Liebling, conductors.
Premiere of *Exeunt*. (See: WB303)

W61c.   November 6, 1983. Alice Tully Hall, Lincoln Center,
New York City. American Composers Orchestra; Dennis
Russell Davies, conductor. New York premiere. (See:
WB304)

BIBLIOGRAPHY

WB303. "World Premieres." *Symphony Magazine* 34:145 (no. 3,
1983)
Notice of the March 22, 1983 premiere
performance. (See: W61b)

WB304. Henahan, Donal. "Concert: 2 Premieres." *New York
Times* November 9, 1983:C24.
Review of the November 6, 1983 New York
premiere performance which also included the premiere
of George Edwards' *Moneta's Mourn*. *Exeunt* is
composed in a strict twelve-tone technique, heavily using
"foreboding string glissando and staccato
bursts...[suggesting] World War III, perhaps?" (See:
W61c)

WB305. Bassin, Joseph Philip. "An Overview of the Third Period
Compositional Output of Lukas Foss, 1976-1983."
Ed.D., Columbia University Teachers College, 1987:70-
79. *Dissertation Abstracts* 48:1573A-1574A (January
1988) UMI# 87-21079.
(See: B216)

W62.   Orpheus and Euridice (1983; Paris: Éditions Salabert.)

For 2 solo violins and chamber orchestra (2 oboes, 2 harps, 2
chimes, piano-strings, strings) with tape delay (electronic
modification).
Dedicated to Yehudi Menuhin and Edna Michell.
Duration: 24 minutes.
Based on *Orpheus* (See: W54). The music follows the story of
the Greek myth and includes stage directions for the
performers.

FIRST PERFORMANCE

W62a.   1985. Gstaad and Lucerne, Switzerland. Yehudi
Menuhin, Edna Michell, violins; Gstaad Orchestra.

BIBLIOGRAPHY

WB306. Bassin, Joseph Philip. "An Overview of the Third Period
Compositional Output of Lukas Foss, 1976-1983."
Ed.D., Columbia University Teachers College, 1987:101-
106. *Dissertation Abstracts* 48:1573A-1574A (January
1988) UMI# 87-21079.
(See: B216)

WB307. Wright, David. Liner notes to New World Records NW
375-2, 1989:4-5. (See: D57)
These program notes include a history of the
work, as well as a description of the programmatic
nature of the music to the story of Orpheus and Euridice.

W63. **Renaissance Concerto** (1985-86; New York: Pembroke, 1986.
Pub. pl. no. PCB126. Solo flute part edited by Carol Wincenc;
piano reduction by Steven Mercurio. Full score and orchestral
parts available on rental.)

For flute and large or small orchestra (minimum 19, maximum 62;
flute (alternating piccolo), oboe, clarinet, bassoon, horn, 2
trumpets, trombone, timpani/percussion (1 or 2 players:
chimes, tambourine, glockenspiel, triangle, Renaissance
drum), harp, optional harpsichord in movement II, violin I (2 to
14 players), violin II (2 to 12 players), viola (2 to 10 players),
violoncello (2 to 8 players), bass (1 to 6 players)).
Contents: I. Intrada -- II. Baroque Interlude (After Rameau) -- III.
Recitative (After Monteverdi) -- IV. Jouissance.
Jointly commissioned by the Barlow Endowment for Music
Composition at Brigham Young University and the Buffalo
Philharmonic Orchestra, Semyon Bychkov, Music Director,
with assistance from the Cameron Baird Foundation and the
Williams Gold Refining Company.
Dedication: "Written for Carol Wincenc, flutist, and the Buffalo
Philharmonic Orchestra."
Duration: 20 minutes.

FIRST PERFORMANCE

W63a. May 9, 1986. Kleinhans Music Hall, Buffalo, New York.
Carol Wincenc, flute; Buffalo Philharmonic Orchestra;
Lukas Foss, conductor. (See: WB308, WB309, WB310)

OTHER PERFORMANCES

W63b. November 1986. Milwaukee, Wisconsin. Carol
Wincenc, flute; Milwaukee Symphony Orchestra; Lukas
Foss, conductor. (See: WB311)

W63c. June 1987. Aldeburgh Festival, England. Carol
Wincenc, flute; English Chamber Orchestra; Lukas Foss,
conductor. 40th Aldeburgh Festival. European premiere;
recorded for BBC Radio. (See: WB111)

W63d.   July 1987. Aspen, Colorado. James Galway, flute; Aspen Festival Orchestra; Lukas Foss, conductor.

W63e.   September 1987. Duisburg, Germany. Carol Wincenc, flute; Indianapolis Symphony Orchestra; John Nelson, conductor. Performed as part of the opening concert of the Duisburg Festival of American Music and recorded for German Radio.

W63f.   February 21, 1988. Carnegie Hall, New York City. Carol Wincenc, flute; American Symphony Orchestra; William Curry, conductor. New York premiere. (See: WB312)

W63g.   July 1989. Tanglewood, Massachusetts. James Galway, flute; Boston Symphony Orchestra; Lukas Foss, conductor.

BIBLIOGRAPHY

WB308. Trotter, Herman. "A Lukas Foss World Premiere." *Buffalo News Gusto* May 2, 1986:10.
        Promotional piece for the May 9, 1986 premiere performance. "[The] new work is intended as an homage to the Renaissance, a handshake across the centuries in which old themes are not just quoted or transcribed, but transformed....The music sort of walks away at the end...like the end of the festivities." (See: W63a)

WB309. Trotter, Herman. "Talents of Foss, Wincenc Make For a Captivating Collaboration." *Buffalo News* May 10, 1986:C10.
        Review of the May 9, premiere performance. "Those who really understand Foss will not be surprised by the unabashed melodiousness, happy ambiance and easy communicativeness of the concerto....This is music that could have been written in no time but our own, but that lovingly captures so much of the essential style and flavor of the Renaissance that is an absolutely captivating listening experience." (See: W63a)

WB310. Trotter, Herman. "Buffalo: Buffalo Philharmonic: Foss *Renaissance Concerto* for Flute." *High Fidelity/Musical America* 36:MA22 (September 1986)
        (See: WB309)

WB311. Strini, Tom. "Foss: Reshaping the Renaissance." *Milwaukee Journal* November 16, 1986:9E.
        Promotional piece for the November 1986 performance in Milwaukee. In an interview, Foss said, "The main thing about the concerto...is the invention of a Renaissance sound that never was. It's not

modernizing the Renaissance, but dreaming yourself back to it and making a piece out of that." (See: W63b)

WB312. Kimmelman, Michael. "Music: A Foss Concerto." *New York Times* February 23, 1988:C17.
Review of the February 21, 1988 New York premiere performance. "[The movements] revolve around sometimes-elaborate adaptations and transformations of Byrd, Rameau, Gesualdo and others. Mr. Foss embellishes and harmonizes these borrowings to give them a curious, refracted, off-kilter quality." (See: W63f)

WB313. Wright, David. Liner notes to New World Records NW 375-1/NW 375-2, 1989:3-4. (See: D57)
Program notes for the piece.

W64.   **Griffelkin Suite** (1986; New York: Carl Fischer; available on rental only.)

For orchestra (2 flutes (2nd doubles piccolo), 2 oboes, clarinet, bass clarinet, 2 bassooms, 2 horns, 2 trumpets, 2 trombones, tuba, timpani, percussion, strings).
Contents: 1. Devil's Ballad (In Hell) -- 2. Piano Deviltry -- 3. On Earth (Dawn) -- 4. Song of the Fountain Statue -- 5. Toyshop Parade -- 6. Chase.
Commissioned by the Oshkosh Symphony Orchestra.
Duration: 25 minutes.
Taken from the opera *Griffelkin* (See: W4).

FIRST PERFORMANCE

W64a.   May 3, 1986. Oshkosh Symphony Orchestra, Henri B. Pensis, conductor. (See: WB314)

OTHER PERFORMANCE

W64b.   Mexico City. UNAM Symphony Orchestra; Lukas Foss, conductor.

W64c.   July 29, 1989. Tanglewood, Lenox, Massachusetts. Lukas Foss, conductor. Performance of the 1989 version of the march only. Written as the opening fanfare for the 1989 season. First performance of this version. (See: WB315; See also: W74k)

BIBLIOGRAPHY

WB314. Francombe, L. "1985-86 Premieres and Season Highlights." *Symphony Magazine* 36:46 (October/November 1985)
Notice of the May 3, 1986 premiere performance. (See: W64a)

WB315. Holland, Bernard. "Tanglewood Offers a Contemporary
Bazaar." *New York Times* August 1, 1989:C16.
  Brief notice of the performance of "a newly
  revised march from [Foss's] early opera *Griffelkin*."
  (See: W64c; See also: WB348).

W65.   Three American Pieces (1986; New York: Carl Fischer;
available on rental.)

For violin/flute and orchestra (flute, clarinet, bassoon, horn,
  trumpet, trombone (optional, movement III only), piano,
  percussion (1 or 2: timpani, tiangle, suspended cymbal, bass
  drum, snare drum), strings/string quintet).
Dedication: none.
Duration: 14 minutes.
Transcription of *Three Pieces* (See: W111). Copyright dictated
  changing *Dedication* and *Composer's Holiday* (originally issued
  by Hargail) to allow them to be issued together with *Early
  Song* by Carl Fischer. All three pieces were orchestrated for
  this reason.

W66.   Concerto No. 2 for Clarinet (1988; New York: Carl Fischer;
available on rental.)

For clarinet and orchestra (flute, oboe, clarinet, horn, trumpet,
  trombone, percussion (1 or 2: timpani, vibraphone,
  xylophone, cymbal, gong), piano, strings/string quintet).
Contents: I. Lento -- II. Allegro -- III. Free -- IV. Allegro.
Commissioned by: Suntori (Tokyo, Japan) International program
  for music composition, in celebration of the 2nd anniversary
  of Suntori Hall 1988.
Dedication: "dedicated to Richard Stoltzman--clarinetist."
Duration: 20 minutes.
Manuscript is located at Carl Fischer, New York City. There is
  also a clarinet-piano version which is marked, "This clarinet-
  piano arrangement is for rehearsal only--L.F."
Based on *Tashi* (See: W95).

FIRST PERFORMANCE

W66a. 1988. Tokyo, Japan. Metropolitan Orchestra.

W67.   For Lenny (Variation on New York, New York) (1988;
manuscript)

For piano obbligato and orchestra.
Written after Bernstein on the occasion of his 70th birthday.
Duration: 4 minutes.

FIRST PERFORMANCE

W67a. 1988. Tanglewood, Massachusetts. Lukas Foss, piano;
  Boston Symphony Orchestra; Seiji Ozawa, conductor.

W68. **Elegy For Anne Frank** (1989; New York: Carl Fischer; photocopy of holograph available on rental.)

For piano obbligato and orchestra (optional winds (2 clarinets/2 muted trumpets, 2 bassoons/2 muted trombones, 1 or 2 horns/trombone/tuba or a combination of these), low drum, strings/string quintet).
Written for the 60th anniversary of the birth of Anne Frank memorial celebration sponsored by the Cathedral of St. John the Divine, the American Friends of the Anne Frank Center, and the International Center for Holocaust Studies of the Anti-Defamation League of B'nai B'rith.
Duration: 5 minutes.
Includes the Nazi hymn in an edited form.

FIRST PERFORMANCE

W68a.   June 12, 1989. Cathedral of St. John the Divine, New York City. Caroline Stoessinger, piano; Brooklyn Philharmonic Orchestra; Lukas Foss, conductor. (See: WB316)

BIBLIOGRAPHY

WB316. Rockwell, John. "New Work by Lukas Foss for Anne Frank." *New York Times* June 14, 1989:C22.
Review of the June 12, 1989 premiere performance as part of the program "Remembering Anne Frank." "The five-minute Foss *Elegy* was overtly programmatic, not to say aurally pictorial, with a broken-off, childlike tune on the piano and sombre string mourning mutating into brutal march music." (See: W68a)

W69. **Guitar Concerto (American Landscapes)** (1989; New York: Carl Fischer, 1990.)

For guitar and large or small orchestra.
Contents: 1. Slow and Free-Allegro Vivace -- 2. Variations on "The Wayfaring Stranger" -- 3. Allegro.
Commissioned by: Carillon Importers, on behalf of Absolut Vodka for Sharon Isbin.
Dedication: "For Sharon Isbin."
Duration: 26 minutes.

FIRST PERFORMANCE

W69a.   November 29, 1989. Avery Fisher Hall, Lincoln Center, New York City. Sharon Isbin, guitar; Orchestra of St. Luke's; Lukas Foss, conductor. (See: WB317)

OTHER PERFORMANCES

W69b.   December 15, 1989. Kleinhans Music Hall, Buffalo, New York. Sharon Isbin, guitar; Buffalo Philharmonic Orchestra; Lukas Foss, conductor. (See: WB318, WB319)

BIBLIOGRAPHY

WB317. Rockwell, John. "Program of Premieres To Benefit Pro Musicis." *New York Times* December 3, 1989:90.
Review of the November 29, 1989 premiere as part of a program entitled "Absolut Concerto," sponsored by Michael Roux's import firm to benefit Pro Musicis, a group which stages concerts in prisons and hospitals. "Mr. Foss's concerto...moved from sometimes evocative but oddly reserved and inconclusive wispiness to a blowsy optimism at the end." (See: W69a)

WB318. Trotter, Herman. "Foss Returns to the Podium He Helped Put on Musical Map." *Buffalo News* December 10, 1989:G3.
Promotional piece for the December 15, 1989 Buffalo performance. Foss's work in Buffalo is outlined, along with information on Sharon Isbin's recent performances. The concerto is referred to by Foss as having "a country fiddle aura" and being full of American folk tunes. (See: W69b)

WB319. McCandless, Michael. "Foss, Guitarist Offer Rare Treat in Concerto." *Buffalo News*, December 16, 1989:C-10.
Review of the December 15, 1989 performance by Sharon Isbin and the Buffalo Philharmonic Orchestra, Lukas Foss, conductor. The piece, written for Isbin, draws its material from American folk music with reminiscences of Copland. "The piece has a zany surface, devoid of self-consciousness and some genuinely beautiful moments....Isbin's performance was nothing short of miraculous." (See: W69b)

CHAMBER MUSIC

W70.   4 Preludes for Flute, Clarinet, and Bassoon (1940; manuscript.)

For flute, clarinet, and bassoon.
Contents: I. Solid -- II. Quiet -- III. Moderate -- IV. Rather Quick.
Dedication: none.
Manuscripts of score and parts are located in the Music Research Division, The New York Public Library; marked "No. V."
Duration: 5 minutes.

W71. **Set of Three Pieces** (1940; New York: G. Schirmer, 1940.
Pub. pl. nos. 38748 (v. 1); 38749 (v. 2); 38750 (v. 3) Published
as three volumes in six parts.)

For two pianos, four hands.
Contents: Vol. 1. March -- Vol. 2. Andante -- Vol. 3. Concertino.
Dedication: "To Edgar M. Levintritt, October, 1938."
Duration: 23 minutes.

FIRST PERFORMANCE

W71a. March 26, 1939. New York? Recital sponsored by the
League of Composers in cooperation with the Society of
Professional Musicians.

BIBLIOGRAPHY

WB320. Rosenfeld, Paul. "Lukas Foss: A New Talent." *Modern
Music* 16:180-182 (March/April 1939)
A 16-year old Lukas Foss performed *Set of Three
Pieces* and *Sonata for Violin and Piano* (See: W96),
among other works for 25 New York and Philadelphia
music experts in the board-room at Schirmer's. His
music was described as similar to Hindemith's harmony,
"with a spontaneity and momentum not unlike that of a
colt which has been let out of its paddock."

WB321. Fine, Irving. "Young America: Bernstein and Foss."
Modern Music 22:241 (May/June 1945)
Brief description of Foss's style in relation to
"March" from *Set of Three Pieces*. It is described as
"[lacking] harmonic refinement [with] an occasional
crude sonority."

W72. **String Quartet No. 1 in G** (1947; New York: Carl Fischer,
1947. Pub. pl. no. O 4242; New York: G. Schirmer, 1949.
(Society for the Publication of American Music) Pub. pl. no.
S.P.A.M.-59.)

For 2 violins, viola, and violoncello.
Contents: I. Andante-Allegro -- II. Theme and Variations.
Prizes: Society for the Publication of American Music Award,
29th season, 1948.
Dedication: "to Serge Koussevitzky."
Duration: 20 minutes.

BIBLIOGRAPHY

WB322. Cazden, Norman. "Music Reviews: Lukas Foss." *Notes*
7:128-129 (December 1949)
Review of the G. Schirmer 1949 publication. "The
idiom of this *Quartet* is that milder species of 1940-
modern identified by a lavish sprinkling of harmonies

containing the minor seventh and a continual tracery of skillful counterpoint about inconsequential material."

W73.   Studies in Improvisation (1959; Charts included in RCA Victor LSC 2558, 1961.)

For clarinet, horn, violoncello, percussion, and piano in various combinations as follows: I. for piano, clarinet, percussion, violoncello; II. for clarinet, percussion, and piano; III. for clarinet, horn, violoncello, percussion, and piano; IV. for clarinet, horn, violoncello, percussion, and piano; V. for piano, clarinet, violoncello, and percussion; VI. for violoncello and percussion; VII. for clarinet, violoncello, percussion, horn, and piano.
Contents: I. Fantasy & Fugue -- II. Music for Clarinet, Percussion and Piano -- III. Variations on a Theme in Unison -- IV. Quintet (Moirai; in three parts: Clotho -- Lachesis -- Atropos) -- V. Encore I (Bagatelle) -- VI. Encore II (Air Antique) -- VII. Encore III (Circus Piece).
Duration: 48 minutes.

FIRST PERFORMANCE

W73a.   March 11, 1962. The New School, New York City. Improvisation Chamber Ensemble (Richard Dufallo, clarinet; Howard Colf, violoncello; Lukas Foss, piano; Charles DeLancey, percussion). (See: WB325, WB326; See also: W32c, W74b)

BIBLIOGRAPHY

WB323. Foss, Lukas and Richard Dufallo. "*Studies in Improvisation*." Pamphlet notes to RCA Victor LM/LSC 2558, 1961. (See: D61)
Foss and Dufallo explain the notations and charts which accompany the recording and make up the score. Included are the theory behind the "compositions," the roles of the performers, and the practice of improvisation. (See also: WB324)

WB324. Foss, Lukas. "Notes on Ensemble Improvisation." Pamphlet notes to RCA Victor LM/LSC 2558, 1961. (See: D61)
In these notes, Foss outlines the history of ensemble improvisation, the way audiences react to the performances, and the function of ensemble improvisation within contemporary music. He concludes by saying, "At the risk of being proven wrong, I should like to predict that in due time, ensemble improvisation, in one form or another, will be studied in conservatories and universities." (See also: WB323)

WB325. Salzman, Eric. "Music: A Foss Afternoon." *New York Times* March 12, 1962:36.

Review of the March 11, 1962 performance at the New School in New York City. "Mr. Foss has borrowed a leaf from jazz, another from the baroque and two or three more from the American and European avant-garde; he has bound them up with some pages of his own to produce his particular and notable performance practice book." Foss's music is generalized as part of the reactions of composers to fight the permanency of electronic music and to opt for music that is constantly changing. (See: W73a; See also: WB160, WB327)

WB326. Helm, Everett. "Foss on Foss." *Musical America* 82:37 (May 1962)

Review of the March 11, 1962 performance by the Improvisation Chamber Ensemble and Adele Addison at the The New School, New York City. "It did not sound improvised....It was as if the ensemble were playing well-rehearsed pieces in a modified post-Webern idiom....The members of the Improvisation Chamber Ensemble have improvised together so often that regular patterns have been established." (See: W73a; See also: WB161, WB328)

W74. **Echoi** (1961-63; New York: Carl Fischer; Mainz: B. Schott's Söhne, 1964. Pub. pl. no. N4338.)

For four soloists (clarinet, violoncello, piano, and percussion (timpano, vibraphone, chimes, glass chimes, antique cymbal, anvil/metal plate, temple blocks, wood blocks, wood chimes, 2 small muffled gongs, suspended deep gong, sandblock, 3 suspended cymbals (sizzle and normal), 3 pipes, bongos, timbali, triangle, claves, snare drum, bass drum, garbage can lid)).
Contents: Echoi I -- Echoi II -- Echoi III (on a childhood tune) -- Echoi IV.
Commissioned by: the Fromm Music Foundation.
Dedication: "For Cornelia."
Duration: 28 minutes.
14 measures of manuscript is located at the Sibley Music Library, Eastman School of Music, Rochester, New York; pencil on yellow paper; gift of Samuel Adler; Inscribed: "For Sam, my dear colleague, or for his favorite wastepaper basket. 1962 Mar. 24."
Composed for the Improvisation Chamber Ensemble. The final three or four minutes of *Echoi IV* involves a pre-recorded tape made by the clarinet and violoncello performers or supplied by the publisher. *Echoi* contains no improvisations.

FIRST PERFORMANCE

W74a. November 11, 1963. McMillin Theater, Columbia University, New York City. Group for Contemporary Music (Arthur Bloom, clarinet; Robert Martin, violoncello; Charles Wuorinen, piano; Raymond Desroches, percussion). Introduced in parts between fall 1961 and 1963. First full performance. (See: WB330, WB332)

OTHER PERFORMANCES

W74b. March 11, 1962. The New School, New York City. Improvisation Chamber Ensemble (Richard Dufallo, clarinet; Howard Colf, violoncello; Lukas Foss, piano; Charles DeLancey, percussion). First performances of parts II and III; sponsored by the Fromm Music Foundation. (See: WB327, WB328, B40; See also: W32c, W73a)

W74c. March 5, 1965. Albright-Knox Art Gallery, Buffalo, New York. Richard Dufallo, clarinet; Lukas Foss, piano; Howard Colf, violoncello; John Bergamo, percussion. (See: D64)

W74d. July 22, 1966. Lincoln Center, New York City. Richard Dufallo, clarinet; Lukas Foss, piano. (See: WB335, WB336)

W74e. September 1967. Warsaw, Poland. Lukas Foss, piano. (See: WB337, WB338)

W74f. March 1, 1968. Université Sir George Williams, Montreal, Quebec. Lukas Foss, piano; Edward Yadzinski, clarinet; Robert Martin, violoncello; Jan Williams, percussion. (See: WB340; See also: W75c)

W74g. 1968. Köln, Germany. (See: WB342)

W74h. November 30, 1979. Alice Tully Hall, Lincoln Center, New York City. Lincoln Center Chamber Music Society; Lukas Foss, piano. (See: WB347)

W74i. December 1, 1979. Kennedy Center Concert Hall, Washington, D.C. Lincoln Center Chamber Music Society; Lukas Foss, piano. (See: WB346)

W74j. June 1987. Aldeburgh Festival, England. European premiere as part of the 40th Aldeburgh Festival. (See: WB111)

W74k. July 1989. Tanglewood, Lenox, Massachusetts. (See: WB348; See also: W64c)

BIBLIOGRAPHY

WB327. Salzman, Eric. "Music: A Foss Afternoon." *New York Times March 12, 1962:36.*
Review of the March 11, 1962 premiere performance of two movements at the New School in New York City. "It had far less motion than most of the

improvisations, a kind of pile-up of static planes." (See:
W74b; See also: WB160, WB325)

WB328. Helm, Everett. "Foss on Foss." *Musical America* 82:37
(May 1962)
Review of the March 11, 1962 premiere of two
sections of *Echoi* (a work in progress). "There were
some fascinating colors and effects." (See: W74b; See
also: WB161, WB326)

WB329. Klein, Howard. "Symposium and Concert at
Tanglewood." *New York Times* August 20, 1963:36.
Three parts of *Echoi* were presented at the final
Fromm Fellow concert of the 1963 Tanglewood season.
The article gives an extensive description of a
symposium on the shortage of violinists facing symphony
orchestras.

WB330. Ericson, Raymond. "Foss's *Echoi* Given First Full
Playing." *New York Times* November 12, 1963:47.
Review of the November 11, 1963 premiere
performance. The details of the work including the use
of prerecorded tape tracks of clarinet and violoncello
parts are given. "[The performance ended] in a brilliant
climactic sound and with a visual effect that brought the
release of laughter from the audience." (See: W74a)

WB331. Foss, Lukas. Liner notes to EPIC LC 3886, 1964. (See:
D62)
Echoi, plural of Echo, is described not as a typical
composition where the composer adds to an idea, but as
a deletion, erasure, arrangement, and choosing of
material which began in abundance. Improvisatory
elements are extremely limited and directed.

WB332. Breuer, Robert. "Die Avantgarde Wirbelt Viel Staub in
New York auf." *Melos* 31:102-103 (March 1964)
Review of the November 1963 first performance.
"The work bears the mark of the sixties, just as its
composer acknowledges. It grows, formed into new
dimensions, to a 'work in the state of progressiveness.'"
(translation) Breuer goes on to mention other
accomplishments of Foss, including his move to Buffalo
to replace Josef Krips as director of the Buffalo
Philharmonic Orchestra. (See: W74a)

WB333. Foss, Lukas. "Work-Notes for *Echoi*." *Perspectives of
New Music* 3:54-61 (Fall/Winter 1964)
These "work-notes" were written from Foss's
recollections of the composition process for *Echoi* which
took him 2 1/2 years to write. It includes excerpts from
the score.

WB334. Chase, Gilbert. "The Eclectics: Toward Improvisation--
and Beyond." In *America's Music from the Pilgrims to
the Present*. Rev. 2d ed. New York: McGraw-Hill,
1966:545-548.
This biographical article centers around Foss's
period of group improvisation and details the composition
of *Echoi*.

WB335. Klein, Howard. "Philharmonic Festival Offers Music
Chosen by Stravinsky." *New York Times* July 23,
1966:13.
Review of the July 22, 1966 performance as part
of the Festival of Stravinsky. "The worst piece was
Lukas Foss's *Echoi*, a verbose potboiler of avant-garde
clichés....Every trick and gimmick was hauled in but no
ideas emerged." (See: W74d; See also: B84, B85,
B86)

WB336. Jacobson, Bernard. "Legacy and Heritage." *Music and
Musicians* 15:32 (November 1966)
Review of the July 22, 1966 performance as part
of the Festival of Stravinsky. "Lukas Foss' *Echoi*
showed real imagination in its hallucinatory and often
moving superimposition of disparate aural and emotional
worlds." (See: W74d)

WB337. Erhardt, Ludwik. "Dziewiec Bogatych Dni." *Ruch
Muzyczny* 11:8-9 (no. 21, 1967)
Review of a performance given by Foss and
members of the University of Buffalo faculty in Poland
which included works by Cardew and Davidovsky as well
as Foss's *Echoi*. "One could blame [Foss] for certain
eclectism, if it were not so impressive from the beginning
to the end, and the capacity to sustain the instumental
invention, color and spontaneous temperament. Foss is
a master musician...what does not happen too often
nowadays." (translation; article in Polish) (See: W74e)

WB338. Fukas, J. "Varsavská Realizace." *Hudebni Rozheldy*
20:604 (no. 19, 1967)
Review of the September 16-24, 1967 Fall festival
held in Warsaw, Poland. Fukas's biggest impression of
the Festival was that of Foss who appeared with three
other performers (who were unnamed in the article).
Echoi was performed, as well as *Non-Improvisation*.
"*Echoi* starts with a bang and continues like this. This
work marks Foss's place in the world." (translation;
article in Czech) (See: W74e)

WB339. Wennerstrom, Mary Hannah. "Parametric Analysis of
Contemporary Musical Form." Ph.D. diss., Indiana
University, 1967:121-148.
A chapter of this dissertation is devoted to a form
and analysis study of *Echoi*.

WB340. Potvin, Gilles. "*Echoi*: Une Expérience Hallucinante."
La Presse (Montreal) March 2, 1968:22.
Review of the March 1, 1968 performance. "The
performance plunged the audience into a quasi-
hallucinagenic state like a psychedelic 'trip.'...With this
work, Foss shows himself to be one of the most
authentic creators of the century." (translation) (See:
W74f; See also: WB352)

WB341. *Lukas Foss on the New Lukas Foss.* New York: Carl
Fischer, 1969:7.
(See: B112)

WB342. Lichtenfeld, Monika. "Neue Musik und ein Jubiläum in
Köln." *Melos* 36:31-32 (January 1969)
Review of a 1968 performance of *Echoi* in Köln.
The reviewer calls this work "astounding" and
"singular....Foss works with contemporary composition
practices in a traditional direction. Elements of his style
include the minute, seamless formation; the naive
coloring of instrumental refinement, and above all, a self-
conscious affirmative optimism." (translation) (See:
W74g)

WB343. Foss, Lukas. "Work Notes for *Echoi*." Liner notes to
Wergo WER 2549 001, 1970. (See: D63)
(See: WB333)

WB344. Dwyer, John. "Ballet Is Clever Lukas Foss Ode."
Buffalo Evening News January 30, 1971:B10.
The music of *Echoi* was used as background for a
filmed ballet by the Company of Man which was a
parody of Foss's tenure in Buffalo. (See also: B131)

WB345. Heindrichs, H.A. "Vielfalt und Konzentration bei den
Wittener Kammermusiktagen 1971." *Melos* 38:301
(July/August 1971)
Heindrichs describes *Echoi* as a "moral work"
which exists in a "spiritual realm....He brings fearful
hallucinations to his listener--will all our quests for a new
order end this way?" (translation)

WB346. Reinthaler, Joan. "Chamber Music Society."
Washington Post December 3, 1979:B12.
Review of the December 1, 1979 concert at the
Kennedy Center. "The piece forces the listener to accept
it on its own terms or not at all, which is fair enough.
Those willing to go along with Foss are treated to a
virtuoso display of creative imagination, wit and musical
craftsmanship....[The] Brahms String Quintet...coming
after the Foss, was hard to concentrate on." (See:
W74i)

WB347. Davis, Peter G. "Music: Foss Plays a Visit." *New York Times* December 4, 1979.

Review of the November 30, 1979 performance at Alice Tully Hall. "*Echoi* reflects may avant-garde tendencies of its time...[but it] sounds just as good now as it did 15 years ago. A score of irrepressible vitality, imagination and flair, the music sustains interest from its first burst of pointillistic cadenzas to the percussionist's final delicate swipe at the lid of a garbage can." (See: W74h)

WB348. Holland, Bernard. "Tanglewood Offers a Contemporary Bazaar." *New York Times* August 1, 1989:C16.

Review of the July 1989 performance as part of the Festival of Contemporary Music at Tanglewood. "[The work is] full of [early 1960s] curiosity over sound effects and its dour introspection. But there is also Mr. Foss's peculiar marriage of intellectual inquiry and sheer love of sonic violence." (See: W74k; See also: WB315)

W75.   Non-Improvisation (1967; exists only in chart form for planned improvisations; no score.)

For four players (clarinet, violoncello, piano/electronic organ, and percussion).
Duration: 12 minutes.
Based on the first movement of Bach's *Concerto for harpsichord in D minor*.

FIRST PERFORMANCE

W75a.   November 7, 1967. Carnegie Recital Hall, New York City. Members of the Center for Creative and Performing Arts (Edward Yadzinski, clarinet; Robert Martin, violoncello; Lukas Foss, piano; Jan Williams, percussion). (See: WB350)

OTHER PERFORMANCES

W75b.   Fall 1967. Warsaw, Poland. Members of the Center for Creative and Performing Arts (Edward Yadzinski, clarinet; Robert Martin, violoncello; Lukas Foss, piano; Jan Williams, percussion). (See: WB351)

W75c.   March 1, 1968. Université Sir George Williams, Montreal, Quebec. Members of the Center for Creative and Performing Arts (Edward Yadzinski, clarinet; Robert Martin, violoncello; Lukas Foss, piano; Jan Williams, percussion). (See: WB352; See also W74f)

W75d.   March 3, 1968. Albright-Knox Art Gallery, Buffalo, New York. Members of the Center for Creative and Performing Arts (Edward Yadzinski, clarinet; Robert

Martin, violoncello; Lukas Foss, piano; Jan Williams, percussion). (See: WB353, D66)

W75e.   March 17, 1970. Kleinhans Music Hall, Buffalo, New York. Buffalo Philharmonic Orchestra; Lukas Foss, conductor. (See: WB354; See also: W53c)

W75f.   July 29, 1971. Temple University Music Festival, Ambler, Pennsylvania. Part of Foss's "rock marathon show." (See: WB355, WB356)

W75g.   March 11, 1972. Brooklyn Academy of Music, Brooklyn, New York. Brooklyn Philharmonia, Lukas Foss, conductor. (See: WB357; See also: W53e, W76i)

BIBLIOGRAPHY

WB349.   "Groups: New Music Ensemble, ONCE Group, Sonic Arts Group, Musica Elettronica Viva." *Source* 2:17 (January 1968)
        In an article primarily by the members of the New Music Ensemble of Davis, California, Foss expresses his views on "anonymous" music, the act of improvisation as compositional style, and how he had returned to composition incorporating improvisation techniques. "I named a recent piece *Non-Improvisation*: tasks so clearly defined that improvisation is ruled out....Ensemble improvisation is always on the verge of disorder, chaos."

WB350.   Davis, Peter G. "Foss: Evenings for New Music." *High Fidelity/Musical America* 18:MA11 (February 1968)
        Review of the first Carnegie Recital Hall "Evenings" concert, November 7, 1967. Though the writer thought of Foss as highly talented, he thought very little of the concert as a whole. Davis refers to *Non-Improvisation* as "a rather silly thing that required four instrumentalists to set up a dense curtain of sound through which one could occasionally hear Mr. Foss at the piano playing a Bach toccata." (See: W75a)

WB351.   Nest'ev, I. "Varshavskie Melodii." *Sovetskaia Muzyka* 32:119-120 (March 1968)
        Review of a performance at a festival in Warsaw in the fall of 1967. "The style is that of pop art, a cheap imitation of the *Mona Lisa*. It reminded me of a circus." (translation; article in Russian) (See: W75b)

WB352.   Potvin, Gilles. "*Echoi*: Une Expérience Hallucinante." *La Presse (Montreal)* March 2, 1968:22.
        Review of the March 1, 1968 performance. "As had been done at the premiere, no composer is named for the *Non-Improvisation*. It is a work of the entire experimental collective...Mr. Foss has organized a sacred

séance of the improvisational collective." (translation)
(See: W75c; See also: WB340)

WB353. Plotkin, Frederick. "Festival of the Arts Today, No. 2."
High Fidelity/Musical America 18:MA24-25 (June 1968)
Review of the festival held in Buffalo, New York,
March 2-17, 1968, including a fine arts display, dance
performances by Merce Cunningham and Company (John
Cage, musical director), and concerts by the Buffalo
Philharmonic Orchestra and the State University of New
York at Buffalo's Center for Creative and Performing
Arts. Foss's works *Non-Improvisation* and *Baroque
Variations* (See: W52d) were performed. "[*Non-
Improvisation* was] an exciting work, generating many
bravos." The festival also saw the premieres of works
by Penderecki, Xenakis, and Pousseur. (See: W75d;
See also: WB223)

WB354. Brennan, James. "Orchestra's Rapport With Rock Bands
Electrifies Audience." *Buffalo Evening News* March 18,
1970:78.
Review of the March 17, 1970 performance
otherwise known as the "Philharmonic Rock Marathon."
(See: W75e; See also: WB257)

WB355. Jacobs, Arthur. "Ambler, Pennsylvania." *The Musical
Times* 112:889-890 (September 1971)
Review of the fourth Temple University Music
Festival in Ambler, Pennsylvania, near Philadelphia. Foss
performed the Bach D minor clavier concerto on piano
with a rock combo added at the end of the concert. He
also conducted the Pittsburgh Symphony Orchestra on
this program. "[Foss's] 'symphonic rock marathon' was
only a pitiable exhibit of what happens when a German-
Jewish ex-Hindemithian gets hung up on Ives, Cage,
electronics and Balinese music." (See: W75f)

WB356. Felton, James. "Temple Festival Gets a Roof Over Its
Head: Foss's Rock Marathon." *High Fidelity/Musical
America* 21:MA19 (November 1971)
Review of "Foss's rock marathon show," July 29,
1971. Included on the program were *Non-Improvisation*,
in which Foss played parts of Bach's clavier concerto in
D minor over and over, *Strategy*, which included rock
bands and symphony players, Cage's *Variations III and
IV*, and Stravinsky's *The Rite of Spring, part I*. "Foss's
marathon was, for all its inequities, the most brilliant and
audacious musical experiment ever held here." (See:
W75f)

WB357. Johnson, Tom. "A Hectic & Haphazard Success."
Village Voice March 16, 1972.

Review of the American Music Marathon at the Brooklyn Academy of Music, March 11, 1972 (See: W75g; See also: WB266, WB367)

W76. **Paradigm** (1968; revised 1969; New York: Carl Fischer; Mainz: B. Schott's Söhne, 1969. Pub. pl. no. N5465. Pub. no. O 4861.)

For percussionist-conductor (musical saw, flexaton, vibraphone, cymbal, gong, snare drum, suspended antique cymbal, tambourine, 5 blocks, superball), electric guitar/electric sitar, 3 instruments (1 each high, middle, low) capable of sustaining a sound, electronics.
Contents: I. Session -- II. Reading -- III. Recital -- IV. Lecture.
Dedication: "for my friends."
Duration: ca. 18 minutes.
Parts I, II, and IV are supplied with English, French, and German texts. The texts are performed by the instrumentalists.

FIRST PERFORMANCE

W76a. October 31, 1968. Hunter College, New York City. Members of the Center of Creative and Performing Arts (Jerry Kirkbride, clarinet; Charles Haupt, violin; Marijke Verberne, violoncello; Jonathan Marcus, guitar; Jan Williams, percussion/conductor).

OTHER PERFORMANCES

W76b. September 3, 1969. Darmstadt 24th International Vacation Course for New Music. Christoph Caskel, percussion/conductor. (See: WB359)

W76c. November 3, 1968. Albright-Knox Art Gallery, Buffalo, New York. Jerry Kirkbride, clarinet; Jonathan Marcus, guitar; Charles Haupt, violin; Marijke Verberne, violoncello; Jon Hassell, Stanley Lunetta, Joseph Romanowski, electronics; Jan Williams, percussion/conductor. (See: D69)

W76d. November 8, 1969. Albright-Knox Art Gallery, Buffalo, New York. Members of the Center of Creative and Performing Arts (Jerry Kirkbride, clarinet; Steven Bell, guitar; Charles Haupt, violin; Marijke Verberne, violoncello; Jan Williams, percussion/conductor). Premiere of the revised version. (See: WB360, WB361, D70)

W76e. November 18, 1969. Maison de la Culture, Bourges, France. (See: WB362)

W76f. March 19, 1970. Carnegie Hall, New York City. New York premiere. Performed as part of an Evenings for New Music Concert. (See: WB364)

W76g.   July 20, 1970. Maeght Festival, St. Paul de Vence.
        First performance of the second version. (See: WB363)

W76h.   1971. Germany. (See: WB365)

W76i.   March 11, 1972. Brooklyn Academy of Music, Brooklyn,
        New York. Jan Williams, percussion/conductor. (See:
        WB366, WB367; See also: W53e, W75g)

W76j.   April 3, 1972. Hamburgische Staatsoper, Hamburg,
        Germany. Scott Douglas, choreographer. First
        performance as a ballet.

W76k.   December 1973(?) Philadelphia Museum of Art and
        Philadelphia Musical Academy, Philadelphia,
        Pennsylvania. Philadelphia premiere. (See: WB368)

W76l.   January 28-March 1, 1974. Tour by Members of the
        State University of New York at Buffalo Center for
        Creative and Performing Arts (Amrom Chodos, clarinet;
        Benjamin Hudson, violin; David Gibson, violoncello; David
        Sussman, guitar; Jan Williams, percussion/conductor;
        Ralph Jones, electronics). Performances were given in
        Dartmouth University; London, England (See: WB369);
        Lisbon, Portugal; Barcelona, Spain; Perugia, Italy; and
        Berlin, Germany.

W76m.   June 14, 1977, Baird Recital Hall, State University of
        New York at Buffalo, Buffalo, New York. Nora Post,
        oboe; Edward Yadzinski, bass clarinet; Don Reinfeld,
        violoncello; Stu Weissman, electric guitar; Jan Williams,
        percussion/conductor. (See: D73)

W76n.   April 18, 1982. Slee Chamber Hall, State University of
        New York at Buffalo. Paul Schlossman, oboe; Edward
        Yadzinski, saxophone; Donald Miller, bass trombone;
        Stuart Weissman, guitar; Jan Williams,
        percussion/conductor. (See: WB370, WB371; See also:
        W109b, W56h, W18d)

W76o.   December 7, 1982. Boston University Concert Hall,
        Boston University School of Music, Boston,
        Massachusetts. Collegium in Contemporary Music;
        Lukas Foss, piano and conductor. (See: D74; See also:
        W18f, W49c, W89b)

W76p.   November 1, 1983. Cooper Union, New York City.
        Bowery Ensemble. (See: B189; See also: W33d, W85f,
        W103c, W109f)

BIBLIOGRAPHY

WB358. *Lukas Foss on the New Lukas Foss.* New York: Carl
        Fischer, 1969:13-14.

(See: B112)

WB359. Siohan, Robert. "Humor and Sarcasm at Darmstadt."
American Musical Digest 1:8-9 (November 1969)
Translated from *Le Monde*, September 5, 1969.
Review of the September 3, 1969 performance.
The humor in the performance came at the end when all
rose to bow except the violoncellist who, with his back
to the audience, continued to play imperturbably. (See:
W76b)

WB360. Putnam, Thomas. "Buffalo Laugh-In." *American Musical
Digest* 1:35 (December 1969) Reprinted from the
Buffalo Courier Express, November 9, 1969.
Review of the revised version of *Paradigm*
November 8, 1969 performance which opened the sixth
season of "Evenings for New Music" in Buffalo, New
York. The performance included Charles Haupt, violinist,
and Jan Williams, conductor. (See: W76d)

WB361. Dwyer, John. "Lukas Foss Finally Lucks Out, Gets Into
Own Way-Out Show." *Buffalo Evening News* November
10, 1969:50.
Review of the November 8, 1969 performance.
Foss was not recognized by the Albright-Knox Art Gallery
guards and was almost not allowed to enter the capacity
filled auditorium for the opening concert of the 1969-70
Evenings for New Music season.
"*Paradigm*...emphasized the musical saw and flexaton in
liquid whippoorwill sounds, and the very clever recitation
by the players..." (See: W76d)

WB362. Gaudibert, Eric. "Bourges: Concert du Domaine
Musical." *Schweizerische Musikzeitung* 110:47
(January/February 1970)
Review of the November 18, 1969 performance.
Paradigm is referred to as a great mixture of voices and
sounds, all very playful and joyful. "The leader gave the
sign to stop, and all but the guitarist did, showing the
hazards of controlled aleatory music." (translation)
(See: W76e)

WB363. "First Performances." *The World of Music* 12:72 (no. 4,
1970)
Listing of the fist performance of the second
version of *Paradigm* on July 20, 1970. (See: W76g)

WB364. Schonberg, Harold C. "The Word." *American Musical
Digest* 1:21-22 (no. 6, 1970) Reprinted from the *New
York Times*, March 20, 1970.
Review of the March 19, 1970 New York premiere
performance. The review explains how composers use
words, vowels, and consonants as sounds rather than as
texts. "*Paradigm* stood out...like a professional's tee

shot against a duffer's. Two of the four brief movements were jazzy, rhythmic, witty, combining old and new techniques, using instruments in a wonderfully outlandish way." (See: W76f)

WB365. Pataki, Ladislaus. "Israeli Musik-Wochen." *Orchester* 19:150-151 (March 1971)
Review of a performance during Israeli Music Week in 1971. "[In *Paradigm*, Foss] gives a lively picture of new American music." (translation) (See: W76h)

WB366. Davis, Peter G. "Philharmonia Puts Focus on Conductor In a Foss Marathon." *New York Times* March 13, 1972:41.
Paradigm was included in this American Music Marathon by the Brooklyn Philharmonia, March 11, 1972. "*Paradigm* is...somewhat spoiled by the trite word games played by the instrumentalists." (See: W76i; See also: WB265)

WB367. Johnson, Tom. "A Hectic & Haphazard Success." *Village Voice* March 16, 1972.
Review of the March 11, 1972 American Music Marathon. Performed was a set of Foss's works, including *Geod* (See: W53e), interrupted by *Non-Improvisation* (See: W75g), and *Paradigm*. "This was a game, with the performers taking cues from each other and from the conductor, although I couldn't figure out exactly what the rules were. There was also a lot of talking and shouting, which didn't communicate much to me. But Williams is a good actor..." (See: W76i; See also: WB266, WB357)

WB368. Chittum, Donald. "Current Chronicle: Philadelphia." *Musical Quarterly* 59:125-133 (January 1973)
Review of the Philadelphia premiere performance presented by the Philadelphia Museum of Art and the Philadelphia Musical Academy. "*Paradigm* is a quasi-theatrical work...The treatment of the text may cause unanticipated literal meanings to emerge which can range from seriousness to parody." (See: W76k)

WB369. Jack, Adrian. "Modern." *Music and Musicians* 22:59 (August 1974)
Review of the February 12, 1974 performance in the Waterloo Room of the Royal Festival Hall in London. *Paradigm* is referred to as "a quest for 'dangerous' music." (See: W76l)

WB370. Putnam, Thomas. "UB Features Foss Creations." *Buffalo Courier Express* April 19, 1982:B6.
Review of the 60th birthday concert at the State University of New York at Buffalo, April 18, 1982.

"*Paradigm's* music suggests a jam session, a literary game...[with] an amusing *Farewell Symphony* finish...Faced with Yadzinski's refusal to give up [playing after all the others had finished], Williams bowed and led his other players off stage."(See: W76n; See also: WB98, WB279, WB447)

WB371. Trotter, Herman. "Influence of Foss Recalled in Program Saluting Composer." *Buffalo Evening News* April 19, 1982:B9.
Review of the April 18, 1982 performance as part of a concert celebrating Foss's 60th year. "Williams conducted mostly from a wildly malleted musical saw or with a flexaton, until Yadzinski was left playing alone, defying the final cutoff." (See: W76n; See also: WB99, WB280, WB448)

W77. **Waves** (1969; lost)

For indeterminate instrumentation.
Composed for the Pro Arte Symphony Orchestra.
Duration: 15 minutes.

FIRST PERFORMANCE

W77a. January 17, 1969. Hofstra University. Pro Arte Symphony Orchestra; Eleazar de Carvalho, conductor.

OTHER PERFORMANCES

W77b. January 20, 1969. Carnegie Recital Hall, New York City. Pro Arte Symphony Orchestra; Eleazar de Carvalho, conductor. (See: WB372)

BIBLIOGRAPHY

WB372. Lowe, Steven. "Pro Arte Symphony (de Carvalho)." *High Fidelity/Musical America* 19:MA23 (April 1969)
Review of the January 20, 1969 Carnegie Hall performance. "Of the Foss piece I can only surmise that it was presented accurately....A constantly repeated ostinato...strangely and disturbingly static, provided a steady base-line [*sic*] over which miscellaneous string timbres were heard." (See: W77b)

W78. **The Cave of the Winds (La Grotte des Vents)** (1972; Paris; New York: Éditions Salabert, 1973. Pub. pl. no. E.A.S.17.112.)

For flute, oboe, clarinet, bassoon, and horn.
Composed while at the Villa Serbelloni, Bellagio, Italy.
Commissioned by and dedicated to: "The Dorian Quintet: Fritz Kraber, flute; Charles Kuskin, oboe; Jerry Kirkbride, clarinet; Jane Taylor, bassoon; Barry Benjamin, horn."
Duration: 15 minutes.

Five scores are used as parts.

FIRST PERFORMANCE

W78a. December 14, 1972. Hunter College Playhouse, New York City. Dorian Quintet (Karl Kraber, flute; Charles Kuskin, oboe; Jerry Kirkbride, clarinet; Jane Taylor, bassoon; Barry Benjamin, horn). (See: WB373)

BIBLIOGRAPHY

WB373. Hughes, Allen. "A New Foss Is Played By Dorian Woodwinds." *New York Times* December 17, 1972.
Review of the December 14, 1972 premiere performance. "The beginning sounds as though Mr. Foss had been influenced chiefly by remembrances of traffic jams in Rome, but its core is a pulsating body of adroitly composed music that achieves its effects in somewhat the same way as steadily blinking bulbs in a flickering-light panel." (See: W78a)

WB374. "Lukas Foss: *The Cave of the Winds* for Wind Quintet (1972)." Pamphlet notes to Vox SVBX 5307, 1977 (See: D75).
Foss comments on his introduction to multiphonics for winds by Larry Singer, William Smith, and Bruno Bartolozzi. "I love these sounds, which enable me to evoke anything from ancient Japanese court music to electronic music, enable me to write for wind quintet without slipping into the inevitable 'pastorale.'"

WB375. Mazurek, R.C. "Compositional Procedures in Selected Woodwind Quintets as Commissioned by the Dorian Quintet." Ph.D. diss., New York University, 1986. *Dissertation Abstracts* 47:3234A (March 1987) UMI #86-25640.
Foss's *Cave of the Winds* is examined along with Berio's *Children's Play* and Druckman's *Delize Contente Che L'Aime Beate*. The study centered on the compositional styles used by each composer and the way the Dorian Quintet interacted in the composition process.

W79. **Ni Bruit Ni Vitesse** (1972; Paris; New York: Éditions Salabert, 1973, c1972. Tape available on rental or may be made by the performers.)

For 2 pianos and 2 percussionists (3 cowbells: large, medium, and small; 3 Japanese bowls; 2 triangle beaters. All percussion parts are played inside the piano), or, piano and prepared piano tape and percussionist and prepared percussion tape.

Commissioned by the New York State Council on the Arts in honor of the 10th anniversary of the Albright-Knox Art Gallery's new wing.

Dedicated to: "The Albright-Knox Art Gallery, Buffalo, New York."

Duration: 13 minutes.

Photocopy of holograph with editing marks by Jan Williams is located in the Music Library, State University of New York at Buffalo.

"For piano keys and piano strings."

FIRST PERFORMANCE

W79a.   February 13, 1972. Albright-Knox Art Gallery, Buffalo, New York. Lukas Foss, piano; Jan Williams, percussion. (See: D76)

OTHER PERFORMANCES

W79b.   February 15, 1972. Carnegie Recital Hall, New York City. Lukas Foss, piano; Jan Williams, percussion. New York premiere.

W79c.   February-March 1974. Lukas Foss, piano; Jan Williams, percussion. Performed on the European tour by the State University of New York at Buffalo Creative Associates. Concerts were given in Paris, Edinburgh, Aberdeen, Glasgow, Rome, Karlsruhe, Warsaw, and Krakow.

W79d.   June 19, 1974. Baird Hall, State University of New York at Buffalo, Buffalo, New York. Dennis Kahle, Jan Williams, percussion. Broadcast live over WBFO-FM, Buffalo, New York.

W79e.   October 7, 1981. Louise Lincoln Kerr Cultural Center, Arizona State University, Tempe, Arizona. New Music Ensemble; Glenn Hackbarth, director. (See: D78; See also: W32f, W85e)

W79f.   March 23, 1982. American Center, Paris. Yvar Mikhashoff, piano; Jan Williams, percussion.

W79g.   April 18, 1982. Albright-Knox Art Gallery Auditorium, Buffalo, New York. Yvar Mikhashoff, piano; Jan Williams, percussion.

BIBLIOGRAPHY

WB376.   Putnam, Thomas. "Walking the Path of New Music." *Buffalo Courier Express Focus* February 13, 1972:1.
Foss took the name for this piece from a traffic sign in France which warned motorists not to blow their horns or speed. He notes "'[*Ni Bruit Ni Vitesse*] is a duet

in the sense that it requires two performers'--but they play on one instrument, and we may hear four performers at work." He jokingly refers to the piece as "'a belated addition to the quasi-extinct piano four-hand literature.'"

WB377. Read, Gardner. "Reviews: Piano Ensemble Music." *Notes* 31:155 (September 1974)
    Review of the Éditions Salabert publication. "The composer's aim seems to be a simple extension of early Cagian pianistic concepts...[with] no insurmountable technical difficulties in the work." Mr. Read also notes that the piece would be interesting to watch as well as hear because of the movements of the performers.

W80.   MAP (Musicians at Play)--A Musical Game (Today) (1970; revised 1977; New York: Pembroke Music, 1978. Pub. pl. no. PCB 109.)

For 4 instrumentalists/virtuosos (4 percussionists or any 4 drawn from these 6 categories: string, woodwind, brass, percussion, plucked instrument, vocalist; each with a variety of instruments from their "family" and each with a bass bow and a superball mallet), tape operator, and referee.
Originally: 5 performer version: string virtuoso (various instruments), [wood]wind virtuoso (various instruments), brass virtuoso (various instruments), percussion virtuoso (various mobile instruments), plucked strings virtuoso (various instruments), auxiliary instruments and bells placed throughout the space, 5 timpani; each player with a bass bow and a superball mallet.
Contents: Prologue -- Rounds: Prelude. Contest I. Contest II. Interlude -- Finale -- Winner's Solo.
Commissioned by: the Foundation Maeght.
Dedication: none.
Duration: 45-75 minutes.
Manuscript is located at the Music Library, State University of New York at Buffalo: 4 performer version, typescript with Foss's editing; 5 performer version.
Actual performance time depends on how long it takes for one of the four contestants [musicians] to be the victor. "A musical game for an entire evening, any 4 [or 5] musicians can play."
The score consists of instructions for recording the tape, game rules, and maps for the tape operator.
The abbreviation *MAP* originally stood for *Men At Play*.

FIRST PERFORMANCE

W80a.   July 16, 1970. St. Paul de Vence, France, in conjunction with the Festival Foundation Maeght. Edward Yadzinski, woodwinds; Charles Haupt, strings; Jan Williams, percussion; Lukas Foss, piano; Joel Chadabe, electronics; Robert Israel, visuals. (See: WB378, WB380, WB381, WB383)

OTHER PERFORMANCES

W80b. December 14, 1970. Metropolitan Museum of Art, New
York City. Stuart Fox, plucked strings; Jim Fulkerson,
brass; Jesse Levine, strings; Jan Williams, percussion;
Edward Yadzinski, woodwinds. American premiere.
(See: WB381, WB382, WB384)

W80c. May 2, 1973. Whitney Museum of American Art, New
York City. Julius Eastman, voice, keyboards,
synthesizer; Petr Kotik, woodwinds; Jesse Levine,
strings; Jan Williams, percussion; Virgil Thomson,
referee; Lukas Foss, score keeper. New York premiere
of the "definitive version." (See: WB385)

W80d. June 14, 1977. Baird Recital Hall, State University of
New York at Buffalo, Buffalo, New York. Edward
Yadzinski, woodwinds; James Kasprowicz, brass; Don
Reinfeld, strings; Jan Williams, percussion; Walter
Gajewski, electronics. Version performed was the 1977
revised version. (See: D79)

BIBLIOGRAPHY

WB378. "Women's Lib, Where are You?" *The Instrumentalist*
25:8 (September 1970)
Mentions the performances in France, Japan, and
New York and describes how the piece is played from
tapes. (See: W80a)

WB379. Putnam, Thomas. "Foss Changed Musical Taste."
Buffalo Courier Express Focus May 31, 1970:28.
Foss describes the composition which was
originally titled *Today* to consist of "12 reels of electronic
music which 'are conceived to be completed by live
performance.'" (See also: B128)

WB380. Schmidt-Faber, W. "In Saint-Paul Experimentelle Musik
bis Mitternacht." *Melos* 37:417-419 (October 1970)
Review of a 1970 summer festival of concerts in
Saint-Paul-de-Vence. *MAP*, described as a "musical
action piece," was inspired by electronic sounds. "The
one surprising effect was when the musicians paused
and froze as the notes of the ensemble stopped. By the
tenth time this happened, however, the initial surprising
effect was long gone." (translation) (See: W80a)

WB381. "Is Avoiding New Music Moral?" *New York Times*
December 13, 1970:II,44.
Description of the unfortunate circumstances of
the collapse of the inflated building where the first
performance of *MAP* was to have taken place in France
and the announcement of the New York premiere on

December 14, 1970 as part of the Composers in Performance series. (See: W80a, W80b)

WB382. Strongin, Theodore. "*MAP*, Foss's Fun-For-All Piece Bows." *New York Times* December 16, 1970:57.
     Review of the December 14, 1970 New York premiere performance. Strongin explains the "game" of *MAP* and the layout of the stage with home territories, dimly lit stage, and bells hanging over the space. "*MAP* is certainly a 'game' for the performers and a 'piece of music' for the listener-viewer. But it is gentle fun and games for the listener-viewer, too. And it is music for the performers...in responding to Mr. Foss's 'game' plan." (See: W80b)

WB383. "Mapping it Out." *Music Educators Journal* 57:88 (February 1971)
     Mentions the preview performance in France with a brief description of how to "play" the game (i.e., composition). (See: W80a)

WB384. DeRhen, Andrew. "Debuts and Reappearances: Lukas Foss's MAP." *High Fidelity/Musical America* 21:MA22 (April 1971)
     Review of the December 14, 1970 American premiere performance. "The game rules require the players to huddle together like doctors at an operating table, take turns conducting, and monkey around with a bull horn and a stringed instrument bow....Towards the end, I noticed that some of them were absent....I think they got bored and left." (See: W80b)

WB385. Henahan, Donal. "'Definitive Version' of Foss's *MAP*." *New York Times* May 6, 1973:70.
     Review of the May 2, 1973 performance of the "definitive version" of *MAP*. Henahan compares this piece to those of Xenakis and Cage from the early 60s. "Like many of Mr. Foss's pieces, then, *MAP* seemed to be more an effort to catch up with the avant-garde than an individual statement." (See: W80c)

WB386. Schwartz, Elliott. "Live Music in an Electronic Climate (Letters and Memos)." In *Electronic Music: A Listener's Guide*. Rev. ed. New York: Praeger, 1975:215-217.
     This article consists of letters and memos written by Foss between March 22, 1971 and August 2, 1971 and follows Foss's progress in learning how to use Joel Chadabe's Supersynthesizer. In this series, Foss follows the development of *MAP* from learning how to use the synthesizer as source material, naming the piece *Today*, turning the work into a game, and renaming it *M.A.P.--Men at Play*.

W81. **Divertissement Pour Mica (String Quartet, No. 2)** (1973;
Paris: Éditions Salabert; New York: G. Schirmer, 1973. Pub. pl.
no. E.A.S. 17.064.)

For 2 violins, viola, and violoncello.
Dedication: for Mica Salabert.
Duration: 3 minutes.
The text of the score is in French and English.

FIRST PERFORMANCE

W81a. November 1972? Kennedy Center, Washington, D.C.
Concord String Quartet (Mark Sokol, Andrew Jennings,
violins; John Kochanowski, viola; Norman Fischer,
violoncello). (See: WB387)

BIBLIOGRAPHY

WB387. Gelles, George. "Festival: The Old & the New." *High
Fidelity/Musical America* 22:MA18+ (December 1972)
Review of the first performance of *Divertissement*
(no date given). The music is described as "pleasant and
easy to take" with its "melodic motto set in a filagreed
texture,...strongly articulated chords,...dissolving in
silence." (See: W81a)

W82. **Chamber Music** (1975)

For percussion and electronics.
Composed jointly with Joel Chadabe.

FIRST PERFORMANCE

W82a. March 22, 1975. Albright-Knox Art Gallery, Buffalo, New
York. Jan Williams, percussion; Joel Chadabe,
electronics. (See: D80)

OTHER PERFORMANCES

W82b. September 24, 1975. Warsaw Festival, Poland. Jan
Williams, percussion; Joel Chadabe, electronics.

W83. **String Quartet No. 3** (1975; Paris: Éditions Salabert; New
York: G. Schirmer, 1976.)

For 2 violins, viola, and violoncello.
Contents: one movement with an appendix of the original version
of the coda which was replaced because of technical
problems for performance.
Commissioned by: Concord Quartet with funds from a New York
State Council on the Arts grant.
Dedication: "Commissioned by the New York State Council of the
Arts."
Duration: 25 minutes.

The piece was expanded as *Quartet Plus* (See: W84).

FIRST PERFORMANCE

W83a.   March 15, 1976. Alice Tully Hall, Lincoln Center, New York City. Concord Quartet (Mark Sokol, Andrew Jennings, violins; John Kochanowski, viola; Norman Fischer, violoncello). (See: WB388, WB389, WB390)

BIBLIOGRAPHY

WB388. Foss, Lukas. "*String Quartet No. 2 [i.e., 3]*, 1974. Program notes, March 15, 1976.
The quartet is incorrectly listed as No. 2 on the program. Foss notes that there is constant activity and constant change. The final major chord "'short circuits'...the rush of patterns, arpeggios and rapid figures...[causing] a sudden stop." (See: W83a)

WB389. "Foss Jets In to Unsnarl Stringmen Fit to Be Tied." *Buffalo Evening News* March 15, 1976:1.
While preparing for their March 15, 1976 concert at Lincoln Center, which included the first performance of *String Quartet No. 3*, the Concord Quartet telephoned Foss in Amsterdam and requested rehearsal help over the phone. Realizing that the work was too complicated to describe over the phone, Foss arranged to leave Amsterdam early and to meet with the group in the Kennedy Airport while waiting for his connecting flight to Kansas City. (See: W83a)

WB390. Putnam, Thomas. "String Quartet Sure Loose, Plays for Foss at Airport." *Buffalo Courier Express* March 16, 1976:6.
"His new quartet is the most taxing quartet in sure endurance...[Foss noted that] it will be a wonder if at the end they have any bow-arms left." (See: W83a)

WB391. Russell, Ann. Liner notes for Composers Recordings Inc. CRI SD 413, 1980. (See: D81)
"*String Quartet No. 3* is Foss' most extreme composition; it is themeless, tuneless, and restless....The sound vision which gave birth to this quartet may be the most merciless in the quartet literature."

W84.   Quartet Plus (1977; manuscript.)

For 2 string quartets (4 violins, 2 violas, 2 violoncellos), narrator, and video presentation.
Text from T.S. Eliot. The work consists of *String Quartet No. 3* with the addition of another string quartet, narration, and video tape (See: W83).

FIRST PERFORMANCE

W84a.   April 29, 1977. "Festival of Modern Combos," Brooklyn
Academy of Music, Brooklyn, New York. Concord
Strings; Larry Rivers, narrator; Ed Emschwiller, video
tape. (See: WB392)

BIBLIOGRAPHY

WB392. Horowitz, Joseph. "Foss's *Quartet Plus* Given Debut by
Concord Strings and Additions." *New York Times* May
1, 1977:70.
Review of the April 29, 1977 premiere
performance as part of the Brooklyn Philharmonia's
Festival of Modern Combos. The video showed
"redundant silhouettes of a man walking." The text
"reflected a Sisyphus-like struggle to move
forward...*Quartet Plus* will have different meanings for
different people, and none at all for a great many." (See:
W84a)

W85.   **Music For Six** (1977; revised 1978; New York: Pembroke,
1978. Pub. pl. no. PCB110.)

For six unspecified treble clef instruments.
Contents: 1st section -- 2nd section -- 3rd section -- Coda.
Commissioned by: Philadelphia Composers' Forum.
Dedication: none.
Duration: 15 minutes (3 min.; 9 min.; 3 min.; 1 min.)

FIRST PERFORMANCE

W85a.   1977. Philadelphia, Pennsylvania. Philadelphia
Composers' Forum.

OTHER PERFORMANCES

W85b.   May 7, 1978. Albright-Knox Art Gallery, Buffalo, New
York. Robert Dick, flute; Nora Post, oboe; Krzysztof
Knittel, piano; Weronika Knittel, violin; Michael Peebles,
violoncello; Jan Williams, percussion. (See: D82)

W85c.   April 19, 1980. State University of New York at Buffalo,
Buffalo, New York. State University of New York at
Buffalo Percussion Ensemble (Jan Williams, Edward
Folger, vibraphones; Bruce Penner, Rick Kazmierczak,
marimbas; Kathryn Kayne, electric piano; James
Calabrese, synthesizer).

W85d.   March 27, 1981. Cooper Union, New York City. State
University of New York at Buffalo Percussion Ensemble
(Marc Copell, Joel Harrod, Edward Folger, Rick
Kazmierczak, David Gordon, Bruce Penner, percussion).

W85e. October 7, 1981. Louise Lincoln Kerr Cultural Center, Arizona State University, Tempe, Arizona. New Music Ensemble; Glenn Hackbarth, director. (See: D84; See also: W32f, W79e)

W85f. November 1, 1983. Cooper Union, New York City. Bowery Ensemble. (See: B189; See also: W33d, W76p, W103c, W109f)

BIBLIOGRAPHY

WB393. Bassin, Joseph Philip. "An Overview of the Third Period Compositional Output of Lukas Foss, 1976-1983." Ed.D., Columbia University Teachers College, 1987:43-50. *Dissertation Abstracts* 48:1573A-1574A (January 1988) UMI# 87-21079.
　　　"[*Music for Six*] is minimal music with a tune at the end that has been hidden." (See: B216)

W86.　Brass Quintet (1978; manuscript)

For 2 trumpets, horn, trombone, and tuba.
Commissioned by: Canadian Brass.
Duration: 17 minutes.
Arranged by the composer for a cappella chorus (See: *Then the Rocks on the Mountain Begin to Shout*, W21) and orchestra (See: *Quintets for Orchestra*, W59).

FIRST PERFORMANCE

W86a. 1978. Canadian Brass (Frederick Mills, Ronald Romm, trumpets; Graeme Page, horn; Eugene Watts, trombone; Charles Daellenbach, tuba).

OTHER PERFORMANCES

W86b. February 11, 1980. Carnegie Recital Hall, New York City. Musical Elements. First American performance. (See: WB394)

BIBLIOGRAPHY

WB394. Ericson, Raymond. "Concert: The Manner of Elements." *New York Times* February 17, 1980:67.
　　　Review of the February 11, 1980 American premiere performance. "Lukas Foss's *Brass Quintet*...sounded simplistic....Attention was held as one wondered if anything interesting was going to happen. Eventually it did, and the composer had some good, even amusing ideas, but there was not really enough movement in the piece to make it seem worthwhile in the end." (See: W86b)

WB395. Bassin, Joseph Philip. "An Overview of the Third Period Compositional Output of Lukas Foss, 1976-1983." Ed.D., Columbia University Teachers College, 1987:120-131. *Dissertation Abstracts* 48:1573A-1574A (January 1988) UMI# 87-21079.
(See: B216)

W87. **Round a Common Center** (1979; New York: Pembroke, 1980. Pub. pl. no. PCB123. Published without the poem "The Runner.")

For piano quartet (violin, viola, violoncello, piano), or quintet (2 violins, viola, violoncello, piano) with or without voice, with or without narration.
Commissioned by: Cantilena Chamber Players for the 1980 Winter Olympics.
Dedication: none.
Duration: 12 minutes.
The reading of the poem "The Runner" by W.H. Auden is optional and is intended to be read during the musical performance. The optional additional violin part was written for Yehudi Menuhin for the first performance.

FIRST PERFORMANCE

W87a. January 30, 1980. Lake Placid Center for Music, Drama, and Art, Lake Placid, New York. Cantilena Chamber Players: Yehudi Menuhin, Edna Michell, violins; Jesse Levine, viola; Stephen Kates, violoncello; Frank Glaser, piano; Lukas Foss, reciter. Performed at the inauguration of the fine arts program at the 1980 Winter Olympics.
(See: WB396, WB397, WB398)

BIBLIOGRAPHY

WB396. "Arts Go Into 'Athletic Drive' for the Olympics." *New York Times* January 31, 1980:C20.
Description of the types of arts displayed and performed in Lake Placid for the 1980 Olympics. The works included Foss's composition as well as visual, theatrical and popular art presentations. "Mr. Foss described the composition's main body in terms of athletic drive' with 'all instruments playing continuously in marathon fashion.'" (See: W87a)

WB397. "Cantilena at Olympics Telecast Nationwide on PBS." *American Ensemble* 3:1 (Winter 1980)
Description of the January 30, 1980 premiere performance. The performance was videotaped for PBS to be broadcast on February 12, 1980 and for international broadcast at a later date. (See: W87a)

WB398. Fleming, Shirley. "Cantilena Chamber Players: Foss Premiere." *High Fidelity/Musical America* 30:MA28 (May 1980)

Review of the January 30, 1980 premiere
performance. "A tight, bright, linear piece built from a
simple basic motivic germ that retains its identity much
of the time...the spirit is definately up-beat....The
Cantilena Chamber Players projected the work with zest
and an air of pleasure." (See: W87a)

W88.   **Curriculum Vitae with Time Bomb** (1980; New York: Carl
Fischer, 1980.)

For accordion and percussion.
"Composed for and in admiration of Jan Williams, percussionist."
Duration: 8 minutes.
Same work as *Curriculum Vitae* (See: W108) "with added
   percussion, 'ticking' away until the final time bomb explodes."
   (Bassin 1987, 119. See: B216) It can be performed with a
   taped accordion part if there is no accordionist available.

FIRST PERFORMANCE

W88a.   March 10, 1981. Det Jydske Musikkonservatorium. Jan
        Williams, percussion; taped accordion (Guy Klucevsek).
        Performed on Williams' European tour.

OTHER PERFORMANCES

W88b.   April 15, 1981. Memorial Auditorium, Edinboro State
        College, Edinboro, Pennsylvania. Jan Williams,
        percussion; taped accordion (Guy Klucevsek).

W88c.   March 1982. Cooper Union, New York City. Guy
        Klucevsek, accordion; Jan Williams, percussion.

W88d.   March 22, 1982. American Center, Paris. Jan Williams,
        percussion; taped accordion (Guy Klucevsek).

W88e.   April 18, 1982. Albright-Knox Art Gallery Auditorium,
        Buffalo, New York. Jan Williams, percussion; taped
        accordion (Guy Klucevsek). (See also: W97b, W103b,
        W109b)

W88f.   October 7, 1982. Composers' Forum, Symphony Space,
        New York City. Guy Klucevsek, accordion; Jan Williams,
        percussion. (See: WB399; See also: W18e, W56i,
        W109e)

BIBLIOGRAPHY

WB399. Holland, Bernard. "Concert: Lukas Foss Works Played
        at Composers' Forum." *New York Times* October 10,
        1982:85.
            Review of the October 7, 1982 performance of
        works by Lukas Foss. "*Curriculum Vitae with Time
        Bomb* was a surly dialogue between accordion and

percussion, with fragments of familiar tunes...fading in and out." (See: W88f; See also: WB100, WB281, WB449)

WB400. Bassin, Joseph Philip. "An Overview of the Third Period Compositional Output of Lukas Foss, 1976-1983." Ed.D., Columbia University Teachers College, 1987:113-119. *Dissertation Abstracts* 48:1573A-1574A (January 1988) UMI# 87-21079.
(See: B216)

W89.   **Solo Observed** (Spring 1982; New York: Pembroke. Score and parts available on rental.)

For piano, harp/violoncello, accordion/electric organ, vibraphone/marimba.
Commissioned by: New World Festival of the Arts in Greater Miami.
This work is an extended version of *Solo* (see: W109), for piano, involving the addition of a coda consisting of vibraphone or marimba, violoncello or harp, and electric organ or accordion reflecting on the pianist's solo which they "observe."

FIRST PERFORMANCE

W89a.   June 7, 1982. First New World Festival of the Arts, Miami, Florida. Lincoln Center Chamber Players; Lukas Foss, piano. (See: WB401, WB402)

W89b.   December 7, 1982. Boston University Concert Hall, Boston University School of Music, Boston, Massachusetts. Collegium in Contemporary Music; Lukas Foss, piano. (See: D86; See also: W18f, W49c, W76o)

W89c.   May 1, 1983. Alice Tully Hall, Lincoln Center, New York City. Lukas Foss, piano; Fred Sherry, violoncello; Charles Wadsworth, electric organ; Richard Fitz, vibraphone. New York premiere. (See: WB403)

BIBLIOGRAPHY

WB401. Kerner, Leighton. "Amid the Sweltering Palms." *Village Voice* June 22, 1982:98.
A report on the first New World Festival of the Arts in Miami, June 4-26, 1982 and review of *Solo Observed*. "Foss has long been an exemplary pianist...and he provided himself with a good showcase this time out." (See: W89a)

WB402. Roos, J. "New World Festival of the Arts: Gould & Foss." *High Fidelity/Musical America* 32:MA26 (November 1982)

Review of the June 7, 1982 premiere performance of *Solo Observed*. "*Solo Observed* [is] a hypnotically flowing solo for piano, colored by the serenest, subtlest sounds of vibraphone and electric organ, urged on by agitated cello." (See: W89a)

WB403. Henahan, Donal. "Concert: Lukas Foss, Pianist and Composer." *New York Times* May 2, 1983:C16.
Review of the May 1, 1983 New York premiere performance by the Chamber Music Society of Lincoln Center. "The work...is vaguely narrative in form...[The pianist seemed] to be stuck in a perseverative groove...After that, the other instruments diffidently joined in and the piece took on a motoric energy." (See: W89c)

WB404. Bassin, Joseph Philip. "An Overview of the Third Period Compositional Output of Lukas Foss, 1976-1983." Ed.D., Columbia University Teachers College, 1987:132-140. *Dissertation Abstracts* 48:1573A-1574A (January 1988) UMI# 87-21079.
(See: B216)

W90. For 200 Cellos (A Celebration) (1982; manuscript)

For 200 violoncellos (or fewer) divided into 4 groups of 50 each.
Commissioned by Mstislav Rostropovich for the International Cello Congress.
Duration: 10 minutes.

FIRST AND LAST PERFORMANCE

W90a.   June 4, 1982. First American Cello Congress, Tawes Theater, University of Maryland, College Park, Maryland. Mstislav Rostropovich, conductor. (See: WB405, WB406, WB407, WB408, WB409)

BIBLIOGRAPHY

WB405. Cera, Stephen. "Piece for 200 Cellos to Highlight Cellists' Congress." *The Sun (Baltimore)* May 30, 1982.
Promotional piece for the June 4, 1982 performance. The history of the composition is presented as well as information about the Congress. "The biggest question mark hovering overhead is not whether so many cellists can be enlisted to take part, but whether so many can actually fit onto the stage of Tawes Theatre....There are very few unison passages...[Foss] wanted to get deeper into what you would do for a lot of cellos that you wouldn't do for a few." (See: W90a)

WB406. McLellan, Joseph. "Cellists in Congress." *Washington Post* June 1, 1982:B1+

Promotional piece for the June 4, 1982
performance in which Rostropovich is interviewed. "'The
ideas in this music we will play on June 4 may not
compete with those of Bach and Brahms,' [Rostropovich]
said, 'but the beauty inherent in the sound will be such
that no one who hears it will ever forget it.'" (See:
W90a)

WB407. McLellan, Joseph. "Jolly Good Cellos." *Washington
Post* June 5, 1982:C1 +
Review of the June 4, 1982 performance at the
first American Cello Congress. "It was the largest cello
orchestra ever assembled, and it produced sounds that
no human ear had ever heard before...The fragments of
sound coalesced into an ensemble of incredible richness.
The prevailing sound conveyed a sense of enormous
depth in a performance that used great power with great
delicacy. (See: W90a)

WB408. Floyd, Jerry. "Cellos of the World Unite at the University
of Md." *Washington Times* June 7, 1982.
Review of the June 4, 1982 performance. "Foss'
15-minute work, written on just three weeks' notice, is a
rouser, scored mostly in 8/8 time, consisting of several
variations on the key of D. The short piece gathers
momentum lika a locomotive...[and then] shifts into
contemporary dissonance before finally resolving itself in
D Major." (See: W90a)

WB409. Cera, Stephen. "200 Cellos Bring College Park Congress
to Rich Finale." *The Sun (Baltimore)* June 7, 1982.
Review of the June 4, 1982 performance.
"Whatever the purely musical, not to mention acoustical,
implications of the event, this grand behemoth of a cello
concert qualified as some sort of happening." (See:
W90a)

WB410. Bassin, Joseph Philip. "An Overview of the Third Period
Compositional Output of Lukas Foss, 1976-1983." Ed.D.
diss., Columbia University Teachers College, 1987:86-
92. *Dissertation Abstracts* 48:1573A-1574A (January
1988) UMI# 87-21079.
Foss is quoted in this dissertation about this
unique work. "This was an interesting assignment
because here I was writing a piece where the first
performance would undoubtedly be the last." (See:
B216)

W91. **Percussion Quartet** (1983; New York: Pembroke, 1983. Pub.
pl. no. PCB 125.)

For 4 percussionists (I. vibraphone (shared with III), timpani (high
G), 2 woodblocks, 1 chime pipe, 1 small bowl; II. vibraphone
(shared with IV), timpani (D), 1 suspended cymbal, 2

cowbells; III. xylophone (shared with IV), timpani (A), 1
muffled cymbal, 1 small muffled gong, 1 tamtam; IV. timpani
(low E), 2 tom toms, 1 crotale).
Contents: 1. Introduction -- 2. Song -- 3. Recitative -- 4.
Monsters -- 5. Dance.
Commissioned by: Claire Heldrich and The New Music Consort
with the assistance of a grant from the New York State
Council on the Arts.
Duration: 16-18 1/2 minutes.
The piece includes two versions of the conclusion depending on
the audience's reaction.

FIRST PERFORMANCE

W91a.   November 5, 1983. Pyramid Art Center, Rochester, New
York. New Music Consort.

BIBLIOGRAPHY

WB411. Goldstein, Perry. Liner notes to New World NW 330,
1985. (See: D88)
In these program notes for the work, Goldstein
describes the various techniques involved, ranging from
chance to competitiveness to polyphonic melodies.

WB412. Bassin, Joseph Philip. "An Overview of the Third Period
Compositional Output of Lukas Foss, 1976-1983."
Ed.D., Columbia University Teachers College, 1987:93-
100. *Dissertation Abstracts* 48:1573A-1574A (January
1988) UMI# 87-21079.
(See: B216)

W92.   Horn Trio (1983; manuscript.)

For horn, violin, and piano.
Duration: 14 minutes.

W93.   Saxophone Quartet (1985; Cherry Hill, N.J.: Roncorp, 1989.)

For soprano saxophone, alto saxophone, tenor saxophone, and
baritone saxophone.
Contents: I. Introduction -- II. Canon -- III. Chorale -- IV. Canon B.
Commissioned by: Amherst Saxophone Quartet.
Duration: 14 minutes.
The breaks between the movements are included in the score.

FIRST PERFORMANCE

W93a.   September 22, 1985. Christ the King Chapel, Canisius
College, Buffalo, New York. Amherst Saxophone
Quartet (Salvatore Andolina, soprano saxophone;
Michael Nascimben, alto saxophone; Steven Rosenthal,
tenor saxophone; Harry Fackelman, baritone saxophone).
(See: WB413)

BIBLIOGRAPHY

WB413. Trotter, Herman. "Foss *Saxophone Quartet* Debuts."
Buffalo News September 23, 1985:C13.
     Review of the September 22, 1985 premiere
performance. "The Foss *Saxophone Quartet* struck this
listener as a major addition to the saxophone
repertoire...." (See: W93a)

W94.   **Embros** (1984-85; New York: Carl Fischer)

For 3 woodwinds, 3 brass, percussion, strings, and electric
     instruments.
Composed on an NEA Consortium Commission.
Duration: 12 minutes.

FIRST PERFORMANCE

W94a.   February 25, 1986. New York City. Musical Elements;
Robert Beaser, conductor. (See: WB414)

BIBLIOGRAPHY

WB414. "Musical Elements." Program notes. February 25,
1986:10.
     "The exact instrumentation is not
specified...[because] under a Consortium Commission
from the National Endowment for the Arts, four different
groups of different instrumentation have commissioned
the work." (See: W94a)

W95.   **Tashi** (1986; New York: Carl Fischer.)

For clarinet, 2 violins, viola, violoncello, and piano.
Contents: I. Lento -- II. Allegro -- III. Free -- IV. Allegro.
Commissioned by: Tashi with funds from the Fortas Fund of the
     Kennedy Center, UCLA Center for the Performing Arts, and
     Carnegie Hall.
Duration: 17 minutes.

FIRST PERFORMANCE

W95a.   February 17, 1987. Terrace Theater, Kennedy Center,
Washington, D.C. Tashi (Richard Stoltzman, clarinet; Ida
Kavafian, Theodore Arm, violins; Steven Tenenbom,
viola; Fred Sherry, violoncello); Lukas Foss, piano. (See:
WB416, WB424)

OTHER PERFORMANCES

W95b.   February 18, 1987. Carnegie Hall, New York City. Tashi
(Richard Stoltzman, clarinet; Ida Kavafian, Theodore
Arm, violins; Steven Tenenbom, viola; Fred Sherry,
violoncello); Lukas Foss, piano. (See: WB417, WB423)

W95c.   February 19, 1987. Northeastern University, Boston,
        Massachusetts. Tashi (Richard Stoltzman, clarinet; Ida
        Kavafian, Theodore Arm, violins; Steven Tenenbom,
        viola; Fred Sherry, violoncello); Lukas Foss, piano. (See:
        WB415, WB418)

W95d.   February 20, 1987. Folly Theater, Kansas City,
        Missouri. Tashi (Richard Stoltzman, clarinet; Ida
        Kavafian, Theodore Arm, violins; Steven Tenenbom,
        viola; Fred Sherry, violoncello); Lukas Foss, piano.

W95e.   February 23, 1987. Chicago Civic Theater, Chicago,
        Illinois. Tashi (Richard Stoltzman, clarinet; Ida Kavafian,
        Theodore Arm, violins; Steven Tenenbom, viola; Fred
        Sherry, violoncello); Lukas Foss, piano. (See: WB419,
        WB420)

W95f.   February 24, 1987. University of Illinois at Champaign-
        Urbana. Tashi (Richard Stoltzman, clarinet; Ida Kavafian,
        Theodore Arm, violins; Steven Tenenbom, viola; Fred
        Sherry, violoncello); Lukas Foss, piano.

W95g.   February 27, 1987. Herbst Theater, San Francisco,
        California. Tashi (Richard Stoltzman, clarinet; Ida
        Kavafian, Theodore Arm, violins; Steven Tenenbom,
        viola; Fred Sherry, violoncello); Lukas Foss, piano.

W95h.   March 1, 1987. Wadsworth Auditorium, University of
        California at Los Angeles. Tashi (Richard Stoltzman,
        clarinet; Ida Kavafian, Theodore Arm, violins; Steven
        Tenenbom, viola; Fred Sherry, violoncello); Lukas Foss,
        piano. (See: WB421, WB422, B212)

BIBLIOGRAPHY

WB415. Pfeifer, Ellen. "Composer Foss Returns to Hub to Debut
        Work." *Boston Herald* February 17, 1987:27.
            Promotional article for the February 19, 1987
        performance in Boston. Foss says "[*Tashi*] combines
        adventurousness with accessibility." (See: W95c)

WB416. McLellan, Joseph. "Foss' Tantalizing *Tashi*."
        Washington Post February 18, 1987:C10.
            Review of the February 17, 1987 premiere
        performance. "This music is too good to remain the
        exclusive property of one ensemble....Last night's
        premiere set a high standard in both composition and
        performance." (See: W95a)

WB417. Holland, Bernard. "Concert: Lukas Foss Is Tashi's Guest
        Soloist." *New York Times* February 22, 1987:I,56.
            Review of the February 18, 1987 New York
        premiere performance. "The subtle and richly sonorous

clarinet playing of Richard Stoltzman [brought the music close to the audience]...One can scarcely lump *Tashi* under the Minimalist heading, but the references... are hard to miss." (See: W95b)

WB418. Tommasini, Anthony. "A Dazzling Performance by Tashi." *Boston Globe* February 23, 1987.
Review of the February 19, 1987 performance. "*Tashi* is the work of a composer who has devoured the musical styles of other composers he loves...and craftily fashioned it all into something personal and original....The performance, like the piece, was an absolute dazzler." (See: W95c)

WB419. Delacoma, Wynne. "Foss Work Packs Lots of Surprises." *Chicago Sun-Times* February 24, 1987.
Review of the February 23, 1987 performance. The piece is described as "a vibrant work." (See: W95e)

WB420. Rhein, John von. "Foss, Tashi Combine to Create a Natural Musical Wonder." *Chicago Tribune* February 24, 1987:II,8.
Review of the February 23, 1987 performance. "Faint, mysterious tendrils of sound emerge...like echoes of Oriental temple chant recalled from a distant past...until...a joyous scherzo bursts forth, alive with a rhythmic bounce as all-American as Stoltzman's debonair virtuosity in the cadenza." (See: W95e)

WB421. Bernheimer, Martin. "*Tashi*--Elegant Foss Premiere." *Los Angeles Times* March 3, 1987:1+
Review of the March 1, 1987 opening performance of the New Music Los Angeles Festival. "Foss' piece offers a beguilingly subtle workout for bravura string quartet, brash clarinet and patriarchal pianist." (See: W95h)

WB422. Swed, Mark. "New Music L.A. Starts off on the Wrong Note." *Los Angeles Herald Examiner* March 3, 1987:C1-2.
Review of the March 1, 1987 performance. "It is a typical Foss piece, which means it is unclassifiable....Foss is also a virtuoso player, as are the members of Tashi, and the performance was an irrepressibly spirited one." (See: W95h)

WB423. Davis, Peter G. "Most Happy Cello." *New York* 20:109 (March 9, 1987)
Review of the February 18, 1987 performance. The work had "a difficult birth" according to Foss. "Four movements...engaged in a fumbling and futile search for the ghost of Poulenc....I have never heard anything from [Foss] quite this feeble." (See: W95b)

WB424. Stearns, David Patrick. "Washington: Tashi: Foss
Tashi." *Musical America* 107:48 (September 1987)
Review of the February 17, 1987 premiere by
Tashi with Lukas Foss, piano. "Throughout the piece,
Foss wisely takes advantage of star clarinetist Richard
Stoltzman's virtuosity, giving him a variety of audacious
cadenzas and spirited solo interjections that he seemed
to relish. The piano part...is curiously
underwritten...[leaving] the group sounding strangely
asymmetrical." (See: W95a)

MUSIC FOR SOLO INSTRUMENTS

W96.   Violin Sonata (1937; manuscript)

For violin and piano.
Duration: 15 minutes.

FIRST PERFORMANCE

W96a.   Spring, 1941. New York City. Eudice Shapiro, violin;
Irene Jacobi, piano. (See: WB426)

BIBLIOGRAPHY

WB425. Rosenfeld, Paul. "Lukas Foss: A New Talent." *Modern
Music* 16:180-182 (March/April 1939)
(See: WB320)

WB426. Fuller, Donald. "Season's Close: New York, Spring,
1941." *Modern Music* 18:257-258 (May/June 1941)
Review of the third concert in the League of
Composers 1941 Young American series, during which
works for violin and piano were featured. "Lukas Foss'
youthful spontaneity is both pleasing and appropriate
though...there is too great a dependence on superficial
and unexciting facility." (See: W96a)

W97.   Four Two-Part Inventions (1938; New York: G. Schirmer,
1938. (Compositions for the piano; 1). Pub. pl. no. 38289; New
York: Carl Fischer, 1967, c1938. Pub. pl. no. N 4889. Pub. no.
P3112.)

For piano.
Contents: I. Introduction -- II. Allegretto -- III. Tranquillo ma
mosso -- IV. Molto vivace.
Dedication: none.
Duration: 8 minutes.
First published composition of Lukas Foss. Issued with *Grotesque
Dance* (See: W98) by G. Schirmer. The G. Schirmer edition
was published with the title *Four Two-Voiced Inventions*.

FIRST PERFORMANCE

W97a. March 24, 1982. American Center, Paris. Lukas Foss, piano.

OTHER PERFORMANCES

W97b. April 18, 1982. Albright-Knox Art Gallery Auditorium, Buffalo, New York. Yvar Mikhashoff, piano. (See also: W88e, W103b, W109b)

BIBLIOGRAPHY

WB427. McPhee, Colin. "Scores and Records." *Modern Music* 17:54 (November/December 1939)
Review of several works published by G. Schirmer including *Grotesque Dance* (See: W98) and *Four Two-Part Inventions* by Foss. McPhee remarks that these works by "the gifted young Lukas Foss...[cannot] be considered significant."

WB428. Fine, Irving. "Young America: Bernstein and Foss." *Modern Music* 22:241 (May/June 1941)
"The earliest work [Foss] cares to acknowledge" is described as clearly influenced by Hindemith harmonically and technically, but with a Haydn-like melodic freshness.

W98. **Grotesque Dance** (1938; New York: G. Schirmer, 1938. (Compositions for the piano, 2) Pub. pl. no. 38290; New York: Carl Fischer, 1967, c1938. Pub. pl. no. N4888.)

For piano.
Dedication: none.
Duration: 3 minutes.
First published composition of Lukas Foss. Issued by G. Schirmer with *Four Two-Part Inventions* (See: W97).

BIBLIOGRAPHY

WB429. McPhee, Colin. "Scores and Records." *Modern Music* 17:54 (November/December 1939)
(See: WB427)

W99. **Sonatina** (1939; manuscript)

For piano.
Duration: 8 minutes.

W100. **Passacaglia** (1941; New York: G. Schirmer, 1941. Pub. pl. no. 39366.)

For piano.
Dedication: "To my Father."

Duration: 4 minutes.

BIBLIOGRAPHY

WB430. Fine, Irving. "Young America: Bernstein and Foss."
Modern Music 22:242 (May/June 1945)
Passacaglia is briefly mentioned as a transitional
piece whose "tendency is away from Hindemith, toward
a more romantic style, with rich almost over-ripe
harmonies."

W101.   Duo (Fantasia) (1941; New York: Hargail Music Publishers,
1941.)

For violoncello and piano.
Duration: 10 minutes.

FIRST PERFORMANCE

W101a. 1943. New York City. A concert sponsored by the
League of Composers devoted to young American
composers. (See: WB431)

BIBLIOGRAPHY

WB431. Fuller, Donald. "Society Notes in New York." *Modern
Music* 20:259 (May/June 1943)
Review of a concert sponsored by the League of
Composers devoted to young Americans. "The *Duo* for
cello and piano...offered Hindemith with some romantic-
impressionistic sidelines." (See: W101a)

W102.   Fantasy Rondo (1944; New York: G. Schirmer, 1946. Pub. pl.
no. 41211; New York: Carl Fischer, 1979, c1946. Pub. pl. no. O
5045.)

For piano.
Dedication: none.
Duration: 8 minutes.

BIBLIOGRAPHY

WB432. Berger, Arthur. "Scores and Records." *Modern Music*
23:135 (Spring 1946)
Review of *Fantasy Rondo* and *Composer's Holiday*
(see: W103) published by G. Schirmer. "The *Fantasy-
Rondo*...has ingenuity, several inspired moments and...a
most pianistic style in its figurations." (See also:
WB435)

W103.   Three Pieces (1944; 1 & 2: New York: Carl Fischer, 1944; New
York: Hargail Music Press, 1945. (Contemporary Music Series)
Pub. pl. nos. H-400 (v. 1); H-401 (v. 2). 3: New York: G.

Schirmer, 1946. Pub. pl. no. 41113; New York: G. Schirmer, 1979, c1946. Pub. pl. no. O5044.)

For violin and piano.
Contents: 1. Dedication -- 2. Early Song -- 3. Composer's
    Holiday.
Commissioned by: Harold Newman.
Dedication: none.
1 & 2: Violin part edited by Roman Totenberg.
These pieces have been arranged for solo flute and piano (see:
    Three Early Pieces, W111) and orchestrated for violin/flute
    and orchestra (See: *Three American Pieces*, W65)

FIRST PERFORMANCE

W103a. November 13, 1944. Carnegie Hall, New York City.
    Roman Totenberg, violin; Lukas Foss, piano. (See:
    WB433, WB434)

OTHER PERFORMANCES

W103b. April 18, 1982. Albright-Knox Art Gallery Auditorium,
    Buffalo, New York. Thomas Halpin, violin; Yvar
    Mikhashoff, piano. (See also: W88e, W97b, W109b)

W103c. November 1, 1983. Cooper Union, New York City.
    Bowery Ensemble. (See: B189; See also: W33d,
    W76p, W85f, W109f)

W103d. January 13, 1986. West Palm Beach Auditorium, West
    Palm Beach, Florida. Itzhak Perlman, violin; Samuel
    Sanders, piano. (See: WB436)

BIBLIOGRAPHY

WB433. Downes, Olin. "Totenberg Heard In Violin Recital." *New
    York Times* November 14, 1944:27.
        Review of the November 13, 1944 performance.
    Totenberg, who was the concertmaster of the City
    Center Symphony Orchestra, was not as well-received in
    recital as he had been as soloist with the Orchestra
    earlier that month, often forcing his tone. "These pieces,
    which we do not find as significant as other of Mr. Foss'
    compositions that we have heard, were warmly received
    and an encore was called for." (See: W103a)

WB434. Fuller, Donald. "Prokofiev and Milhaud, Winter of
    1944." *Modern Music* 22:106 (January/February 1945)
        Brief review of the November 13, 1944 premiere
    performance. "Foss lets changing eighth notes do much
    of his fast, vigorous work, but his slow passages show
    deep lyrical feeling." (See: W103a)

WB435. Berger, Arthur. "Scores and Records." *Modern Music*
23:135 (Spring 1946)
Reviews of *Fantasy Rondo* (see: W102) and
Composer's Holiday published by G. Schirmer. "The
Americanisms, as in other of his pieces of this period, are
too deliberate." (See also: WB432)

WB436. Brink, Bob. "Itzhak Perlman Proves He Has Few Equals."
Palm Beach Post (West Palm Beach, Fla.) January 14,
1986:C1.
Review of the January 13, 1986 performance
before a capacity audience. "The lines of *Dedications*
[*sic*] were ever so flowing...*Composer's Holiday* was
much like a hoedown..." (See: W103d)

W104. Capriccio (1948; New York: G. Schirmer, 1948. Pub. pl. no.
41651; New York: Carl Fischer, 1979, c1948. Pub. pl. no.
05043.)

For violoncello and piano.
Commissioned by: Koussevitzky Music Foundation, Inc., Lenox,
Massachusetts in memory of Natalie Koussevitzky.
Dedication: "In memory of Natalie Koussevitzky."
Duration: 5 minutes.
Violoncello part edited by Gregor Piatigorsky.

BIBLIOGRAPHY

WB437. Thorolfson, Frank. "Review of New Music." *Music
News* 41:22 (January 1949)
Review of the G. Schirmer edition. "*Capriccio*...is
an extended work requiring a first-rate cellist. Excellent
concert material."

WB438. "Review: The Strings." *Musicology* 2:318 (April 1949)
Review of the G. Schirmer publication.
"*Capriccio*...is one of the numerous works half-way
between competence and mediocrity that concert
'cellists...for some unfathomable reason insist on
including in their working repertoires."

W105. Prelude in D (1949; New York: Hargail Music Press, 1951.
(Contemporary Music Series) Pub. pl. no. H-716.)

For piano.
Dedication: "For 10 o'clock in the morning at South Chatham and
Ellie."
Duration: 3 minutes.

BIBLIOGRAPHY

WB439. "Music Reviews: Keyboard Music." *Notes* 9:495 (June
1952)

Review of the Hargail Press publication. "This remains a rather unimaginative piece of music making use of clichés unworthy of Mr. Foss' talent."

W106. **Scherzo Ricercato** (1953; New York: Carl Fischer, 1953, 1961. Pub. pl. no. N 3596-10. Pub. no. P3022.)

For piano.
Commissioned by: Composed for the Young Pianists Competition sponsored by the Wichita Falls Symphony, 1953.
Dedication: none.
Duration: 4 minutes.
Published with *Fantasy Rondo* (See: W102).

W107. **Etudes for Organ** (1967; Mainz: B. Schott's Söhne; New York: Carl Fischer, 1973, c1967. Pub. pl. no. N 5674. Pub. no. O4759; *Source: Music of the Avant-Garde* 2:29-33 (July 1968).

For organ (with 2 optional registration assistants).
Contents: Etude I -- Etude II -- Etude III -- Etude IV.
Commissioned by: Cornell College, Mount Vernon, Iowa on the occasion of the installation of their 65-rank Möller pipe organ in King Memorial Chapel.
Dedication: none.
Duration: 15 minutes.
The B. Schott's Söhne/Carl Fischer edition includes sample realizations.

FIRST PERFORMANCE

W107a. November 14, 1967. King Memorial Chapel, Cornell College, Mount Vernon, Iowa. Robert F. Triplett, organ. (See: WB440)

BIBLIOGRAPHY

WB440. Houkom, Alf S. "Lukas Foss and Chance Music." *Music/The A.G.O. Magazine* 2:10 (February 1968)
Review of the November 14, 1967 premiere performance. "Foss has created a work not only well suited to the instrument, but one that by utilizing only particular aspects of aleatoricism for each etude avoids the monotony and anonymity which could easily arise from such a technique." (See: W107a)

WB441. "*Etudes for Organ*." *Source: Music of the Avant-Garde* 2:29-33 (July 1968)
Includes a brief biography with the score.

WB442. *Lukas Foss on the New Lukas Foss.* New York: Carl Fischer, 1969:12-13.
(See: B112)

WB443. Haller, William. "Organ Works of the Avant-Garde."
Clavier 13:33-36 (April 1974)
Discussion of many avant-garde organ works and
how they are performed. Included in this article are
Etudes for Organ and *Baroque Variations* (See: W52),
the latter of which "concludes with a duel for organ and
percussion." He describes *Etudes* as a piece notated as
groups of ideas, allowing the performer certain creative
powers.

WB444. Little, Jeanie Rebecca. "Serial, Aleatoric, and Electronic
Techniques in American Organ Music Published Between
1960 and 1972." Ph.D. diss., University of Iowa,
1975:178-184. *Dissertation Abstracts* 36:7722A (June
1976), UMI# 76-13412.
"The purpose of this investigation is to single out
effective American organ music that makes use of serial,
aleatoric, and electronic techniques." Foss's *Four Etudes
for Organ* is included in the list of compositions analyzed.
The analysis focuses on the viewpoint of the performer,
mentioning the performance techniques and the organ
stops involved in playing the work.

W108.   Curriculum Vitae (1977; New York: Pembroke Music, 1978.
Pub. pl. no. PCB108.)

For accordion.
Commissioned by: American Accordionists Society.
Dedication: none.
Duration: 8 minutes.
Edited by Guy Klucevsek.
Percussion was added to this composition to create *Curriculum
Vitae With Time Bomb* (See: W88).

FIRST PERFORMANCE

W108a. November 1, 1977. New York City. William Schimmel,
accordion. Performed at the American Accordionists
Society Conference.

OTHER PERFORMANCE

W108b. September 27, 1985. St. Cuthbert's, Hamilton, Ontario.
Joseph Petric, accordion. (See: WB445)

BIBLIOGRAPHY

WB445. Fraser, Hugh. "Artsound 3 Proves Itself The Cutting
Edge." *Hamilton Spectator* September 28, 1985:C6.
Review of the September 27, 1985 performance.
"Meaningful quotes from Brahms *Lullaby*, Mozart's
Turkish March and the Horst *Wessel Lied* are tortured
and twisted by the ebbing and flowing terror of blaring
train whistle blasts, frantic, scurrying flight cut short by

dissonant chords of brutal violence. It all recedes into the distance as escape is made." (See: W108b)

WB446. Bassin, Joseph Philip. "An Overview of the Third Period Compositional Output of Lukas Foss, 1976-1983." Ed.D., Columbia University Teachers College, 1987:113-119. *Dissertation Abstracts* 48:1573A-1574A (January 1988) UMI# 87-21079.
(See: B216)

W109. Solo (1981; New York: Pembroke, 1982. Pub. pl. no. PCB 122.)

For piano.
Commissioned by: Yvar Mikhashoff through the American Music Center with the assistance of the State University of New York at Buffalo and Cambiata, Inc., Emiol MacKay, President.
Dedication: none.
Duration: 14 minutes. This was Foss's first piano composition in 28 years. It was extended and titled *Solo Observed*, for piano and three accompanying instruments. (See: *Solo Observed*, W89, for further information.)

FIRST PERFORMANCE

W109a. March 24, 1982. American Center, Paris. Yvar Mikhashoff, piano.

OTHER PERFORMANCES

W109b. April 18, 1982. Slee Concert Hall, State University of New York at Buffalo. Yvar Mikhashoff, piano. American premiere. Repeated that evening at the Albright-Knox Art Gallery Auditorium, Buffalo, New York. (See: WB447, WB448; See also: W18d, W56h, W76n, W88e, W97b, W103b)

W109c. May 19, 1982. Vienna. Yvar Mikhashoff, piano.

W109d. July 6, 1982. Chicago Public Library Cultural Center, Chicago, Illinois. Yvar Mikhashoff, piano.

W109e. October 7, 1982. Composers' Forum, Symphony Space, New York City. Yvar Mikhashoff, piano. New York premiere. (See: WB449; See also: W18e, W56i, W88f)

W109f. November 1, 1983. Cooper Union, New York City. Bowery Ensemble. (See: B189; See also: W33d, W76p, W85f, W103c)

BIBLIOGRAPHY

WB447. Putnam, Thomas. "UB Features Foss Creations." *Buffalo Courier Express* April 19, 1982:B6.

Review of the 60th birthday concert at the State University of New York at Buffalo, April 18, 1982. "Mikhashoff gave a wonderfully steady, strongly shaded performance...*Solo* is dry but not bloodless." (See: W109b; See also: WB98, WB279, WB370)

WB448. Trotter, Herman. "Influence of Foss Recalled in Program Saluting Composer." *Buffalo Evening News* April 19, 1982:B9.

Review of the April 18, 1982 American premiere performance. "[The twelve-note motif changes through] an inexorable metamorphosis during the course of which one suddenly notices that the dynamic level has changed or there has been a drift to a lower keyboard register...until, without warning, there are a couple of forte chords, a few agitated passages and a sudden, quizzical conclusion, almost as though some prankster had pulled the plug." (See: W109b; See also: WB99, WB280, WB371)

WB449. Holland, Bernard. "Concert: Lukas Foss Works Played at Composers' Forum." *New York Times* October 10, 1982:85.

Review of the October 7, 1982 performance of works by Lukas Foss. "*Solo*...created a perpetual-motion device in which phrases held fast to certain patterns but detail within this movement blurred and changed." (See: W109e; See also: WB100, WB281, WB399)

WB450. Bassin, Joseph Philip. "An Overview of the Third Period Compositional Output of Lukas Foss, 1976-1983." Ed.D., Columbia University Teachers College, 1987:132-140. *Dissertation Abstracts* 48:1573A-1574A (January 1988) UMI# 87-21079.
(See: B216)

W110.   Curriculum Vitae Tango (1983; Quadrivium Music Press, 1985-86.)

For piano.
Commissioned by: Yvar Mikhashoff through the Quadrivium Music Press.
Duration: ca. 3 minutes.
Published as part of the International Tango Collection, conceived in 1983 by Yvar Mikhashoff, to include 88 tangos by composers from 30 nations, none of which exceed three minutes in duration. The tango is taken from *Curriculum Vitae* (See: W108).

FIRST PERFORMANCE

W110a. April 14, 1985. Hallwalls Art Gallery, Buffalo, New York. Yvar Mikhashoff, piano. (See: WB451)

BIBLIOGRAPHY

WB451. Stiller, Andrew. "Mikhashoff, At Piano, Shows It Takes More Than Two to Tango." *Buffalo Evening News* April 15, 1985:B10.
Review of Mikhashoff's program entitled "Elastic Roses: The International Piano Tango Marathon" which was part of the 1985 North American New Music Festival, sponsored by the State University of New York at Buffalo. The four-hour performance included the performance of 46 tangos, interspersed with slide presentations depicting the history of the tango. Foss's tango is not mentioned in the review. (See: W110a)

W111. Three Early Pieces (1986; New York: Carl Fischer, 1990.)

For flute and piano.
Contents: 1. Early Song -- 2. Dedication -- 3. Composer's Holiday.
Duration: 13 minutes.
Arranged at the request of Carol Wincenc for flute and piano from the original 1944 version, *Three Pieces* (See: W103) for violin and piano by Lukas Foss. The published version is edited by Carol Wincenc and includes both the violin and flute parts on the same score. This was also arranged for violin and orchestra (See: *Three American Pieces*, W65).

FIRST PERFORMANCE

W111a. August 23, 1986. National Flute Association Convention, New York City. Carol Wincenc, flute; Eric Larsen, piano.

OTHER PERFORMANCES

W111b. October 12, 1987. Indiana University School of Music, 1987. Carol Wincenc, flute; James Tocco, piano. (See: D98)

W112. Central Park Reel (1987; New York: Carl Fischer. Available on rental.)

For violin and piano.
Commissioned by the United States Information Agency for the winners of their 1986-87 Artistic Ambassador music competition, Kathleen Winkler, violin and Deborah Berman, piano.
Duration: 11 minutes.

FIRST PERFORMANCE

W112a. June 17, 1987. Victoria Concert Hall, Singapore. Kathleen Winkler, violin; Deborah Berman, piano.

OTHER PERFORMANCES

W112b. July 5, 1987. Great Hall, Arts Centre, Toronto, Ontario, Canada. Kathleen Winkler, violin; Deborah Berman, piano. (See: WB452, WB453)

W112c. October 5, 1987. Town Hall, New York City. Philip Johnson, violin; Kenneth Bowen, piano. (See: WB454)

BIBLIOGRAPHY

WB452. "American Duo in *Central Park*." *The Press (Toronto)* July 1, 1987:21.
Promotional piece for the July 5, 1987 performance and includes biographical information an Foss, Winkler, and Berman. "Foss wrote the piece in his New York apartment, basing the music on the classic American bluegrass fiddle style." (See: W112b)

WB453. "Special Work at Recital." *Star (Toronto)* July 2, 1987.
Promotional article for the July 5, 1987 performance by the Winkler/Berman Duo. The article explains the commission of the work from the United States Information Agency for the duo's tour to New Zealand, Korea, Indonesia, Malaysia, and Singapore. "Foss has based the music on the classic American bluegrass fiddle style and has considerable fun, at its expense, turning the repetitive sound of the bluegrass into a distorted expression of New York as the piece evolves." (See: W112b)

WB454. "A Tribute To Lukas Foss at Town Hall." *New York Times* October 5, 1987:C17.
Announcement of a 65th birthday celebration concert in Foss's honor. Included was the New York premiere of *Central Park Reel.* (See: W112c)

W113.   Chaconne (1987; *Guitar Review* no. 73:5-12 (Spring 1988))

For guitar.
Contents: Moderato -- Slow -- Agitato -- Lo Stesso Tempo.
Commissioned by: Albert Augustine, Ltd.
Dedication: "Written for David Starobin."
Duration: 9 minutes.
A tape delay joins the soloist in the fourth section which can be performed by a pre-recorded tape or a second guitarist. The work is written in one movement with four sections.

FIRST PERFORMANCE

W113a. November 8, 1987. New York City. David Starobin, guitar. (See: WB455)

BIBLIOGRAPHY

WB455. Starobin, David. "Lukas Foss." *Guitar Review* no.73:2-
12 (Spring 1988)
Interview with Lukas Foss by the dedicatee of
Chaconne. The article includes a biographical sketch of
Foss's education and a discussion of his use of the guitar
in various compositions including *Baroque Variations*
(See: W52). The score to *Chaconne* is included at the
end of the interview. (See: W113a)

ADAPTATIONS

W114.   Rameau, Jean-Philippe. *Les Fêtes d'Hébé*.

W115.   Mozart, Wolfgang Amadeus. *The Impressario*. Recitatives.

W116.   Mozart, Wolfgang Amadeus. *Don Giovanni*. Overture and music
for 3 orchestras.

W117.   Wagner, Richard. *Parsifal Symphony*. (See: B168)

W118.   Beethoven, Ludwig van. *Military Marches for Winds*. (See also:
D51)

DISCOGRAPHY

This list includes commercially available recordings of works by Foss, performances by Foss, and works conducted by Foss. It also includes non-commercially available recordings which are archivally significant performances of works by Foss, performances by Foss, or works conducted by Foss. The numbers preceded by "DB" in the "See" references in this section refer to item numbers in the "Discography Bibliography" section.

FOSS AS COMPOSER

OPERAS

The Jumping Frog of Calaveras County (Der Held von Calaveras)

D1.   The Orchard Collection, Indiana University (tape reel, stereo) Unnamed performers.
        Donated by Robert Orchard to Indiana University.

D2.   Lyrichord LL 11 (mono); LLST 711 (stereo), 1953?. After Dinner Opera Company (Smiley: Burton Trimble, tenor; Stranger: Paul Ukena, bass-baritone; Uncle Henry: Elvin Campbell, baritone; Lulu: Ruth Biller, soprano; Guitar Player: Ralph Cavalucci, baritone; Crap Shooters: Karl Brock, tenor, Ahti Tuuri, bass); Frederic Kurzweil, piano; Richard Flusser, director. (See: DB1, DB2)

D3.   College of Musical Arts, Bowling Green, Ohio (cassette, stereo), 1985. Todd Graber, Lance Ashmore, baritones; Ruth Cunningham, soprano; Eric Perkins, tenor; Robert Spano, musical director; Terry Eder, chorus director.

Recorded at Bowling Green State University College of Musical Arts, Kobacker Hall, November 15, 1985. With: Weill, Kurt. *Down in the Valley*.

Introductions and Goodbyes

D4.   The Orchard Collection, Indiana University (tape reel, mono) Unnamed performers.
        Donated by Robert Orchard to Indiana University.

CHORAL MUSIC

The Prairie

D5.   Turnabout TV-S 34649 (stereo), 1976. Jeanne Distell, soprano; Ani Yervanian, mezzo soprano; Jerold Norman, tenor; Harlan Foss, baritone; Gregg Smith Singers; Long Island Symphonic Choral Association; Brooklyn Philharmonia; Lukas Foss, conductor.

Behold! I Build an House

D6.   Composers Recordings CRI SD 123 (stereo), 1958. Roger Wagner Chorale; James MacInnes and Lukas Foss, pianos; Roger Wagner, conductor.
        A recording of the 1957 American Academy of the National Institute of Arts and Letters award winners. With: Foss. *Psalms* (See: D13); Shifrin, Seymour. *Serenade for Five Instruments*. (See: DB3, DB4, DB5)

D7.   *America Sings, v. 5: The 20th Century American Masters (1920-1950)*. Vox SVBX 5353, 1977. Gregg Smith Singers; Gregg Smith, conductor.
        With: Schuman, William. *Prelude*; Carter, Elliott. *Musicians Wrestle Everywhere, Defense of Corinth*; Riegger, Wallingford. *Who Can Revoke*; Seeger, Ruth Crawford. *Chant*; Sessions, Roger. *Turn O Southern Hymns*; Thompson, Randall. *Alleluia*; Piston, Walter. *Psalm and Prayer of David*; Cowell, Henry. *Luther's Carol to His Son*; Barber, Samuel. *A Stopwatch and an Ordinance Map*; Fine, Irving. *The Choral New Yorker*; Talma, Louise. *Let's Touch the Sky*; Bernstein, Leonard. *Choruses from the Lark*; Gershwin, George. *Two Madrigals*; Ives, Charles. *Two Election Songs*.

D8.   *Music of Lukas Foss*. Oshkosh Symphony Orchestra, Inc. KM 14002 (stereo), 1986. University of Wisconsin Oshkosh Choral Union; Oshkosh Symphony Orchestra; Henri B. Pensis, conductor.
        With: Foss. *Gift of the Magi. Suite* (i.e., *Pantomime*; See: D37), *Griffelkin. Suite* (See: D58).

A Parable of Death (Ein Märchen vom Tod)

D9.   Columbia ML 4859 (mono), 195-? Vera Zorina, narrator; Farrold
      Stephens, tenor; Louisville Orchestra; Robert Whitney, conductor.
      (*Columbia Masterworks*)
            Reissued as Special Service Records CML 4859 (See: D11)
      and Columbia Special Products AML 4859 (See: D12). With:
      Martinu, Bohuslav. *Intermezzo*; Milhaud, Darius. *Kentuckiana*.
      (See: DB6, DB7, DB8, DB9)

D10. Educo ECM 4002 (mono), 1954? Marvin Hayes, narrator; Richard
      Robinson, tenor; Pomona College Glee Club; Lukas Foss,
      conductor.
            Recording of the chamber version. (See: DB10)

D11. Special Service Records CML 4859 (mono), 197-? (*Collector's
      Series*)
            Reissue of Columbia ML 4859, 195-? (See: D9)

D12. Columbia Special Products AML 4859 (mono), 1974.
            Reissue of Columbia ML 4859, 195-? (See: D9)

Psalms

D13. Composers Recordings CRI SD 123 (stereo), 1958. Claire Gordon,
      Richard Levitt, vocal solos in *Psalms*, pt. 1; Keith Wyatt, vocal solo
      in *Psalms*, pt. 2; Roger Wagner Chorale; James MacInnes, Lukas
      Foss, pianos; Roger Wagner, conductor.
            A recording of the 1957 American Academy of the National
      Institute of Arts and Letters award winners. With: Foss. *Behold! I
      Build an House* (See: D6); Shifrin, Seymour. *Serenade for Five
      Instruments*. (See: DB11, DB12)

D14. Pro Arte (digital, stereo) PAD 169 (phonodisc); CDD 169 (compact
      disc); PCD 169 (cassette), 1984. Wisconsin Conservatory
      Symphony Chorus; Margaret Hawkins, director; Milwaukee
      Symphony Orchestra; Lukas Foss, conductor.
            Recorded May 26, 27, 29, 1983 in Uihlein Hall, Milwaukee,
      Wisconsin with grant funds from the Milwaukee Symphony
      Women's League. With: Stravinsky, Igor. *Symphony of Psalms*;
      Ives, Charles. *Psalm 67*. (See: DB13, DB14, DB15)

Fragments of Archilochos

D15. State University of New York at Buffalo, Evenings for New Music
      114, 1968. Robert Betts, countertenor; Miriam Abramowitsch,
      Melvin Strauss, speakers; Crane Collegiate Singers (State
      University of New York College at Potsdam); Oswald Rantucci,
      mandolin; Jonathan Marcus, guitar; Jan Williams, Edward
      Burnham, Lynn Harbold, percussion; Lukas Foss, conductor.

Recorded March 3, 1968, Albright-Knox Art Gallery, Buffalo, New York. (See: W17b)

D16.   Wergo WER 60 040 (stereo), 1969? Robert Betts, countertenor; Miriam Abramowitsch, Melvin Strauss, speakers; Crane Collegiate Singers (State University of New York College at Potsdam); Oswald Rantucci, mandolin; Jonathan Marcus, guitar; Jan Williams, Edward Burnham, Lynn Harbold, percussion; Brock McElheran, conductor.
Recorded May 1968, Buffalo, New York. With: Foss. *Echoi* (See: D63), *Non-Improvisation* (See: D67).

D17.   Heliodor (stereo) 2549 001 (phonodisc); 3313 001 (cassette), 1970. Re-release of Wergo WER 60 040 (See: D16)

Three Airs for Frank O'Hara's Angel
(Trois Airs Pour l'Ange de Frank O'Hara)

D18.   State University of New York at Buffalo, Evenings for New Music 237, 1972. Sylvia Dimiziani, soprano; Fredonia Chamber Singers (State University of New York College at Fredonia); William Graf, director; Dennis Kahle, percussion; Lukas Foss, piano; Oswald Rantucci, mandolin; Guy Klucevsek, accordion; tape.
Recorded December 3, 1972, Albright-Knox Art Gallery, Buffalo, New York. (See: W18b)

D19.   *America Sings: American Choral Music After 1950: The Non-Traditionalists.* Turnabout TV 34759 (stereo), 1980. Gregg Smith Singers; Gregg Smith, conductor.
Recorded March 1976. With: Brown, Earle. *Small Pieces for Large Chorus*; Reynolds, Roger. *The Emperor of Ice Cream*; Richards, Eric. *Though Under Medium.*

D20.   *Music of the Twentieth Century.* Boston University School of Music, (tape reel, stereo), December 7, 1982. Marjorie McDermott, soprano; Collegium in Contemporary Music; Lukas Foss, piano.
Recorded in concert in Boston University Concert Hall. With: Foss. *Elytres* (See: D45); *Paradigm* (See: D74); *Solo Observed* (See: D86). (See: W18f)

Lamdeni

D21.   State University of New York at Buffalo, Evenings for New Music 292, 1975. State University of New York at Buffalo Choir; Dennis Kahle, Donald Knaack, Jan Williams, Margaret Knaack, percussion; Joseph Kubera, harpsichord; Harriet Simons, conductor.
Recorded March 22, 1975, Albright-Knox Art Gallery, Buffalo, New York. (See: W19b)

With Music Strong

D22. Koss Classics KC-1004 (digital, stereo), 1990. Milwaukee
Symphony Orchestra; Lukas Foss, conductor.
With: Foss. *Song of Songs* (See: D25), *Ode* (See: D36).

MUSIC FOR SOLO VOICE

Song of Songs

D23. Columbia ML 5451 (mono); MS 6123 (stereo), 1962. Jennie
Tourel, mezzo soprano; New York Philharmonic Orchestra; Leonard
Bernstein, conductor.
Recorded under the auspices of the Naumburg Foundation
from whom it won the 1957 Naumburg Recording Award. Deleted
from Columbia's catalog and re-released by CRI (See: D24). With:
Ben-Haim, Paul. *Sweet Psalmist of Israel.* (See: DB16, DB17,
DB18, DB19, DB20, DB21)

D24. Composers Recordings CRI SD 284E (mono); CRI SD 284 (stereo),
1972. Jennie Tourel, mezzo soprano; New York Philharmonic;
Leonard Bernstein, conductor.
"Recorded under the auspices of the Walter W. Naumburg
Foundation American Recording Awards Program." Originally
released in 1962 by Columbia and subsequently deleted from their
catalog (See: D23). With: Riegger, Wallingford. *Symphony no. 3*,
op. 42.

D25. Koss Classics KC-1004 (digital, stereo), 1990. Carolyn Page,
soprano; Milwaukee Symphony Orchestra; Lukas Foss, conductor.
With: Foss. *Ode* (See: D36), *With Music Strong* (See:
D22).

Time Cycle (Orchestral version)

D26. Columbia ML 5680 (mono); MS 6280 (stereo), 1962. Adele
Addison, soprano; Improvisation Chamber Ensemble (Richard
Dufallo, clarinet; Howard Colf, violoncello; Lukas Foss, piano;
Charles DeLancey, percussion); Columbia Symphony Orchestra;
Leonard Bernstein, conductor.
"First recording." Reissued as Columbia Special Products
AMS 6280 (stereo); CMS 6280 (See: D27). (See: DB22, DB23,
DB24, DB25, DB26, DB27)

D27. Columbia Special Products AMS 6280 (stereo); CMS 6280, 197-?
Reissue of Columbia MS 6280, 1962. (See: D26)

D28. *The International Contemporary Music Exchange, Inc. Presents the
Outstanding Contemporary Orchestral Compositions of the United
States.* ICME 1 (mono), 1975.

"A sampler and comprehensive survey." With: Brown, Earle. *Available Forms II*; Carter, Elliott. *Concerto for Orchestra*; Copland, Aaron. *Appalachian Spring*; Crumb, George. *Echoes of Time and the River*; Harris, Roy. *Symphony No. 3*; Ives, Charles. *Symphony No. 4*; Ruggles, Carl. *Sun-Treader*; Schuman, William. *Symphony No. 6*; Sessions, Roger. *Symphony No. 3*; Barber, Samuel. *Knoxville: Summer of 1915*; Cowell, Henry. *Synchrony*; Druckman, Jacob. *Windows*; Harrison, Lou. *Symphony on G*; Hovhaness, Alan. *Mysterious Mountain*; Riegger, Wallingford. *Symphony No. 3*, op. 42; Rochberg, George. *Symphony No. 2*; Schuller, Gunther. *Seven Studies on Themes of Paul Klee*; Thomson, Virgil. *The Plow that Broke the Plains*; Varèse, Edgard. *Arcana*; Wuorinen, Charles. *Piano Concerto*.

Time Cycle (Chamber version)

D29.   *Two Record Premieres: Commissioned by the Fromm Music Foundation*. Epic LC 3886 (mono); BC 1286 (stereo), 1964. Grace-Lynne Martin, soprano; Improvisation Chamber Ensemble (Richard Dufallo, clarinet; Lukas Foss, piano/celesta; Howard Colf, violoncello; Charles DeLancey, percussion).
   With: Foss. *Echoi* (See: D62). (See: DB28, DB29, DB30, DB31, DB32, DB33, DB34)

D30.   State University of New York at Buffalo, Evenings for New Music 39, 1965. Sylvia Dimiziani, soprano; Sherman Friedland, clarinet; Jay Humeston, violoncello; Frederic Myrow, piano; Jan Williams, percussion; Richard Dufallo, conductor.
   Recorded May 9, 1965, Albright-Knox Art Gallery, Buffalo, New York. (See: W32e)

D31.   *Chamber Music of Lukas Foss*. Tempe, AZ: Arizona State University, (tape reel, stereo), October 7, 1981. New Music Ensemble; Glenn Hackbarth, director; Lukas Foss, conductor.
   Recorded during performance in the Louise Lincoln Kerr Cultural Center. With: Foss. *Ni Bruit Ni Vitesse* (See: D78); *Music for Six* (See: D84). (See: W32f)

D32.   *American Composers*. Contemporary Recording Studios CRS 8219 (stereo), 1982. Janice Kestler, soprano; John Russo, clarinet; Lori Barnet, violoncello; John Dulik, piano/celesta; Glenn Steele, percussion; Lukas Foss, conductor.
   With: Levinson, Gerald. *Trio for Clarinet, Cello, and Piano*; Russo, John. *Four Riffs for Clarinet and Percussion*.

D33.   *Time as a Structural Metaphor: A Study of Tonal, Proportional and Textual Relationships in Time Cycle....* Indiana University School of Music, (tape reel, stereo), 1983. Virginia Palmer, soprano and lecturer; Marlene Macomber, clarinet; Timothy Mutschlecner, violoncello; William Crowle, piano; Rebecca Kite, percussion.
   Recorded April 25, 1983 in the Music Annex, Indiana University (See: W32g). Contents: v. 1. *Time Cycle* -- v. 2. Lecture by Virginia Palmer.

Thirteen Ways of Looking at a Blackbird

D34.   Composers Recordings CRI SD 442 (stereo), 1981. Rose-Marie
         Freni, mezzo soprano; Robert Dick, flute; Jan Williams, percussion;
         Yvar Mikhashoff, piano. (*American Contemporary*)
             Recorded in New York City, April 1980. With: Mollicone,
         Henry. *The Face on the Barroom Floor*. Winner of the American
         Composers Alliance Recording Award. (See: DB35, DB36)

Measure for Measure

D35.   Gramavision GR 7005 (stereo), 1983. Frank Hoffmeister, tenor;
         Brooklyn Philharmonic Orchestra; Lukas Foss, conductor.
             With: Foss. *Night Music for John Lennon* (See: D54), *Solo
         Observed* (See: D87).

ORCHESTRAL MUSIC

Ode

D36.   Koss Classics KC-1004 (digital, stereo), 1990. Milwaukee
         Symphony Orchestra; Lukas Foss, conductor.
             With: Foss. *Song of Songs* (See: D25), *With Music Strong*
         (See: D22).

Pantomime

D37.   *Music of Lukas Foss*. Oshkosh Symphony Orchestra, Inc. KM
         14002 (stereo), 1986. Oshkosh Symphony Orchestra; Henri B.
         Pensis, conductor.
             With: Foss. *Griffelkin. Suite* (See: D58), *Behold! I Build an
         House* (See: D8).

Concerto for Oboe

D38.   Crystal S 851 (stereo), 1971. Bert Gassman, oboe; Crystal
         Chamber Orchestra (Louise DiTullio Dussman, flute; David Atkins,
         clarinet; David Breidenthal, bassoon; Robert Henderson, horn;
         Thomas Stevens, trumpet; Bryon Peebles, trombone; Harold
         Dicterow, Lyndl Christ, violins; Albert Falkove, viola; Mary Louise
         Zeyen, violoncello; Milton Nadel, bass); Akira Endo, conductor.
             This recording uses the string quintet version of the string
         parts. With: Stevens, Halsey. *Concerto for Clarinet & String
         Orchestra*. (See: DB37, DB38, DB39, DB40)

Concerto No. 2 for Piano

D39.   Decca DL 9889 (mono), 1957. Lukas Foss, piano; Los Angeles
Festival Orchestra; Franz Waxman, conductor.
The poor sound quality of this recording was remastered and
improved for the Varèse/Sarabande release. (See: D40, DB41,
DB42, DB43, DB44)

D40.   *Waxman Conducts Waxman; Foss Plays Foss.* Varèse/Sarabande
VC 81052E (mono), 1978. Lukas Foss, piano; Los Angeles
Festival Orchestra; Franz Waxman, conductor.
Reissue of Decca DL 9889, remastered with improved sound
quality (See: D39). With: Waxman, Franz. *Sinfonietta for Strings
and Timpani.*

Symphony of Chorales

D41.   Recording Guarantee Project, American International Music Fund,
Koussevitzky Music Foundation 35/5 (tape reel, mono), 1958.
Boston Symphony Orchestra; Lukas Foss, conductor.
Limited edition; recorded live for radio broadcast, October
31, 1958 in Symphony Hall, Boston, Massachusetts. (See: W47b
WB187)

Elytres

D42.   Recording Guarantee Project, American International Music Fund,
Koussevitzky Music Foundation (tape reel, mono), 1966. Julius
Baker, flute; John Corigliano, Frank Gullino, violins; New York
Philharmonic Orchestra; Lukas Foss, conductor.
Limited edition; recorded live April 14-15, 1966 in
Philharmonic Hall, Lincoln Center, New York City. (See also:
W49b)

D43.   Turnabout TV-S 34514 (stereo), 1972. John Wummer, flute; Felix
Galimir and Hiroko Yajima Rhodes, violins; Robert Levin, piano;
Members of the New York Philomusica Chamber Ensemble; Lukas
Foss, conductor. (*The Contemporary Composer in the U.S.A.*)
With: Foss. *Paradigm* (See: D72), *Ni Bruit Ni Vitesse* (See:
D77); Williams, Jan. *Dream Lesson.* (See: DB45)

D44.   *Verehrter Meister, Lieber Freund: Begegnungen mit Komponisten
Unserer Zeit.* Deutsche Grammophon 0629 027--0629 031
(stereo), 1977-1978. Unnamed performers.
Issued with Heinrich Strobel's book of the same title. With:
Stravinsky, Igor. *Agon*; Hindemith, Paul. *Symphonic
Metamorphosis of Themes by C.M. von Weber*; Messiaen, Olivier.
Réveil des Oiseaux; Krenek, Ernst. *From Three Make Seven*;
Liebermann, Rolf. *Concerto für Jazzband und Sinfonieorchester*;
Boulez, Pierre. *Polyphonie X*; Britten, Benjamin. *Sinfonia da
Requiem*, op. 20; Berio, Luciano. *Chemins*; Ligeti, György.

Lontano; Stockhausen, Karlheinz. *Punkte 1952/62*; Penderecki, Kryzysztof. *Sonata für Violoncello und Orchester*; Nono, Luigi. *Varianti*; Haubenstock-Ramati, Roman. *Credentials*; Hartmann, Karl Amadeus. *Concerto for Piano and Band*; Dallapiccola, Luigi. *An Mathilda*; Zimmermann, Bernd Alois. *Konzert für Oboe und Orchester*.

D45. *Music of the Twentieth Century*. Boston University School of Music (tape reel, stereo), December 7, 1982. Collegium in Contemporary Music; Lukas Foss, conductor.

Concert presented in the Boston University Concert Hall (See: W49c). With: Foss. *Solo Observed* (See: D86); *Paradigm* (See: D74); *Three Airs for Frank O'Hara's Angel* (See: D20)

Cello Concert

D46. Recording Guarantee Project, American International Music Fund, Koussevitzky Music Foundation, (tape reel, mono), 1966-67. Mstislav Rostropovich, violoncello; Buffalo Philharmonic Orchestra; Lukas Foss, conductor.

Limited edition; recorded live 1966-67 in Kleinhans Music Hall, Buffalo, New York. (See: W51b)

Baroque Variations

D47. Nonesuch (stereo) H 71202 (phonodisc); N5-1202 (cassette), 1968. Buffalo Philharmonic Orchestra; Lukas Foss, conductor.

Re-released as part of Nonesuch 71416 (See: D48). First recordings of *Baroque Variations I* and *II*. Recorded at Kleinhans Music Hall, Buffalo, New York, March 1968 during the 2nd Buffalo Festival of the Arts. With: Cage, John. *Concerto for Prepared Piano and Chamber Orchestra*. (See: DB46, DB47, DB48, DB49, DB50, DB94; See also: W52d, D49)

D48. Nonesuch (stereo) 71416 (phonodisc); 71416-4 (cassette), 1985. Buffalo Philharmonic; Lukas Foss, conductor.

Reissue in part of Nonesuch H 71202 (See: D47) and Nonesuch HC 73030 as part of the 300th anniversary of Bach, Handel, and Scarlatti. *Baroque Variations* recorded March 1968 in Kleinhans Music Hall, Buffalo, New York. With: Bach, Johann Sebastian. *Sinfonia* from the 29th Cantata, *Wir Danken Dir, Gott, Wir Danken Dir*; *Prelude from Partita in E Major for Solo Violin*; Scarlatti, Domenico. *Sonata in E, L. 23*; Handel, George Frideric. *Larghetto* from *Concerto Grosso, op. 6, no. 12*. (See: DB51)

Baroque Variations. Phorion

D49. *Bernstein Conducts Music of Our Time*. Columbia ML 6452 (mono); MS 7052 (stereo), 1967. New York Philharmonic; Leonard Bernstein, conductor. (*Columbia Masterworks; Music of Our Time*, v. 2)

"First recordings." Recording of movement III, *Phorion*, only.
With: Denisov, Edison. *Crescendo e Diminuendo*; Schuller,
Gunther. *Triplum*. (See: DB52, DB53)

Geod

D50.   Candide CE 31042 (stereo), 1969. Buffalo Philharmonic Orchestra;
Lukas Foss, conductor.
Recorded under a subsidy by the American International
Music Fund.

Salomon Rossi Suite

D51.   Indiana University School of Music Program, 1977-1978, no. 91,
1977. Indiana University Festival Orchestra; Lukas Foss,
conductor.
Recorded at the Indiana University School of Music, July 29,
1977. With: Beethoven, Ludwig van. *Military Marches for Winds*
(See: W118). (See: W58b)

D52.   *Orchestral Works by Lukas Foss*. New World Records (digital,
stereo) NW375-1 (phonodisc); NW375-2 (compact disc), 1989.
Brooklyn Philharmonic Orchestra; Lukas Foss, conductor.
Recorded September 27, 1988 in the Great Hall, Cooper
Union, New York City. "Recording made possible with grants from
the Mary Flagler Cary Charitable Trust, Francis Goelet, the Rita and
Stanley H. Kaplan Foundation, Joseph Machlis, The National
Endowment for the Arts, the New York State Council on the Arts,
Arnold L. Sabin, and Starrett City Housing Corporation." With:
Foss. *Renaissance Concerto* (See: D57), *Orpheus and Euridice*
(See: D56). (See: DB54, DB55, DB56, DB57)

Quintets for Orchestra

D53.   Indiana University School of Music Program, 1979-1980, no. 454
(tape, stereo), 1980. Indiana University Symphony Orchestra;
Thomas Baldner, conductor.
This work comprises v. 2. Recorded February 6, 1980.
(See: W59b)

Night Music for John Lennon

D54.   Gramavision GR 7005 (stereo), 1983. Wilmer Wise, Neil Balm,
trumpets; Brooks Tillotson, horn; Jonathan Taylor, trombone;
Andrew Seligson, tuba; Brooklyn Philharmonic Orchestra; Lukas
Foss, conductor.
With: Foss. *Solo Observed* (See: D87), *Measure for
Measure* (See: D35).

Exeunt

D55.   Indiana University School of Music Program, 1981-1982, no. 31
(tape reel, stereo), 1981. Indiana University Festival Orchestra;
Lukas Foss, conductor.
Recording of the July 2, 1981 premiere performance, under
the title *Dissertation* (See: W61a). With: Berlioz, Hector. *Le
Carnaval Romain Overture*; Ives, Charles. *Decoration Day*; Ravel,
Maurice. *Daphnis et Chloé, Suite No. 2.*

Orpheus and Euridice

D56.   *Orchestral Works by Lukas Foss.* New World Records (stereo,
digital) NW375-1 (phonodisc); NW375-2 (compact disc), 1989.
Yehudi Menuhin, Edna Michell, violins; Brooklyn Philharmonic
Orchestra; Lukas Foss, conductor.
Recorded May 12, 1988 in the Great Hall, Cooper Union,
New York City. "Recording made possible with grants from the
Mary Flagler Cary Charitable Trust, Francis Goelet, the Rita and
Stanley H. Kaplan Foundation, Joseph Machlis, The National
Endowment for the Arts, the New York State Council on the Arts,
Arnold L. Sabin, and Starrett City Housing Corporation." With:
Foss. *Renaissance Concerto* (See: D57), *Salomon Rossi Suite* (See:
D52). (See: DB58, DB59, DB60)

Renaissance Concerto

D57.   *Orchestral Works by Lukas Foss.* New World Records (stereo,
digital) NW375-1 (phonodisc); NW375-2 (compact disc), 1989.
Carol Wincenc, flute; Brooklyn Philharmonic Orchestra; Lukas Foss,
conductor.
Recorded September 27, 1988 in the Great Hall, Cooper
Union, New York City. "Recording made possible with grants from
the Mary Flagler Cary Charitable Trust, Francis Goelet, the Rita and
Stanley H. Kaplan Foundation, Joseph Machlis, The National
Endowment for the Arts, the New York State Council on the Arts,
Arnold L. Sabin, and Starrett City Housing Corporation." With:
Foss: *Salomon Rossi Suite* (See: D52), *Orpheus and Euridice* (See:
D56). (See: DB61, DB62, DB63, DB64)

Griffelkin Suite

D58.   *Music of Lukas Foss.* Oshkosh Symphony Orchestra, Inc. KM
14002 (stereo), 1986. Oshkosh Symphony Orchestra; Henri B.
Pensis, conductor.
With: Foss. *Pantomime* (See: D37), *Behold! I Build an
House* (See: D8).

CHAMBER MUSIC

String Quartet No. 1 in G

D59.   Columbia ML 5476 (mono), 1960. American Art Quartet (Eudice Shapiro, Robert Sushel, violins; Virginia Majewski, viola; Victor Gottlieb, violoncello). (*Columbia Masterworks; Modern American Music Series*)
      With: Bergsma, William L. *Quartet 3*. Reissued as Columbia Special Products AML 5476 (See: D60). (See: DB65, DB66)

D60.   Columbia Special Products AML 5476 (mono), 1973. (*Columbia Records Collector's Series*)
      Reissue of Columbia ML 5476, 1960 (See: D59).

Studies in Improvisation

D61.   *Studies in Improvisation*. RCA Victor LSC 2558 (mono); LM 2558 (stereo), 1961. Improvisation Chamber Ensemble (Richard Dufallo, clarinet; Lukas Foss, piano; Howard Colf, violoncello; Charles DeLancey, percussion); David Duke, horn.
      First recorded performance of the Improvisation Chamber Ensemble. (See: DB67, DB68, DB69, DB70, DB71, DB72)

Echoi

D62.   *Two Record Premieres: Commissioned by the Fromm Music Foundation*. Epic LC 3886 (mono); BC 1286 (stereo), 1964. Group for Contemporary Music at Columbia University (Arthur Bloom, clarinet; Robert Martin, violoncello; Charles Wuorinen, piano; Raymond Desroches, percussion).
      With: Foss. *Time Cycle* (chamber version) (See: D29). (See: DB74, DB75, DB76, DB77, DB78, DB79, DB80)

D63.   Wergo WER 60 040 (stereo), 1969? Edward Yadzinski, clarinet; Douglas Davis, violoncello; Lukas Foss, piano; Jan Williams, percussion.
      "Recording supervised by the composer." Re-released as Heliodor 2549 001 (See: D65). With: Foss. *Non-Improvisation* (See: D67), *Fragments of Archilochos* (See: D16). Recorded May 1968, Buffalo, New York.

D64.   State University of New York at Buffalo, Evenings for New Music 23, 1965. Richard Dufallo, clarinet; Lukas Foss, piano; Howard Colf, violoncello; John Bergamo, percussion.
      Recorded March 5, 1965, Albright-Knox Art Gallery, Buffalo, New York. (See: W74c)

D65.   Heliodor (stereo) 2549 001 (phonodisc); 3313 001 (cassette), 1970. Re-release of Wergo WER 60 040 (See: D63)

Non-Improvisation

D66.   State University of New York at Buffalo, Evenings for New Music
115, 1968. Edward Yadzinski, clarinet and percussion; Robert
Martin, violoncello; Lukas Foss, piano; Jan Williams, electric organ.
   Recorded March 3, 1968, Albright-Knox Art Gallery, Buffalo,
New York. (See: W75d)

D67.   Wergo WER 60 040 (stereo), 1969? Edward Yadzinski, clarinet;
Douglas Davis, violoncello; Lukas Foss, piano; Jan Williams,
percussion. Re-released as Heliodor 2549 001 (See: D68)
   Recorded May 1968, Buffalo, New York. With: Foss. *Echoi*
(See: D63), *Fragments of Archilochos* (See: D16)

D68.   Heliodor (stereo) 2549 001 (phonodisc); 3313 001 (cassette),
1970. Re-release of Wergo WER 60 040 (See: D67)

Paradigm

D69.   State University of New York at Buffalo, Evenings for New Music
135, 1968. Jerry Kirkbride, clarinet; Jonathan Marcus, guitar;
Charles Haupt, violin; Marijke Verberne, violoncello; Jon Hassell,
Stanley Lunetta, Joseph Romanowski, electronics; Jan Williams,
percussion/conductor.
   Recorded November 3, 1968, Albright-Knox Art Gallery,
Buffalo, New York. (See: W76c)

D70.   State University of New York at Buffalo, Evenings for New Music
162, 1969. Jerry Kirkbride, clarinet; Steven Bell, guitar; Charles
Haupt, violin; Marijke Verberne, violoncello; Jan Williams,
percussion/conductor.
   Recorded November 8, 1969, Albright-Knox Art Gallery,
Buffalo, New York. (See: W76d)

D71.   Deutsche Grammophon 2543 005 (mono); 2561 042 (stereo),
1971. Members of the State University of New York at Buffalo
Center for Creative and Performing Arts (Jerry Kirkbride, clarinet;
Steven Bell, guitar; Charles Haupt, violin; Marijke Verberne,
violoncello; Jan Williams, percussion/conductor; George Ritscher,
electronics; Lukas Foss, musical supervision). (*Avant Garde*)
   With: Hiller, Lejaren. *Algorithms I, Versions I & IV*;
Schwartz, Elliott. *Signals*. (See: DB81, DB82)

D72.   Turnabout TV-S 34514 (stereo), 1972. Ronald Roseman, oboe;
Jesse Levine, viola; Lukas Foss, electric harpsichord; Stanley
Silverman, electric guitar; Jan Williams, percussion/conductor.
(*The Contemporary Composer in the U.S.A.*)
   With: Foss. *Elytres* (See: D43), *Ni Bruit Ni Vitesse* (See:
D77); Williams, Jan. *Dream Lesson*. (See: DB83)

D73.   State University of New York at Buffalo, June In Buffalo, JB123,
1977. Nora Post, oboe; Edward Yadzinski, bass clarinet; Don

Reinfeld, violoncello; Stuart Weissman, electric guitar; Jan Williams, percussion/conductor.
> Recorded June 14, 1977, Baird Recital Hall, Buffalo, New York. (See: W76m)

D74. *Music of the Twentieth Century.* Boston University School of Music (tape reel, stereo), December 7, 1982. Collegium in Contemporary Music; Lukas Foss, piano/conductor.
> Recorded in concert in the Boston University Concert Hall (See: W76o). With: Foss. *Elytres* (See: D45); *Solo Observed* (See: D86); *Three Airs for Frank O'Hara's Angel* (See: D20)

The Cave of the Winds (La Grotte des Vents)

D75. *The Avant Garde Woodwind Quintet in the USA: 20th Century American Music for Woodwind Quintet.* Vox SVBX 5307 (stereo), 1977. Dorian Quintet (Karl Kraber, flute; Charles Kuskin, oboe; Jerry Kirkbride, clarinet; Barry Benjamin, horn; Jane Taylor, bassoon).
> With: Barber, Samuel. *Summer Music*; Berger, Arthur. *Quartet in C Major for Woodwinds*; Carter, Elliott. *Woodwind Quintet*; Berio, Luciano. *Children's Play for Wind Quintet Opus Number ZOO*; Fine, Irving. *Partita*; Davidovsky, Mario. *Synchronisms, No. 8*; Druckman, Jacob. *Delizie Contente Che l'Alme Beate*; Schuller, Gunther. *Woodwind Quintet*; Husa, Karel. *Deux Préludes Pour Flûte, Clarinette et Basson*.

Ni Bruit Ni Vitesse

D76. State University of New York at Buffalo, Evenings for New Music 221, 172. Lukas Foss, piano; Jan Williams, percussion.
> Recording of the premiere performance February 13, 1972, Albright-Knox Art Gallery, Buffalo, New York. (See: W79a)

D77. Turnabout TV-S 34514 (stereo), 1972. Lukas Foss, piano; Jan Williams, percussion. (*The Contemporary Composer in the U.S.A.*)
> With: Foss. *Elytres* (See: D43), *Paradigm* (See: D72); Williams, Jan. *Dream Lesson*. (See: DB84)

D78. *Chamber Music of Lukas Foss.* Tempe, Arizona: Arizona State University (tape reel, stereo), October 7, 1981. New Music Ensemble; Glenn Hackbarth, director.
> Recorded during performance at the Louise Lincoln Kerr Cultural Center, Arizona State University (See: W79e). With: Foss. *Music for Six* (See: D84), *Time Cycle* (See: D31).

MAP (Musicians at Play)--A Musical Game

D79. State University of New York at Buffalo, June in Buffalo, JB124, 1977. Edward Yadzinski, winds; James Kasprowicz, brass; Don

Reinfeld, strings; Jan Williams, percussion; Walter Gajewski, electronics.
Recorded June 14, 1977, Baird Recital Hall, Buffalo, New York. Version performed was the 1977 revised version. (See: W80d)

Chamber Music

D80. State University of New York at Buffalo, Evenings for New Music 293, 1975. Jan Williams, percussion; Joel Chadabe, electronics.
Recording of the March 22, 1975 premiere performance. (See: W82a)

String Quartet No. 3

D81. *Music by Lukas Foss*. Composers Recordings CRI SD 413 (stereo), 1980. (*American Contemporary*) Columbia Quartet (Benjamin Hudson, Carol Zeavin, violins; Janet Lyman Hill, viola; André Emelianoff, violoncello).
With: Foss. *Music for Six* (See: D83), *Curriculum Vitae* (See: D95).

Music for Six

D82. State University of New York at Buffalo, Evenings for New Music 371, 1978. Robert Dick, flute; Nora Post, oboe; Krzysztof Knittel, piano; Weronika Knittel, violin; Michael Peebles, violoncello; Jan Williams, percussion.
Recorded May 7, 1978, Albright-Knox Art Gallery, Buffalo, New York. (See: W85b)

D83. *Music by Lukas Foss*. Composers Recordings CRI SD 413 (stereo), 1980. State University of New York at Buffalo Percussion Ensemble (Jan Williams, Edward Folger, vibraphones; Bruce Penner, Rick Kazmierczak, marimbas; Kathryn Kayne, electric piano; James Calabrese, synthesizer). (*American Contemporary*)
With: Foss. *Curriculum Vitae* (See: D95), *String Quartet no. 3* (See: D81).

D84. *Chamber Music of Lukas Foss*. Tempe, Arizona: Arizona State University, (tape reel, stereo), 1981. New Music Ensemble; Glenn Hackbarth, director.
Recorded October 7, 1981 at the Louise Lincoln Kerr Cultural Center (See: W85d). With: Foss. *Ni Bruit Ni Vitesse* (See: D78), *Time Cycle* (See: D31)

Round a Common Center

D85. Intersound Pro Arte Pro (stereo, digital) PAD 120 (phonodisc); CDD 120 (compact disc), 1982. Orson Welles, narrator; Yehudi

Menuhin, violin; Elaine Bonazzi, voice; Cantilena Chamber Players
(Edna Michell, violin; Philipp Naegele, viola; Marcy Rosen,
violoncello; Frank Glaser, piano).
   With: Copland, Aaron. *Quartet for Piano and Strings*;
Wyner, Yehudi. *Intermezzi for Piano Quartet*. (See: DB85)

Solo Observed

D86. *Music of the Twentieth Century*. Boston University School of
   Music, (tape reels, stereo), December 7, 1982. Collegium in
   Contemporary Music; Lukas Foss, piano.
      Recorded in concert in the Boston University Concert Hall
   (See: W89b). With: Foss. *Elytres* (See: D45), *Paradigm* (See:
   D74), *Three Airs for Frank O'Hara's Angel* (See: D20)

D87. Gramavision GR 7005 (stereo), 1983. Lukas Foss, piano; Lincoln
   Center Chamber Music Society (Fred Sherry, violoncello; Richard
   Fitz, vibraphone; Charles Wadsworth, electric organ).
      With: Foss. *Night Music for John Lennon* (See: D54),
   Measure for Measure (See: D35).

Percussion Quartet

D88. *Double Music: Works for Percussion and Strings*. New World
   Records NW 330 (stereo), 1985. Members of the New Music
   Consort (Joseph Grable, Kory Grossman, James Preiss, William
   Trigg, percussion).
      With: Cage, John. *Second Construction*; Cage, John and
   Lou Harrison. *Double Music*; Sollberger, Harvey. *The Two and the
   One*.

Tashi

D89. *Rendezvous with Tashi*. RCA Victor 7901-2-RC, 1989. Tashi
   (Richard Stoltzman, clarinet; Ida Kavafian, Theodore Arm, violins;
   Steven Tenenbom, viola; Fred Sherry, violoncello); Lukas Foss,
   piano.
      With: Hindemith, Paul. *Quintet, op. 30*; Shulman, Alan.
   Rendezvous; Gershwin, George. *Promenade, Bess, You Is My
   Woman, Who Cares?, Liza, I Got Rhythm*.

MUSIC FOR SOLO INSTRUMENTS

Three Pieces. Dedication

D90. Hargail MW 300 (mono), 194-? E. Ortenberg, violin; Lukas Foss,
   piano.
      With: Hindemith, Paul. *Violin Sonata in E*.

Fantasy Rondo

D91.   Concert Hall CH-B9 (mono), 194-? Lukas Foss, piano.

Capriccio

D92.   RCA Victor Red Seal LM 2940 (mono); LSC 2940 (stereo), 195-?
        Stephen Kates, violoncello; Samuel Sanders, piano.
            With: Boccherini, Luigi. *Sonata for Cello in C*; Tchaikovsky,
        Petr Il'ich. *Nocturne*, op. 19, no. 4, *Pizzo Capriccioso*, op. 62;
        Banshchikov, Gennadi. *Four Fugitives*; Faure, Gabriel. *Après un
        Rêve*; Bach, Johann Sebastian. *Adagio* from *Organ Toccata in C*;
        Granados, Enrique. *Orientale*. (See: DB88, DB89, DB90, DB91)

D93.   RCA Victor LM 2293 (mono); LSC 2293 (stereo), 1959. Gregor
        Piatigorsky, violoncello; Lukas Foss, piano.
            Re-released as part of New World Records NW 281 (See:
        D94). With: Stravinski, Igor. *Suite Italienne*; Debussy, Claude.
        Sonata in D Minor; Busoni, Ferruccio. *Kleine Suite*, op. 23,
        Sostenuto ed espressivo. (See: DB86, DB87)

D94.   *Chamber Music by Lou Harrison, Ben Weber, Lukas Foss, Ingolf
        Dahl.* New World Records NW 281, 1976. Gregor Piatigorsky,
        violoncello; Lukas Foss, piano. *(Recorded Anthology of American
        Music)*
            Re-release in part of RCA Victor LSC 2293 (See: D93).
        With: Harrison, Lou. *Suite for Cello & Harp*; Weber, Ben. *Sonata
        da Camera*; Dahl, Ingolf. *Concertino a tre.*

Curriculum Vitae

D95.   *Music by Lukas Foss.* Composers Recordings CRI SD 413 (stereo),
        1980. Guy Klucevsek, accordion. *(American Contemporary)*
            With: Foss. *Music for Six* (See: D83), *String Quartet No. 3*
        (See: D81).

Curriculum Vitae Tango

D96.   Music & Arts Program CD-604 (digital, stereo), 1989. Ursula
        Oppens, piano.
            With: Carter, Elliot. *Night Fantasies*; Adams, John. *Phrygian
        Gates*; Nancarrow, Conlon. *Tango?* Bolcom, William. *The Death
        Moth Tango*; Sahl, Michael. *Exiles' Cafe Tango*; Hemphill.
        Parchment; Jaggard, David. *Tango.*

Three Early Pieces

D97.   *Carol Wincenc: Music of Griffes, Copland, Barber, Del Tredici,
        Foss and Cowell.* Nonesuch (digital, stereo) 79114 (phonodisc);

79114-4 (cassette); 79114-2 (compact disc), 1985. Carol
Wincenc, flute; Lukas Foss, piano.
 Recorded June 1-5, 1984, at the American Academy and
Institute of Arts and Letters, New York City. With: Griffes,
Charles. *Poem*; Cowell, Henry. *Two Bits*; Del Tredici, David.
Acrostic Song; Barber, Samuel. *Canzone*; Copland, Aaron. *Duo for
Flute and Piano*. (See: DB92)

D98.   *Faculty Recital*. Indiana University School of Music 1987-1988,
no. 175, v. 3 (tape reel, stereo), 1987. Carol Wincenc, flute;
James Tocco, piano.
 Recorded in recital October 12, 1987 (See: W111b). With:
Beethoven, Ludwig van. *Serenades in D Major*, op. 25.

FOSS AS CONDUCTOR

MUSIC BY OTHER COMPOSERS

D99.   Siena Records S 100-2 (mono); Unicorn UNLP 1037 (mono), 1956.
Zimbler Sinfonietta; Lukas Foss, conductor.
 Recorded in Symphony Hall, Boston. Re-released in stereo
as Turnabout TV 34154S. Contents: Bartok, Béla. *Divertimento
for String Orchestra*; Ives, Charles. *The Unanswered Question*;
Milhaud, Darius. *Symphonies pour Petit Orchestre, No. 4*;
Skalkottas, Nikos. *Little Suite for Strings*. (See: D107)

D100. Unicorn UN LP 1039 (mono), 1960? Lukas Foss, piano; James
Pappoutsakis, flute; George Zazovsky, violin; Zimbler Sinfonietta;
Lukas Foss, piano/conductor.
 Contents: Bach, Johann Sebastian. *Brandenburg Concerto
No. 5*.

D101. *The World of Bartok*. Vox VSPS 11 (stereo), 196-? Zimbler
Sinfonietta; Lukas Foss, conductor.
 A five disc collection of the music of Béla Bartok. Foss
conducts Bartok's *Divertimento for String Orchestra* (See: D99).

D102. Recording Guarantee Project, American International Music Fund,
Koussevitzky Music Foundation (tape reel, stereo), 1965.
Emmanuel Temple Chorale; Buffalo Philharmonic Orchestra; Lukas
Foss, conductor.
 Limited edition; recorded February 28, 1965 in Kleinhans
Music Hall, Buffalo, New York. Contents: Feldman, Morton. *The
Swallows of Salangen*.

D103. Recording Guarantee Project, American International Music Fund,
Koussevitzky Music Foundation (tape reel, mono), 1965. Francis
Pierre, harp; Buffalo Philharmonic Orchestra; Lukas Foss,
conductor.
 Limited edition; American premiere. Recorded live December
12, 1965 in Kleinhans Music Hall, Buffalo, New York. Contents:
Berio, Luciano. *Chemins 1*.

D104. Recording Guarantee Project, American International Music Fund, Koussevitzky Music Foundation (tape reel, mono), 1965. Grant Johannessen, piano; Buffalo Philharmonic Orchestra; Lukas Foss, conductor.

Master copy at the New York Public Library. Recording of the world premiere performance, December 12, 1965, Kleinhans Music Hall, Buffalo, New York. Contents: Talma, Louise. *Dialogues for Piano and Orchestra.*

D105. Recording Guarantee Project, American International Music Fund, Koussevitzky Music Foundation (tape reel, mono), 1966. Tossy Spivakovsky, violin; Buffalo Philharmonic Orchestra; Lukas Foss, conductor.

Limited edition; master tape. Recorded live January 16 and 23, 1966 in Kleinhans Music Hall, Buffalo, New York. Contents: Schuman, William. *Concerto for Violin.*

D106. Recording Guarantee Project, American International Music Fund, Koussevitzky Music Foundation (tape reel, stereo), 1966. New York Philharmonic Orchestra; Lukas Foss, conductor.

Limited edition; recorded live March 25-26, 1966 in Philharmonic Hall, Lincoln Center, New York City. Contents: Kilar, Wojciech. *Riff 62.*

D107. *Lukas Foss Conducts the Zimbler Sinfonietta.* Turnabout TV 34154S (stereo), 1967? Zimbler Sinfonietta; Lukas Foss, conductor.

Re-mastered for stereo. Originally released as Siena S-100-2 (See: D99).

D108. Recording Guarantee Project, American International Music Fund, Koussevitzky Music Foundation (tape reel, mono), 1967. Charles Wuorinen, piano; Buffalo Philharmonic Orchestra; Lukas Foss, conductor.

Limited edition; recorded October 1, 1967, Kleinhans Music Hall, Buffalo, New York. Contents: Wuorinen, Charles. *Concerto for Piano and Orchestra.*

D109. Audio Center (tape reel, mono), 1967. Buffalo Philharmonic Orchestra; Lukas Foss, conductor.

Limited edition; recorded September 24, 1967, Kleinhans Music Hall, Buffalo, New York. Recorded and distributed by the Recording Guarantee Project, American International Music Fund, Koussevitzky Music Foundation. Contents: Thorne, Francis. *Lyric Variations for Orchestra.*

D110. Recording Guarantee Project, American International Music Fund, Koussevitzky Music Foundation (tape reel, mono), 1967. Buffalo Philharmonic Orchestra; Lukas Foss, conductor.

Limited edition; recorded September 24, 1967, Kleinhans Music Hall, Buffalo, New York. Contents: Persichetti, Vincent. *Symphony No. 7, op. 80 (Liturgic).*

D111.   Nonesuch H 71201 (stereo), 1968. Buffalo Philharmonic
Orchestra; Lukas Foss, conductor.
Recorded March 1968, Kleinhans Music Hall, during the
second Buffalo Festival of the Arts Today. Contents: Penderecki,
Krzysztof. *De Natura Sonoris, Capriccio for Violin*; Xenakis, Iannis.
Akrata, Pithoprakta. (See: DB46, DB47, DB94, DB95, B103)

D112.   Nonesuch H 71203 (stereo), 1968. Buffalo Philharmonic
Orchestra; Lukas Foss, conductor.
Recorded March 1968, Kleinhans Music Hall, Buffalo, New
York, during the second Buffalo Festival of the Arts Today.
Contents: Sibelius, Jean. *Four Legends from The Kalevala*. (See:
DB46, B103)

D113.   Recording Guarantee Project, American International Music Fund,
Koussevitzky Music Foundation (tape reel, mono), 1968. Leo Smit,
piano; Buffalo Philharmonic Orchestra; Lukas Foss, conductor.
Limited edition; world premiere; recorded November 26,
1968, Kleinhans Music Hall, Buffalo, New York. Contents: Smit,
Leo. *Concerto for Piano and Orchestra*.

D114.   Recording Guarantee Project, American International Music Fund,
Koussevitzky Music Foundation, (tape reel, mono), 1969. Buffalo
Philharmonic Orchestra; Lukas Foss, conductor.
Limited edition; world premiere. Recorded December 8 and
10, 1969, Kleinhans Music Hall, Buffalo, New York. Contents:
Sapp, Allen. *Second Suite in Four Movements*.

D115.   *Americana, v. 1*. Turnabout TV-S 34398 (stereo), 1970. Buffalo
Philharmonic Orchestra; Lukas Foss, conductor.
Contents: Copland, Aaron. *Quiet City*; Ruggles, Carl. *Men
and Mountains, Angels*; Ives, Charles. *From the Steeples and the
Mountains*; Mason, Daniel Gregory. *String Quartet on Negro
Themes in G Minor*, op. 19. (See: DB96, DB97)

D116.   Recording Guarantee Project, American International Music Fund,
Koussevitzky Music Foundation (tape reel, stereo), 1970. Buffalo
Philharmonic Orchestra; Lukas Foss, conductor.
Limited edition; recorded "from Turnabout TV-S 34398"
(See: D115). Contents: Ruggles, Carl. *Men and Mountains* (1941
rev. version).

D117.   *The Contemporary Composer in the USA*. Turnabout TV-S 34428
(stereo), 1972. Buffalo Philharmonic Orchestra; Lukas Foss,
conductor.
Contents: Subotnick, Morton. *Laminations*; Eaton, John.
Concert Piece; Bergsma, William L. *Concerto for Violin*. (See:
DB96)

D118.   Vox Turnabout TV-S 34614 (stereo), 1974. Jerusalem Symphony
Chamber Orchestra: Lukas Foss, piano/conductor.
Contents: Bach, Johann Sebastian. *Concerti for Harpsichord
and String Orchestra*, BWV 1052, D Minor; BWV 1056, F Minor.

D119. Turnabout (stereo) TV 34675 (phonodisc); Vox CT 2154 (cassette), 1977. Rosalyn Barak, Adi Etzion-Zak, sopranos; Oemer Demirkazik, Joerg Kuhn, tenors; Ron Greiner, Willy Haparnass, basses; Jerusalem Symphony Orchestra; Lukas Foss, conductor. Music for Westchester Symphony Orchestra; Siegfried Landau, conductor.
  Recorded in 1974 and 1975. Contents: Weill, Kurt. *Mahogonny Songspiel, Kleine Dreigroschenmusik (Suite from the Three Penny Opera).*

D120. *The Art of Fuguing.* Town Hall Album S20, (stereo, multiple microphone version), 1978. Ensemble of [40] Los Angeles string, woodwind, and percussion players; Lukas Foss, conductor.
  Recorded May 25-26, 1977, First Presbyterian Church of Hollywood. Contents: Bach, Johann Sebastian. *Der Kunst der Fuge*, arranged by William Malloch. (See: DB98, DB99; See also: D121)

D121. *The Art of Fuguing.* Town Hall Records S21 (stereo; single microphone version), 1978. Ensemble of [40] Los Angeles string, woodwind and percussion players; Lukas Foss, conductor.
  Recorded May 25-26, 1977, First Presbyterian Church of Hollywood. Contents: Bach, Johann Sebastian. *Der Kunst der Fuge*, arranged by William Malloch. (See: DB98, DB99; See also: D120)

D122. Indiana University Music Center (tape reel, stereo), 1979. Buffalo Philharmonic Orchestra; Lukas Foss, conductor.
  Contents: Iturriaga, Enrique. *Vivencias, I-IV.*

D123. Indiana University Music Center (tape reel, stereo), 1979. Buffalo Philharmonic Orchestra; Lukas Foss, conductor.
  Contents: Garrido-Lecca, Celso. *Laudes.*

D124. *Listen.* Side 19. CBS Inc. AS15390 (stereo), 1980. Zimbler Sinfonietta; Lukas Foss, conductor.
  A collection of recordings to accompany Joseph Kerman's textbook of the same name. Foss conducts *The Unanswered Question* by Charles Ives.

D125. *Music of Irving Fine.* Composers Recordings CRI SD 460 (stereo), 1981. Janet Lyman Hill, viola; Alyssa Hess, harp; Brooklyn Philharmonia; Lukas Foss, conductor. (*American Historic*)
  Recorded March 1981, in New York. Contents: Fine, Irving. *Notturno for Strings and Harp, Childhood Fables for Grownups, Fantasia for String Trio.*

D126. *American Festival.* Pro Arte (digital; stereo) CDD-102 (compact disc); PAD-102 (phonodisc); PCD-102 (cassette), 1983. Milwaukee Symphony Orchestra; Lukas Foss, conductor.
  Recorded May 26, 27, and 29, 1983 in Uihlein Hall, Milwaukee, Wisconsin. Contents: Copland, Aaron. *Fanfare for the Common Man, Variations on a Shaker Melody* (from *Appalachian Spring*); Barber, Samuel. *Adagio for Strings*; Cowell, Henry.

Saturday Night at the Firehouse; Ives, Charles. *Circus Band March, The Unanswered Question*; Bernstein, Leonard. *Overture to Candide;* Schuman, William. *Newsreel;* Ruggeri, Roger. *If...Then.* (See: DB100)

D127. *Brooklyn Philharmonic Symphony Orchestra.* Gramavision GR 7006 (stereo); GRC 7006 (cassette), 1983. Brooklyn Philharmonic Orchestra; Lukas Foss, conductor.
Recorded at Cooper Union Great Hall. Contents: Harrison, Lou. *At the Tomb of Charles Ives*; Ussachevsky, Vladimir. *Divertimento for Electronic Valve, Tape and Orchestra*; Cage, John, Henry Cowell, Lou Harrison, Virgil Thomson. *Party Pieces*; Smit, Leo. *Academic Graffiti.* (See: DB101)

D128. *Zeitgenössische Musik in der Bundesrepublik Deutschland, Nr. 5, 1960-1970.* Deutsche Harmonia Mundi DMR 1013--DMR1015 (stereo), 1983. Michael W. Ranta, percussion; Radio-Sinfonie-Orchester des Hessischen Rundfunks; Lukas Foss, conductor.
A collection of music by German composers; Foss conducts *Air, für Grosses Orchester und Schlagzeug-Solo* by Helmut Lachenmann.

D129. Composers Recordings Inc. CRI SD 554 (digital, stereo), 1988. Tobias Picker, Michael Barrett, pianos; Brooklyn Philharmonic Orchestra; Lukas Foss, conductor.
Recorded January 7, 1985 and January 26, 1986 in the Manhattan Center. Contents: Picker, Tobias. *Keys to the City*; Blitzstein, Marc. *Piano Concerto.*

MUSIC BY FOSS

CHORAL MUSIC

The Prairie

D130. Turnabout TV-S 34649 (stereo), 1976. (See: D5)

A Parable of Death (Ein Märchen vom Tod)

D131. Educo ECM 4002 (mono), 1954? (See: D10)

Psalms

D132. Pro Arte PAD 169 (stereo); CDD 169 (digital); PCD 169 (cassette), 1984. (See: D14)

Fragments of Archilochos

D133.   State University of New York at Buffalo, Evenings for New Music 114, 1968. (See: D15)

With Music Strong

D134.   Koss Classics KC-1004 (digital, stereo), 1990. (See: D22)

MUSIC FOR SOLO VOICE

Song of Songs

D135.   Koss Classics KC-1004 (digital, stereo), 1990. (See: D25)

Time Cycle (Chamber version)

D136.   *Chamber Music of Lukas Foss*. Tempe, Arizona: Arizona State University, October 7, 1981. (See: D31)

D137.   *American Composers*. Contemporary Recording Studios CRS 8219 (stereo), 1982. (See: D32)

Measure for Measure

D138.   Gramavision GR 7005 (stereo), 1983. (See: D35)

ORCHESTRAL MUSIC

Ode

D139.   Koss Classics KC-1004 (digital, stereo), 1990. (See: D36)

Symphony of Chorales

D140.   Recording Guarantee Project, American International Music Fund, Koussevitzky Music Foundation 35/5 (tape reel, mono), 1958. (See: D41)

Elytres

D141.   Recording Guarantee Project, American International Music Fund, Koussevitzky Music Foundation (tape reel, mono), 1966. (See: D42)

D142.   Turnabout TV-S 34514 (stereo), 1972. (See: D43)

D143.   *Music of the Twentieth Century.* Boston University School of Music (tape reel, stereo), December 7, 1982. (See: D45)

Cello Concert

D144.   Recording Guarantee Project, American International Music Fund, Koussevitzky Music Foundation, 1966-67. (See: D46)

Baroque Variations

D145.   Nonesuch (stereo) H 71202 (LP); N5-1202 (cassette), 1968. (See: D47)

D146.   Nonesuch (stereo) 71416 (LP); 71416-4 (cassette), 1985. (See: D48)

Geod

D147.   Candide CE 31042 (stereo), 1969. (See: D50)

Salomon Rossi Suite

D148.   Indiana University School of Music Program, 1977-1978, no. 91, 1977. (See: D51)

D149.   *Orchestral Works by Lukas Foss.* New World Records (stereo, digital) NW375-1 (phonodisc); NW375-2 (CD), 1989. (See: D52)

Night Music for John Lennon

D150.   Gramavision GR 7005 (stereo), 1983. (See: D54)

Exeunt

D151.   Indiana University School of Music Program, 1981-1982, no. 31, 1981. (See: D55)

Orpheus and Euridice

D152.   *Orchestral Works by Lukas Foss.* New World Records (stereo, digital) NW375-1 (phonodisc); NW375-2 (CD), 1989. (See: D56)

Renaissance Concerto

D153.   *Orchestral Works by Lukas Foss.* New World Records (stereo, digital) NW375-1 (phonodisc); NW375-2 (CD), 1989. (See: D57)

CHAMBER MUSIC

Paradigm

D154.   *Music of the Twentieth Century.* Boston University School of Music, December 7, 1982. (See: D74)

FOSS AS PERFORMER

WORKS BY OTHER COMPOSERS

D155.   Hargail Records, 194-? Verna Osborne, voice; Lukas Foss, piano. Contents: Milhaud, Darius. *Cinq Chansons.* (See: DB93)

D156.   Decca DL 9634 (mono), 195-? Lukas Foss, piano. (*Decca Gold Label Series*)
        Contents: Bach, Johann Sebastian. *15 Three-Part Inventions.*

D157.   *The Age of Anxiety.* Columbia ML 4325 (mono), 1950. New York Philharmonic-Symphony Orchestra; Lukas Foss, piano; Leonard Bernstein, conductor. (*Columbia Masterworks*)
        Contents: Bernstein, Leonard. *Symphony No. 2 (The Age of Anxiety).*

D158.   *Theme and Four Variations: The Four Temperaments.* Decca DL 7501 (mono), 1950. Lukas Foss, piano; Josef Zimbler, violoncello; Zimbler String Sinfonietta.
        Contents: Hindemith, Paul. *Theme and Variations According to the Four Temperaments.*

D159.   Period SPLP 508 (mono), 195-?. Lukas Foss, Walter Hendl, piano.
        Contents: Mozart, Wolfgang Amadeus. *Piano Sonata for Four Hands in F*, K. 497; *Rondo for Piano in A Minor*, K. 511; *Minuet in D for Piano*, K. 355; *Gigue for Piano in G*, K. 574.

D160.   Decca DL 9601 (mono), 1952. Lukas Foss, piano; Zimbler String Sinfonietta.
        Contents: Bach, Johann Sebastian. *Concertos for Harpsichord and String Orchestra*, BWV 1052 and BWV 1056.

D161.   *Beethoven Sonatas for 'Cello and Piano (Complete); Beethoven Variations.* RCA Victor LM 6120-1 (mono), 1955? Gregor Piatigorsky, violoncello; Lukas Foss, piano.

Contents: Beethoven, Ludwig van. *Twelve Variations on a Theme from Handel's Judas Maccabaeus, Twelve Variations on a Theme from Mozart's The Magic Flute, Seven Variations on a Theme from Mozart's The Magic Flute.*

D162.   Unicorn UNLP 1039 (mono), 1960? (See: D100)

D163.   Contemporary Records M6009 (mono), 1961. American Art Quartet; Lukas Foss, piano. (*Contemporary Composers Series*)
Contents: Vincent, John. *String Quartet No. 1 in G, Consort for Piano & Strings.*

D164.   *Bach & 20th Century Composers.* Center for Cassette Studies 33355-33356, (2 cassettes, mono), 1973. Rosalyn Tureck, piano; Lukas Foss, Arthur Berger, Benjamin Lees, Eric Salzman, lecturers.
Recorded at a congress of the International Bach Society.
Contents: Contemporary Composers Explore Bach's Influence; Eminent Composers Discuss Bach in Relation to Contemporary Music.

D165.   Vox Turnabout TV-S 34614 (stereo), 1974. (See: D118)

D166.   *Serge Koussevitsky* [*sic*] *Remembered.* Minnesota Public Radio B-002, 1974. Richard Burgin, Lukas Foss, Leonard Bernstein, Aaron Copland, and Seiji Ozawa, speakers.
Recorded December 10, 1974 at a weekend Tanglewood symposium held at the Berkshire Music Center on the observance of the anniversary of music conductor Serge Koussevitzky. It was broadcast on National Public Radio.

D167.   Deutsche Grammophon 2530 969 (stereo), 1978. Lukas Foss, piano; Israel Philharmonic Orchestra; Leonard Bernstein, conductor.
Recorded August 1977 at the Berlin Music Festival.
Reissued as Deutsche Grammophon 415 964-2. (See: D167)
Contents: Bernstein, Leonard. *Symphony No. 2 (The Age of Anxiety)* (revised version of 1965).

D168.   *Lukas Foss on His Music.* Boston (tape reel, stereo), 1980. Lukas Foss, speaker. (*Composers' Forum Series, 1980-1981*)
Recorded October 28, 1980. Tape is located at Boston University.

D169.   *Music for Piano.* Pro Arte (digital, stereo) PAD 183 (phonodisc); PCD 183 (cassette); CDD 183 (compact disc), 1984. James Tocco, piano; Lukas Foss, 2nd piano on *Danzón Cubano.*
(*American Artists Series*)
Recorded at Ein Festeburg-Kirche, Frankfurt, and the Manhattan School of Music. Contents: Copland, Aaron. *Three Piano Excerpts from Our Town, Four Episodes from Rodeo, Piano Variations, Four Piano Blues, Danzón Cubano.* (See: DB102, DB104)

D170.   *Baroque Confessions.* Lawrence University (2 cassettes, mono), 1985. Lukas Foss, speaker.

Recorded on October 1, 1985 at the Lawrence University (Appleton, Wisconsin) Convocation.

D171. Deutsche Grammophon (stereo) 415 964-2 (compact disc), 1986. Lukas Foss, piano; Israel Philharmonic Orchestra; Leonard Bernstein, conductor.
Reissue of Deutsche Grammophon 2530 969. (See: D163, DB103)

D172. AS DISC 553 (digital, stereo), 1989. Lukas Foss, piano; Boston Symphony Orchestra; Serge Koussevitzky, conductor.
Recording of a November 4, 1947 radio broadcast.
Contents: Mendelssohn, Felix. *Concerto No. 1 in G Minor* for Piano and Orchestra, op. 25; *A Midsummer's Night Dream; Scherzo*, op. 61; *Symphony No. 4 in A*, op. 90. Foss performs only on the *Concerto*. (See: DB106)

MUSIC BY FOSS

CHORAL MUSIC

Behold! I Build an House

D173. Composers Recordings CRI SD 123 (stereo), 1958. (See: D6)

Psalms

D174. Composers Recordings CRI SD 123 (stereo), 1958. (See: D13)

Three Airs for Frank O'Hara's Angel
(Trois Airs Pour l'Ange de Frank O'Hara)

D175. *Music of the Twentieth Century.* Boston University School of Music (tape reel, stereo), December 7, 1982. (See: D20)

MUSIC FOR SOLO VOICE

Time Cycle (Orchestral version)

D176. Columbia ML 5680 (mono); MS 6280 (stereo), 1962. (See: D26)

D177. Columbia Special Products (stereo) AMS 6280; CMS 6280, 197-? (See: D27)

Time Cycle (Chamber version)

D178.   *Two Record Premieres: Commissioned by the Fromm Music Foundation.* Epic LC 3886 (mono); BC 1286 (stereo), 1964. (See: D29)

ORCHESTRAL MUSIC

Concerto No. 2 for Piano and Orchestra

D179.   Decca DL 9889 (mono), 1957. (See: D39)

D180.   *Waxman Conducts Waxman; Foss Plays Foss.* Varèse/Sarabande VC 81052E (mono), 1978. (See: D40)

CHAMBER MUSIC

Studies in Improvisation

D181.   *Studies in Improvisation.* RCA Victor LSC 2558 (mono); LM 2558 (stereo), 1961. (See: D61)

Echoi

D182.   Wergo WER 60 040 (stereo), 1969? (See: D63)

D183.   State University of New York at Buffalo, Evenings for New Music 23, 1965. (See: D64)

Non-Improvisation

D184.   State University of New York at Buffalo, Evenings for New Music 115, 1968. (See: D66)

D185.   Wergo WER 60 040 (stereo), 1969? (See: D67)

D186.   Heliodor 2549 001 (stereo), 1970. Re-release of Wergo WER 60 040. (See: D68)

Paradigm

D187.   Turnabout TV-S 34514 (stereo), 1972. (See: D72)

D188.   *Music of the Twentieth Century.* Boston University School of Music, December 7, 1982 (See: D74).

Ni Bruit Ni Vitesse

D189.   Turnabout TV-S 34514 (stereo), 1972. (See: D77)

Solo Observed

D190.   *Music of the Twentieth Century*. Boston University School of
Music, December 7, 1982. (See: D86)

D191.   Gramavision GR 7005 (stereo), 1983. (See: D87)

Tashi

D192.   *Rendezvous with Tashi*. RCA Victor 7901-2-RC, 1989. (See:
D89)

MUSIC FOR SOLO INSTRUMENTS

Three Pieces. Dedication

D193.   Hargail MW 300, 194-? (See: D90)

Fantasy Rondo

D194.   Concert Hall CH-B9, 194-? (See: D91)

Capriccio

D195.   RCA Victor LM 2293 (mono); LSC 2293 (stereo), 1959. (See:
D93)

D196.   *Chamber Music by Lou Harrison, Ben Weber, Lukas Foss, Ingolf
Dahl*. New World Records NW 281, 1976. (See: D94)

Three Early Pieces

D197.   *Carol Wincenc*. Nonesuch (digital; stereo) 79114 (phonodisc);
79114-4 (cassette); 79114-2 (compact disc), 1985. (See: D97)

DISCOGRAPHY
BIBLIOGRAPHY

The numbers preceded by "D" in the "See" references in this section refer to item numbers in the "Discography" section.

FOSS AS COMPOSER

OPERAS

The Jumping Frog of Calaveras County

DB1.   Berger, Arthur. "Spotlight On the Moderns." *Saturday Review* 34:63 (May 26, 1951)
        Review of Lyrichord LL 11/LLST 711. The work is compared to its staged and orchestrated version and is criticized for its "fairly rough performance by the After Dinner Opera Company...It suffers in being transplanted from the stage." (See: D2)

DB2.   "Foss: *The Jumping Frog of Calaveras County*." *The New Records* 19:10 (July 1951)
        Review of Lyrichord LL 11/LLST 711. Lyrichord is both praised for releasing this item with a small demand for it and criticized for not including a libretto and for the poor balance between the piano and singers. (See: D2)

CHORAL MUSIC

Behold! I Build an House

DB3.   "Foss: *I Build an House...*" *Saturday Review* 41:42
         (July 26, 1958)
                 Review of CRI SD 123. "[The two-piano
         accompaniment] is much less satisfying, aurally, than
         when heard with orchestra." (See: D6)

DB4.   Jones, Ralph E. "Foss: (3) *Psalms...Foss: Behold! I
         Build an House...*" *The New Records* 26:9 (September
         1958)
                 Review of CRI SD 123. (See: D6; See also:
         DB11)

DB5.   "Modern and Baroque." *New York Times* September 14,
         1958:X19.
                 Review of CRI SD 123. "The cantata, *Behold! I
         Build an House*, is a sonorous and effective piece." (See:
         D6; See also: DB12)

A Parable of Death

DB6.   "Foss: *A Parable of Death...*" *The New Records* 22:13
         (May 1954)
                 Review of Columbia ML 4859 that praises Foss's
         accomplishment of the difficult task of merging narrative
         with music. "Vera Zorina's reading of the narrative is a
         work of art that, through its simplicity and transparent
         beauty, holds one spellbound." (See: D9)

DB7.   Schonberg, Harold C. "Records: Two-Piano." *New
         York Times* May 2, 1954:X9.
                 Review of Columbia ML 4859. "This choral
         work...is a sensitive setting, fairly modern in technique,
         not too original in ideas, but altogether an honest,
         sincere effort." (See: D9)

DB8.   Haggin, B. H. "Records." *The Nation* 178:430-431
         (May 15, 1954)
                 Review of Columbia ML 4859. "In the twenty-five
         minutes of manipulation...I heard not one phrase of
         music that had any interest in itself or in relation to the
         narrative." (See: D9)

DB9.   Berger, Arthur. "Harrison, Weber, Foss, and Other
         Americana." *Saturday Review* 37:48-49 (May 29, 1954)
                 Review of Columbia ML 4859. "Foss seems...to
         have developed an enormous control over the
         notes....There is, too, a remarkable professional finish in
         the timing and interweaving of the various constituents."
         (See: D9)

DB10. Adler, Paul. "Records in Review: Foss, Lukas. *A Parable of Death*." *High Fidelity* 5:62 (February 1955)
Review of Educo ECM 4002. Adler prefers the original Columbia recording performances to this more casual chamber version. (See: D10)

Psalms

DB11. Jones, Ralph E. "Foss: (3) *Psalms*...Foss: *Behold! I Build an House*..." *The New Records* 26:9 (September 1958)
Review of CRI SD 123. "Mr. Foss' settings of three of the most familiar Psalms seem to us to be unimaginative and not particularly capable of establishing a mood corresponding to their texts." The recording as a whole is criticized because of the piano accompaniments rather than the original orchestral versions. (See: D13; See also: DB4)

DB12. "Modern and Baroque." *New York Times* September 14, 1958:X19.
Review of CRI SD 123. (See: D13; See also: DB5)

DB13. McCardell, Charles. "Record Reviews (Stravinsky: *Symphony of Psalms*; Foss: *Psalms*; Ives: *Psalm 67*)." *High Fidelity/Musical America* 34:MA47-48 (October 1984)
Review of Pro Arte PAD 169/PCD 169, the first orchestral recording of Foss's *Psalms*. "The recording...has a tubby, bass-heavy quality that disturbs the balance between instruments and voices." (See: D14)

DB14. Freed, Richard. "Stravinsky: *Symphony of Psalms*. Foss: *Psalms*..." *Stereo Review* 49:104 (November 1984)
Review of Pro Arte PAD 169/PCD 169. "The performance must be regarded as definitive, but the recording balance, with the chorus rather in the background, seems to keep the work from making its strongest effect." (See: D14)

DB15. Salzman, Eric. "Foss: *Psalms*..." *Ovation* 5:56 (January 1985)
Review of Pro Arte PAD 169/PCD 169. "This is a striking and highly successful work from Foss' neo-Classical period and its joyful noise makes as fine a hymn of celebration as I can think of." (See: D14)

MUSIC FOR SOLO VOICE

Song of Songs

DB16.   Ericson, Raymond. "Disks: Oddities." *New York Times* June 17, 1962:12X.
        Review of Columbia ML 5451/MS 6123. "It is a lyrical, fresh, uncomplicated score...with bristling, lively figurations...[and] long, floating melismatic lines....It is a very personal, individual work." (See: D23)

DB17.   "First for Foss." *Saturday Review* 45:52 (July 28, 1962)
        Review of Columbia ML 5451/MS 6123. "It is a vocal effort in which Miss Tourel may well take pride...Bernstein leads an orchestral performance beautifully complementary to the soloist." (See: D23)

DB18.   Jones, Ralph E. "Foss: *Song of Songs*." *The New Records* 30:12 (July 1962)
        Brief review of Columbia ML 5451/MS 6123. "[*Song of Songs*] is a moody piece, marked...by Jennie Tourel's fine vocalism." (See: D23)

DB19.   Miller, Philip L. "Foss: *Song of Songs*..." *Library Journal* 87:2879 (September 1, 1962)
        Review of Columbia ML 5451/MS 6123. The work is equally suited for both lyric soprano (Ellabelle Davis, by whom the work was premiered) and mezzo soprano (Jennie Tourel of the present recording). "[Tourel] is in good form, making the most of both the words and Foss' grateful, somewhat conservative music." (See: D23)

DB20.   Flanagan, William. "Foss: *The Song of Songs*..." *HiFi/Stereo Review* 9:74+ (September 1962)
        Review of Columbia ML 5451/MS 6123. "[*Song of Songs*] takes us back to an era in American music where clarity, precision, and the sort of simplicity that is so hard to come by these days were the desired elements in new music....Both Miss Tourel and Mr. Bernstein have done us a great service in bringing it so convincingly to discs." (See: D23)

DB21.   Ardoin, John. "Foss: *Song of Songs*..." *Musical America* 82:114 (September 1962)
        Review of Columbia ML 5451/MS 6123. "Tourel has rarely sounded finer than in this superb recording of Foss's moving cantata." (See: D23)

Time Cycle (Orchestral version)

DB22. Helm, Everett. "Breath of Fresh Air." *Musical America* 82:23-24 (March 1962)
Review of Columbia MS 6280/ML 5680. The orchestra is incorrectly identified as the New York Philharmonic. Adele Addison's "pitch even in the most difficult passages, is true and clean, her characterization convincing and her changes of pace brilliant....Columbia's engineers also have made a handsome contribution to this outstanding recording." (See: D26)

DB23. Flanagan, William. "Foss: *Time Cycle*." *HiFi/Stereo Review* 8:67-68 (April 1962)
Review of Columbia MS 6280/ML 5680. "Columbia's presentation of the cycle is surely its composers dream come true. Adele Addison...negotiates the treacherous vocal line as if it were a Puccini aria, and Bernstein has made the most of the dazzling array of sounds produced by Foss's orchestral conception." (See: D26)

DB24. Jones, Ralph E. "Foss: *Time Cycle*." *The New Records* 30:4 (April 1962)
Review of Columbia MS 6280/ML 5680. "Interesting? Yes. Musically exciting? Occasionally. Lasting? We wonder." (See: D26)

DB25. Hart, Philip. "Lucas Foss' *Time Cycle*: Four 'Songs' in Two Languages." *Musical Courier* 164:42-43 (April 1962)
Review of Columbia ML 5680/MS 6280. "Foss has produced a fascinating new work of major stature." (See: D26)

DB26. Salzman, Eric. "Disks: Lukas Foss: Composer Revives Improvisatory Art as Foundation for His Technique." *New York Times* May 13, 1962:II,14.
Review of Columbia ML 5680/MS 6280. "Foss...has taken contemporary ideas and even avant-garde notions, merged them and turned them into an elegant, simple, enormously effective music, a little theatrical, but of a direct literary, dramatic and psychological impact." (See: D26)

DB27. "Free Ways: Foss and Britten." *Harper's Magazine* 224:96 (April 1962)
Review of Columbia ML 5680/MS 6280. "Conservative listeners...should be warned that the score is wild and dissonant. However, it is the product of a brilliant musician, and it very much expresses a contemporary attitude toward tone and life, in quite personal terms." (See: D26)

Time Cycle (Chamber version)

DB28. "Foss: *Echoi...*" *Saturday Review 47:66 (September 26, 1964)*
Review of Epic LC 3886/BC 1286. The performance of *Time Cycle* is preferred over *Echoi* (See: D62), although the reviewer misses the orchestral colors in this chamber version. "Miss Addison...is a more resourceful vocalist and a more imaginative artist than Miss Martin." (See: D29; See also: DB74)

DB29. Miller, Philip L. "Two 'Firsts' for Lukas Foss." *American Record Guide* 31:236-237 (November 1964)
Review of Epic LC 3886/BC 1286. "The performances on both records [the original orchestral Columbia MS 6280 (See: D26) and the present chamber version] are superb; modern music enthusiasts and students of contemporary trends will certainly want to own both versions." (See: D29; See also: DB75)

DB30. Henahan, Donal. "Comments on Classics." *Down Beat* 31:28 (November 5, 1964)
Review of Epic LC 3886/BC 1286. The recording is referred to as "fascinating and worth close study." (See: D29; See also: DB76)

DB31. Strongin, Theodore. "Haphazard Treatment." *New York Times* November 29, 1964:X24.
Review of Epic LC 3886/BC 1286. "*Time Cycle...*has some of the haunting quality of *Echoi*, but, it is a calmer work....Mr. Foss uses the haman voice in it in very contemporary fashion, with difficult leaps and rhythms. But he fits it so well to the text that all sounds natural." (See: D29; See also: DB77)

DB32. Susa, Conrad S. "Foss/Clocks and Echoes." *Musical America* 84:266 (December 1964)
Review of Epic LC 3886/BC 1286. "The new version--not an arrangement of the 1961 original, but a re-thinking of the sonorities--seems to gain in strength and focus without the sprawling colors of the orchestral version....Foss has finally arrived at random composition..." The performance is rated as "very accomplished." (See: D29; See also: DB78)

DB33. Shupp, Enos E., Jr. "Foss: *Echoi.*" *The New Records* 33:9 (March 1965)
Review of Epic LC 3886/BC 1286. Shupp didn't know quite how to react to *Time Cycle* stating, "We are in no position to pass judgment on the performances, but since Foss produced the record they must be all right with him." (See: D29; See also: DB79)

DB34. Miller, Philip L. "Foss. *Echoi.*" *Library Journal* 90:2536
(June 1, 1965)
Brief review of Epic LC 3886/BC 1286 which
explains that these are record premieres. (See: D29;
See also: DB80)

Thirteen Ways of Looking at a Blackbird

DB35. "Henry Mollicone: *The Face on the Barroom Floor.*
Lukas Foss: *Thirteen Ways of Looking at a Blackbird.*"
Tribune/Today (Oakland, Calif.) August 2, 1981.
Review of CRI SD 442. "Foss's setting...is often
excessively dramatic, burying the texts in sudden
irrelevant outbursts, repeating texts far too much,
throwing the poem-cycle out of balance." (See: D34)

DB36. Dalheim, Eric L. "Record Reviews: Henry Mollicone. *The
Face on the Barroom Floor*; Lukas Foss. *Thirteen Ways of
Looking at a Blackbird.*" *American Music* 1:110-111 (no.
3, 1983)
Review of CRI SD 442. "Foss, in fashioning a
musical tapestry of evocative threads and hues states
that stylistically, the work is an odd combination of the
tonal lyricism of his early music and the experimental
sonorities of his recent work....*Thirteen Ways* has been
given a superbly realized performance here." (See: D34)

ORCHESTRAL MUSIC

Concerto for Oboe

DB37. Shupp, Enos E., Jr. "Foss: *Concerto for Oboe and
Orchestra...*" *The New Records* 27:5 (March 1971)
Review of Crystal S 851. "The oboe concerto
enjoys the playing of one of the best oboists around,
Bert Gassman, whose suave handling of this material is
balm for the ear." (See: D38)

DB38. "Stevens: *Concerto...*Foss: *Concerto.*" *Saturday
Review* 54:72 (March 27, 1971)
Review of Cyrstal S 851. "The Foss work...is neo-
Baroque in its clarity, simplicity, and balance. It is
beautifully performed by Gassman." (See: D38)

DB39. Stevenson, Gordon. "Lukas Foss. *Concerto for Oboe
and Orchestra.*" *Library Journal* 96:1245 (April 1, 1971)
Review of Crystal S 851. "I doubt that it will find
a permanent place in the repertory, but it does have its
moments..." (See: D38)

DB40. Trimble, Lester. "Foss: *Concerto for Oboe and
Orchestra...*" *Stereo Review* 27:84+ (July 1971)

Review of Crystal S 851. "The playing of Bert Gassman...is an absolute miracle. His tone is unforgettably subtle and attractive; his rhythmic poise and phrase-shaping are a constant joy." (See: D38)

Concerto No. 2 for Piano

DB41.   "Foss: *Concerto No. 2.*" *The New Records* 25:6 (March 1957)
Review of Decca DL 9889. "The present recording may be said to be definitive, for the composer, a first-rate artist, is at the keyboard." (See: D39)

DB42.   "Comment in Brief." *New York Times* April 7, 1957:X15.
Review of Decca DL 9889. "The Foss score...is strongly Stravinsky-derived, and its content wears thin after a couple of hearings. (See: D39)

DB43.   "Waxman...Foss: *Concerto for Piano.*" *Saturday Review* 40:42 (June 29, 1957)
Review of Decca DL 9889. "Two works of uncommon appeal, provided with an authentic interpretation though the participation of the composer in both...The Foss [is] a little overstated." (See: D39)

DB44.   Miller, Philip L. "Foss *Piano Concerto No. 2...*" *Library Journal* 82:2778 (November 1, 1957)
Brief review of Decca DL 9889. "The Foss concerto is composed in the grand style, with a fat, showy solo part but is essentially without meaning--a string of clichés in the modern manner." (See: D39)

Elytres

DB45.   Morgan, Robert P. "Contemporary American Chamber Music--With a Classical Bent." *High Fidelity/Musical America* 23:96 (September 1973)
Review of Turnabout TV-S 34514. "[*Elytres*] consists of twelve phrases, each of which is played twice to complete the piece....The result...has little real character, although it is certainly pleasant and innocuous enough." (See: D43; See also: DB83, DB84)

Baroque Variations

DB46.   Gelatt, Roland. "Xenakis, Penderecki... and Buffalo." *High Fidelity/Musical America* 18:20 + (June 1968)
Review of the Nonesuch recording sessions held during the second Festival of the Arts Today, Buffalo, New York. Nonesuch came to Buffalo to record new works by Penderecki and Xenakis as well as works by Cage, Foss, and Sibelius. Three records were produced from the sessions. (See: D47, D111, D112)

DB47. Kolodin, Irving. "Foss and Feathers." *Stereo Review* (October 26, 1968):75.
    Review of Nonesuch H-71201 and H-71202. "[*Baroque Variations* is] a breach of the peace by Lukas Foss, in which the likes of Handel, Scarlatti, and Bach are subjected to his bad-boy antics. To judge from the quality of performance here, the Buffalo Philharmonic may take rank as the fist symphony orchestra to gain fame from its playing of non-music." (See: D47, D111)

DB48. Shupp, Enos E., Jr. "Xenakis: *Akrata*..." *The New Records* 36:2-3 (November 1968)
    Review of the Nonesuch Buffalo recording sessions. "Foss' *Variations* is a wonderful listening experience." (See: D47, D111, D112; See also: DB94)

DB49. Strongin, Theodore. "Too Loud? Too Soft? Sometimes You Can't Win." *New York Times* November 10, 1968:D25.
    Review of Nonesuch H 71202. "[John Cage's *Concerto for Prepared Piano*] is better heard live. The human ear is more flexible than electronic listening and recording equipment....The effect of [*Baroque Variations* is] a sensation, and one guaranteed to make you sit up and take notice....The *Variations* are a high-class set of tricks, expert and astonishing..." (See: D47)

DB50. Salzman, Eric. "Contemporary Music: Two Unquiet Streams." *Stereo Review* 22:106 (February 1969)
    Review of Nonesuch H 71202. "Most of the music is elegant and even beautiful--like an intentionally distorted and filtered photograph of a cathedral. Only the end is destructive and even this can have a meaning...No praise is too high for these performances by the Buffalo Orchestra under Foss' knowledgeable direction." (See: D47)

DB51. Canby, Edward Tatnall. "Lost & Found Sound: Lukas Foss *Baroque Variations*: Music of Bach, Scarlatti, Handel." *Audio* 69:108-110 (December 1985)
    Review of Nonesuch 71416. Along with the original Buffalo Philharmonic performance are performances of the works which were used as the basis of *Baroque Variations*. "These recordings, spread out from 1967 to 1985, are remarkably equal in sonic quality." (See: D48)

Baroque Variations. Phorion

DB52. Shupp, Enos E., Jr. "*Music of Our Time* (Vol. 2)..." *The New Records* 35:3 (January 1968)

Brief review of Columbia ML 6452/MS 7052.
"This ten-minute work is a fascinating thing, occasionally
noisy, often appealing." (See: D49)

DB53.   Flanagan, William. "Foss: *Phorion...*" *HiFi/Stereo
         Review* 20:86+ (April 1968)
                 Review of Columbia ML 6452/MS 7052. "Lukas
         Foss should go stand in the corner for composing
         Phorion....[The work] sounds a little like a horror-movie
         background score--one in which a vampire, perhaps,
         plays Bach on the organ in an echo-chamber." (See:
         D49)

Salomon Rossi Suite

DB54.   Pincus, Andrew L. "All Sounds Blend In a Rich American
         Mainstream." *New York Times* August 20, 1989:II,29.
                 (See: D52, DB61, DB105)

DB55.   Ditsky, John. "Foss: *Renaissance Concerto for Flute
         and Orchestra. Salomon Rossi Suite. Orpheus and
         Eurydice* [*sic*]..." *Fanfare* 13:204 (September/October
         1989)
                 Review of New World NW375-1/NW375-2. "It is
         happily reminiscent of a number of Stravinsky reworkings
         of older music." (See: D52; See also: DB58, DB62)

DB56.   "Foss: *Renaissance Concerto for Flute and Orchestra.
         Salomon Rossi Suite. Orpheus and Euridice.*"
         Gramophone 67:657 (October 1989)
                 Review of New World NW375-1/NW375-2. "Foss
         presents us with a straight case of re-composition--his
         scoring as deft as it is novel." (See: D52; See also:
         DB59, DB63)

DB57.   Miller, K. "Foss: *Orpheus and Euridice; Renaissance
         Flute Concerto; Salomon Rossi Suite.*" *American Record
         Guide* 52:55 (September/October 1989)
                 Review of New World NW375-1/NW375-2. "The
         performances are quite good....The Brooklyn
         Philharmonic does a terrific job. Overall this is an
         excellent release." (See: D52; See also: DB60, DB64)

Orpheus and Euridice

DB58.   Ditsky, John. "Foss: *Renaissance Concerto for Flute
         and Orchestra. Salomon Rossi Suite. Orpheus and
         Eurydice* [*sic*]..." *Fanfare* 13:204 (September/October
         1989)
                 Review of New World NW375-1/NW375-2. The
         work is in a single, sustained dramatic movement. The
         scoring is imaginative and also allows for a certain
         amount of freedom for the players..." (See: D56; See
         also: DB55, DB62)

DB59. "Foss: *Renaissance Concerto for Flute and Orchestra. Salomon Rossi Suite. Orpheus and Euridice.*" *Gramophone* 67:657 (October 1989)
 Review of New World NW375-1/NW375-2. The reviewer mentions that the aural effects suffer greatly by the lack of the visual effects. "It is only when Euridice awakens and the violins begin their ecstatic but short-lived union that the piece makes real music." (See: D56; See also: DB56, DB63)

DB60. Miller, K. "Foss: *Orpheus and Euridice; Renaissance Flute Concerto; Salomon Rossi Suite.*" *American Record Guide* 52:55 (September/October 1989)
 Review of New World NW375-1/NW375-2. "It is full of musical gestures associated with the avant-garde of the 1970s coupled with moments of conservative lyricism." (See: D56; See also: DB57, DB64)

Renaissance Concerto

DB61. Pincus, Andrew L. "All Sounds Blend In a Rich American Mainstream." *New York Times* August 20, 1989:II:29.
 Review of New World NW375-1/NW375-2 in the context of 20th century American symphonic music. "The flute concerto and the *Rossi Suite* combine Renaissance and modern elements--Monteverdian aria and bent tones coexist happily--to create music of elegance and shimmering contrasts." (See: D57; See also: DB54, DB105)

DB62. Ditsky, John. "Foss: *Renaissance Concerto for Flute and Orchestra. Salomon Rossi Suite. Orpheus and Eurydice* [*sic*]..." *Fanfare* 13:204 (September/October 1989)
 Review of New World NW375-1/NW375-2. "The *Renaissance Concerto* is a delicious amalgam of authentic period materials and contemporary developmental approaches." (See: D57; See also: DB55, DB58)

DB63. "Foss: *Renaissance Concerto for Flute and Orchestra. Salomon Rossi Suite. Orpheus and Euridice.*" *Gramophone* 67:657 (October 1989)
 Review of New World NW375-1/NW375-2. "[The *Renaissance Concerto* could] build itself quite a following among deprived flautists in search of worthwhile new repertoire. It is showy, grateful and varied for the instrument; and exceedingly 'audience-friendly.'" (See: D57; See also: DB56, DB59)

DB64. Miller, K. "Foss: *Orpheus and Euridice; Renaissance Flute Concerto; Salomon Rossi Suite.*" *American Record Guide* 52:55 (September/October 1989)

Review of New World NW375-1/NW375-2. "In the *Renaissance Concerto* Foss returns to his early romantic compositional style....The *Concerto* is conservative, rather light and diverting in character. It is a delightful combination of his earlier compositional style and gestures and thematic elements borrowed from the Renaissance." (See: D57; See also: DB57, DB60)

CHAMBER MUSIC

String Quartet No. 1 in G

DB65.   "Foss: *Quartet No. 1* (1947)..." *The New Records* 28:7 (July 1960)
Review of Columbia ML 5476. It took the reviewers three hearings to begin to understand the work and hear things that are not obvious. (See: D59)

DB66.   DeMotte, Warren. "Bergsma: *Quartet No. 3*; Foss: *Quartet No. 1*." *HiFi/Stereo Review* 5:85 (December 1960)
Brief review of Columbia ML 5476. "The performances are brilliant as well as authentic." (See: D59)

Studies in Improvisation

DB67.   Jones, Ralph E. "*Studies in Improvisation*." *The New Records* 29:9 (November 1961)
Review of RCA Victor LSC 2558/LM 2558. Though Jones doubts whether classical improvisation has much of a future, he feels that it is interesting nonetheless. "Aided by close study, this disc provides an almost unique penetration into the working mind of a performing musician." (See: D61)

DB68.   Hart, Philip. "Improvising Moderns on Records." *Musical Courier* 163:21 (December 1961)
Review of RCA Victor LSC 2558/LM 2558. Since aleatory music is supposed to be different every time it is performed, the author here questions the validity of recordings of these works. Of Foss's group improvisations, he states, "[They] seem to me to be closely related to jazz...but without the characteristic blues melodic basis, and certainly with a much greater sophistication." (See: D61)

DB69.   Rorem, Ned. "Lukas' Latest." *Musical America* 81:53 (December 1961)
Review of RCA Victor LSC 2558/LM 2558. "If the prime function and appeal of these studies lie in unpredictability and lucky accidents which should be heard live...[this release] offers nothing unpredictable

after one hearing....In themselves [Foss's experiments] are smaller than the sum of their parts." (See: D61)

DB70. Daniel, Oliver. "Foss and His Improvisers." *Saturday Review* 44:49 (December 2, 1961)
Review of RCA Victor LSC 2558/LM 2558. "The most impressive aspect is perhaps the vitality and absorption of each player. It would be refreshing indeed if other performing groups...could approach their art with such identification....Foss is reactivating one of the most fascinating and needed aspects of music." (See: D61)

DB71. Flanagan, William. "Foss: *Studies in Improvisation*." *HiFi/Stereo Review* 8:70 (January 1962)
Review of RCA Victor LSC 2558/LM 2558. This recording's interest is listed as "long-hair improvisation." "What Foss has done...is extend the principal of four-hand piano improvisation that every composer has engaged in with a sympathetic colleague within the confines of a conservatory practice studio." Flanagan continues by mentioning that "interesting effects are achieved...but they often emerge from stretches of otherwise unabated noodling." (See: D61)

DB72. Salzman, Eric. "Disks: Lukas Foss: Composer Revives Improvisatory Art as Foundation for His Technique." *New York Times* May 13, 1962:II,14.
Review of RCA Victor LM 2558/LSC 2558. "In spite of this [cold, canned form] a great impression of freshness and excitement still remains." (See: D61)

DB73. Thacker, Eric. "Signals for Spontaneity: the Lucas Foss Improvisation Group." *Jazz Monthly* 11:17-18 (December 1965)
Review and comment on a BBC Third Programme broadcast based on the album *Studies in Improvisation* (See: D61). Thacker gives a brief background on the use of improvisation in classical music before trying to describe Foss's contemporary improvisatory music. Five pieces (three studies and two duets) were performed. He described the broadcast as "interesting" and continued, "Two things...compelled attention and discouraged impatience....First, the evident skill and technical authority of the four musicians, and, second, the unpompous nature of the whole enterprise."

Echoi

DB74. "Foss: *Echoi*..." *Saturday Review* 47:66 (September 26, 1964)
Review of Epic BC 1286/LC 3886. Brief mention of *Echoi* as "non-sequential tonal patterns." (See: D62; See also: DB28)

DB75. Miller, Philip L. "Two 'Firsts' for Lukas Foss." *American Record Guide* 31:236-237 (November 1964)
Review of Epic BC 1286/LC 3886. "*Echoi* is not serial in the accepted sense of the word. Series for pitches, durations, entrances, etc., serve to obtain a 'raw material,' a scaffold which in the process of composition is gradually eliminated, destroyed." (See: D62; See also: DB29)

DB76. Henahan, Donal J. "Comments on Classics." *Down Beat* 31:28 (November 5, 1964)
Review of Epic BC 1286/LC 3886 which also includes *Time Cycle*. Henahan had attended a live performance of *Echoi* and explains how the recording falls short when it comes to the "visual" aspects of the work. (See: D62; See also: DB30)

DB77. Strongin, Theodore. "Haphazard Treatment." *New York Times* November 29, 1964:X24.
Review of Epic BC 1286/LC 3886. The recording and performance qualities are rated as spectacular. "It is a strange, but compelling concatenation of halts, skips, clusters, strange timbres. At times it mounts to almost hysterical excitement. At other times, it has a haunting beauty." (See: D62; See also: DB31)

DB78. Susa, Conrad S. "Foss/Clocks and Echoes." *Musical America* 84:266 (December 1964)
Review of Epic BC 1286/LC 3886. "It is by virtue of his technique that Foss saves this piece from pure chaos....The sounds are extremely pleasant, and the rhythms full of unexpected tensions and balances." The performance is rated as "very accomplished." (See: D62; See also: DB32)

DB79. Shupp, Enos E., Jr. "Foss: *Echoi.*" *The New Records* 33:9 (March 1965)
Review of Epic BC 1286/LC 3886. "*Echoi*...is an experimental work and will sound to many like a work in process [*sic*] that needs some more finishing." (See: D62; See also: DB33)

DB80. Miller, Philip L. "Foss. *Echoi.*" *Library Journal* 90:2536 (June 1, 1965)
Review of Epic BC 1286/LC 3886 (See: D62, DB34)

Paradigm

DB81. Henahan, Donal. "Completing the Stravinsky Jigsaw." *New York Times* October 3, 1971:D26.
Review of Deutsche Grammophon 2543 005. "The Foss is high-spirited and full of interlocking

complexities that the performers may enjoy more than the listener." (See: D71)

DB82. Bronston, Levering. "Foss: *Paradigm...*" *The New Records* 39:12-13 (November 1971)
Brief review of Deutsche Grammophon 2543 005 stating that the work is "a masterpiece of musical emesis." (See: D71)

DB83. Morgan, Robert P. "Contemporary American Chamber Music--With a Classical Bent." *High Fidelity/Musical America* 23:96 (September 1973)
Review of Turnabout TV-S 34514. "Two of the four movements...generate an extraordinary amount of rhythmic impetus...and manage to achieve real excitement." (See: D72; See also: DB45, DB84)

Ni Bruit Ni Vitesse

DB84. Morgan, Robert P. "Contemporary American Chamber Music--With a Classical Bent." *High Fidelity/Musical America* 23:96 (September 1973)
Review of Turnabout TV-S 34514. "The work is very simply, though effectively, constructed....Some thirteen minutes in duration, the work hangs together very well and evokes most effectively the sense of the title (literally 'neither noise nor speed')." (See: D77; See also: DB45, DB83)

Round a Common Center

DB85. Moor, Paul. "Foss, Copland, Wyner: Bonazzi, Menuhin." *High Fidelity* 37:67 (October 1987)
Review of Pro Arte PAD 120/CDD 120. "*Round a Common Center*...shows once again Lukas Foss's weathervane swiftness to trim his musical conscience to the fashion of the times." (See: D85)

MUSIC FOR SOLO INSTRUMENTS

Capriccio

DB86. "Piatigorsky With Foss." *Saturday Review* 42:35 (December 26, 1959)
Review of RCA Victor LM 2293/LSC 2293. Foss's performance is referred to as a "flexible, always well-shaded pianistic performance." Piatigorsky's performance is mentioned as "among the best of recent... performances...[for] beauty of sound and strength of statement." (See: D93)

DB87. Lewis, Richard. "Stravinsky: *Suite Italienne*...Foss:
        Capriccio for Cello and Piano." *Musical America* 80:244
        (February 1960)
        Review of RCA Victor LM 2293/LSC 2293.
        Piatigorsky's performance is described as having
        "deftness and zest." The recording is rate as "excellent"
        overall and in addition to the Stravinsky work, it contains
        "three brief but exciting works." Foss's *Capriccio* is not
        mentioned by the reviewer. (See: D93)

DB88. "Stravinsky: *Suite Italienne*..." *The New Records* 27:9
        (February 1960)
        Brief review of RCA Victor LM 2940/LSC 2940.
        The recording is recommended to students of the
        violoncello as "examples of magnificent technique
        in...most difficult music." (See: D92)

DB89. "Boccherini: *Sonata in C*...Foss (ed. Piatigorsky):
        Capriccio..." *Saturday Review* 50:70 (March 25, 1967)
        Review of RCA Victor LM 2940/LSC 2940. "Kates
        has a fluent command of cellistic problems [and] a fine
        flowing sound... however, he appears to be stimulated
        more by pieces that challenge his technical resources
        than those in which the problems are primarily musical
        and interpretative." (See: D92)

DB90. Shupp, Enos E., Jr. "Violoncello Recital." *The New
        Records* 35:5 (April 1967)
        Brief review of RCA Victor LM 2940/LSC 2940.
        "The repertoire is a widely diversified group of eight
        short works that display versatility....Kates plays with
        great vitality...[although] the recording sounds as though
        the mike were put inside the 'cello." (See: D92)

DB91. Kipnis, Igor. "Young Artists in the Recording Studio."
        HiFi/Stereo Review 19146-147 (October 1967)
        Review of RCA Victor LM 2940/LSC 2940. The
        review centers around Kates's playing and does not
        mention Foss's *Capriccio*. (See: D92)

Three Early Pieces

DB92. Scherer, Barrymore L. "The Many Colors of Music for
        Winds." *New York Times* August 16, 1987:H23.
        Review of Nonesuch 79114-2/79114-1/79114-4.
        "*Three Pieces*...evince the composer's early assimilation
        of American folk-dance rhythms and melodic turns of
        phrase....Ms. Wincenc plays with her characteristic grace
        throughout..." (See: D97)

FOSS AS PERFORMER AND CONDUCTOR

DB93. Berger, Arthur. "Scores and Records." *Modern Music* 23:213 (Summer 1946)
Review of the Hargail Records recording of Foss accompanying singer Verna Osborne on Milhaud's *Cinq Chansons*. The pieces are "Gallic, folkish tunes [with] highly pianistic accompaniments." (See: D155)

DB94. Shupp, Enos E., Jr. "Xenakis: *Akrata...*" also "Cage: *Concerto for Prepared Piano and Orchestra...*" *The New Records* 36:2-3 (November 1968)
Reviews of Nonesuch H 71201 and H 71202. "The [Buffalo Philharmonic] Orchestra plays all of this music with amazing agility, and the sound is excellent." (See: D47, D111; See also: DB48)

DB95. Grueninger, Walter F. "Xenakis: *Akrata* and *Pithoprakta...*" *Consumers Bulletin* 52:16 (January 1969)
Review of Nonesuch H 71201. The artistry of this recording is favored, however the engineering is criticized for lack of "presence, clarity, and body." (See: D111)

DB96. "Orchestra Records 12-Hour Session of American Pieces." *Buffalo Evening News* April 9, 1970:67.
Review of the Buffalo Philharmonic Orchestra recording session which produced Turnabout TV-S 34398 and Turnabout TV-S 34428. It lists works recorded, how much money was spent, and from where the money came. (See: D115, D117)

DB97. Maconie, Robin. "Recordings." *Tempo* 103:54-55 (December 1972)
Review of Turnabout TV-S 34398. The only remark made about the performance is that Ives's *From the Steeples and the Mountains* is taken at too fast a speed to be effective. (See: D115)

DB98. Monson, Karen. "Bach-Malloch: *Art of Fuguing.*" *Chicago* 28:148 (February 7, 1979)
Review of the Town Hall Records recordings of William Malloch's Bach-Malloch *Art of Fuguing* with Lukas Foss conducting a group of 40 California instrumentalists, and the California Boys' Choir. "The music is alive, vital, vibrant. You'll either rush to shut it off, or you'll have a grand old time. Lukas Foss was obviously the ideal leader for this excellent group. (See: D120, D121)

DB99. Payne, Ifan. "10 Favorite Recordings: Sonic Spectaculars of the Last 25 Years: Bach-Malloch: *The*

Art of Fuguing." *American Record Guide* 42:5 (August 1979)

Review of the Town Hall S-20 and S-21 recordings. "Not only is this wonderful music-making, but it is also a fascinating demonstration of the opposing sides of recording philosophies: multi-mike versus single mike." (See: D120, D121)

DB100. Smoley, Lewis M. "American Festival." *American Record Guide* 47:58-59 (May 1984)

Review of ProArte PAD-102/PCD-102. "While the quality of the performances is high, the level of involvement is as uneven as the music is diverse." (See: D126)

DB101. Schwarz, K. Robert. "Recitals and Miscellany: Brooklyn Philharmonic Symphony Orchestra." *High Fidelity* 34:75-76 (June 1984)

Review of Gramavision GR 7006/GRC 7006. "This record contains not one really substantial work--that it is in essence an album of curiosities, each piece having some sort of extramusical gimmick....The playing is excellent throughout." (See: D127)

DB102. Freed, Richard. "Copland: *Our Town, Three Pieces*; *Rodeo, Four Episodes*; *Piano Variations*; *Four Piano Blues*; *Danzón Cubano*." *Stereo Review* 50:89 (January 1985)

Review of ProArte PAD 183/PCD 183/CDD 183. "The two-piano version of the *Danzón Cubano*...is given a persuasive reading with Lukas Foss on the second instrument." (See: D169)

DB103. Moore, David W. "Bernstein's Bernstein on DG Compact Discs." *American Record Guide* 50:74-75 (March/April 1987)

Review of Deutsche Gramophone 415 964-2. The revised version of *Symphony No. 2* includes a lengthy piano cadenza. "Foss is a much more persuasive proponent than was Entremont in the Columbia recording, now out of print." (See: D171)

DB104. Koldys, Mark. "Copland: Three Piano Excerpts from *Our Town*; Four Episodes from *Rodeo*; *Piano Variations*; *Four Piano Blues*; *Danzón Cubano*." *American Record Guide* 48:29 (November/December 1987)

Review of Pro Arte PAD 183/PCD 183/CDD 183. "[The two-piano version of *Danzón Cubano*] which has been performed and recorded before, albeit infrequently, actually sounds more at home here than in its instrumental incarnation." (See: D169)

DB105. Pincus, Andrew L. "All Sounds Blend In a Rich American Mainstream." *New York Times* August 20, 1989:II,29.

Review of CRI SD 554 in the context of American symphonic music. (See: D129; See also: DB54, DB61)

DB106. Tuska, Jon. "Mendelssohn: *Concerto No. 1 in G Minor* for Piano and Orchestra, op. 25..." *Fanfare* 13:230-231 (March/April 1990)
Review of AS DISC 553. "In the piano concerto, Foss performs with rapt grace and deep feeling, while Koussevitzky's accompaniment is supercharged..." (See: D172)

GENERAL
BIBLIOGRAPHY

The numbers preceded by "W," or "WB" in the "See" and "See also" references in this section refer to item numbers in the "Works and Performances" section.

B1.   Fine, Irving. "Boston Opens an Exciting Season."
       Modern Music 22:43-45 (November/December 1944)
            Review and outline of the Boston Symphony's
       season. Announced is the performance of Hindemith's
       *Theme and Variations According to the Four
       Temperaments* which Foss premiered as piano soloist
       with the Boston Symphony, Richard Burgin, conductor,
       in the summer of 1944.

B2.   Fine, Irving. "Young America: Bernstein and Foss."
       Modern Music 22:238-243 (May/June 1945)
            In this early article on the beginnings of the
       careers of Foss and Bernstein, they are referred to as
       "the twin prodigies, the fair-haired boys of the
       contemporary musical scene." It continues by outlining
       the early works by Foss and his influences by Hindemith
       and Copland.

B3.   Reis, Claire R. "Lukas Foss." In *Composers in America:
       Biographical Sketches of Contemporary Composers with
       a Record of Their Works*. revised and enlarged ed. New
       York: Macmillan, 1947:126-127.
            This brief biographical sketch of Foss outlines his
       major accomplishments to 1947. It also includes a
       classified catalog of his compositions to that date with
       durations, publishers, and dates of composition.

B4.   Copland, Aaron. "New School of American Composers."
       New York Times Magazine March 14, 1948:18 +

Brief biographical essays on Foss and six of his contemporaries, their styles, and musical accomplishments to 1948. "It is impossible not to admire the spontaneity and naturalness of [Foss's] musical flow, the absolute clarity in texture, and the clean and easy handling of large formal problems."

B5.   Ewen, David. "Lukas Foss, 1922- ." In *American Composers Today: A Biographical and Critical Guide*. New York: H.W. Wilson, 1949:94-95.
         This biographical sketch includes a principal works list.

B6.   Saleski, Gdal. "Lukas Foss." In *Famous Musicians of Jewish Origin*. New York: Bloch, 1949:56-57.
         This biographical article centers around Foss's many accomplishments as the "wonder-boy of the modern music world" and outlines his premieres, commissions, and awards. Among these, it is mentioned that he was the youngest composer to ever be awarded a Pulitzer Fellowship and a Guggenheim Fellowship.

B7.   Taylor, Betty. "Youth Should Be Heard." *Christian Science Monitor* October 17, 1950:13.
         Brief biographical piece listing many of the awards Foss had received for his music up until he was 28 years old.

B8.   Kyle, Marguerite Kelly. "AmerAllegro: Lukas Foss." *Pan Pipes* 43:119 (December 1950)
         Announcement of Foss's resignation as pianist of the Boston Symphony and his intention to spend the season at the American Academy in Rome as a result of his Fulbright Fellowship and his Prix de Rome for 1950-51; listings of the premieres of *The Jumping Frog of Calaveras County* (See: W3a), *Song of Anguish* (See: W28a), *Behold! I Build an House* (See: W14a), and *Concerto for Oboe* (See: W43a); other performances of *The Prairie* and *Song of Songs*; and the preparation/publication of *Song of Songs, String Quartet in G, Wanderers Gemütsruhe, Where the Bee Sucks, Concerto for Oboe, Behold! I Build an House, The Jumping Frog of Calaveras County,* and *Adon Olom.*

B9.   Kyle, Marguerite Kelly. "AmerAllegro: Lukas Foss." *Pan Pipes* 46:39 (January 1954)
         Listings of the March 11, 1953 premiere performance of *A Parable of Death* (See: W15a) by the Louisville Orchestra; other performances of *Parable, The Jumping Frog of Calaveras County, Piano Concerto No. 2, Song of Songs,* and *Song of Anguish*; the publication of the vocal score to *A Parable of Death, Piano Concerto No. 2,* and the preparation of *Song of Anguish* by Carl Fischer; the recordings of *A Parable of Death* and *String*

Quartet No. 1 in G; and the announcement of Foss's appointment as associate professor at U.C.L.A.

B10.   Taubman, Howard. "Jazz Pianist Digs the Sonata Form." *New York Times* August 6, 1954:10.
        Describes how Lukas Foss worked with jazz pianist Joe Bushkin on composition while Foss was teaching at Tanglewood during the summer of 1954.

B11.   Taubman, Howard. "Lipkin is Soloist at Lenox Festival." *New York Times* August 7, 1954:7.
        Review of the August 6, 1954 performance at Tanglewood by the Boston Symphony Orchestra, Seymour Lipkin, pianist, and Lukas Foss, conductor. Performed were Mozart's *B Flat Major Concerto*, K. 450, excerpts from Mozart's *Idomeneo*, and Stravinsky's *Pulcinella*. "Mr. Foss conducted the *Idomeneo* excerpts with affection and verve."

B12.   Gräter, Manfred. "Lukas Foss--ein Amerikanischer Musiker." *Melos* 21:340-341 (December 1954)
        "Spontaneity of expression, honesty and the warmth of sensitivity, the clarity of an alert connoisseur and a sure mastery of a composer's craft--are the concepts upon which his music is judged." (translation) Foss also discusses his German and American compositional influences (Bach, Hindemith, Copland) stating that composition is his primary focus, while performing and conducting are necessary outlets for his musical temperament. Includes a list of works.

B13.   Berger, Arthur. "Stravinsky and the Younger American Composers." *The Score and I.M.A. Magazine* no. 12:38-46 (June 1955)
        Originally influenced by Hindemith, Foss was led to Stravinsky's style through a desire to search and develop his composition technique. He is included here as a part of the "Boston Group" and "Stravinsky School" of composers along with Copland, Shapero, Haieff, Berger, Lessard, and Fine.

B14.   Darack, Arthur. "This Week's Soloist: Lukas Foss, Pianist." *Cincinnati Symphony Orchestra Programs* February 22, 1957:549.
        Biographical sketch which appears in the program notes for Foss's solo performance of Mozart's *Concerto in G Major* for piano and orchestra, K. 453.

B15.   Foss, Lukas. "Does Contemporary Music Really Profit from Performances by Community Orchestras?" *American Composers Alliance Bulletin* 6:13+ (Winter 1957) Reprinted from the *American Symphony Orchestra League Newsletter*.

Address given at the 11th annual convention of the American Symphony Orchestra League, June 14-16, 1956 at Providence, Rhode Island. Aimed at community orchestra directors, Foss remarks that not enough new music is given a fair chance by young composers, conductors, or the musicians.

B16.   Kyle, Marguerite Kelly. "AmerAllegro: Lukas Foss." *Pan Pipes* 50:53 (January 1958)
Listings of the premiere performances of *Psalms* (See: W16a) and *Symphony of Chorales* (See: W47b), the German premiere of *The Jumping Frog of Calaveras County* (See: W3f); Foss's fourteenth performance with a major orchestra of *Concerto No. 2 for Piano*; the publication of *Psalms* by Carl Fischer for chorus and two pianos; recordings of *Concerto No. 2 for Piano* (See: D39), *String Quartet No. 1 in G* (See: D59), *Psalms* (See: D13), and *Behold! I Build an House* (See: D6); and announcements of receipt of a Naumburg Recording Award, $1000 grant from the National Institute of Arts and Letters, Southern Campus Award (UCLA) and the receipt of an Honorary Doctorate of Music from the Los Angeles Conservatory of Music.

B17.   Foss, Lukas. "A Beginning." *Juilliard Review* 5:12-16 (Spring 1958)
Foss describes why he began the Improvisation Chamber Ensemble. Through group improvisation, he hoped to create a new area for future masterworks, create a fresh approach to performance away from the printed note, and to bridge the gap between composer and performer.

B18.   Kyle, Marguerite Kelly. "AmerAllegro: Lukas Foss." *Pan Pipes* 51:62 (January 1959)
Listings of the premiere of the revised version of *Ode* (See: W41b); the performances of *Symphony of Chorales* in Pittsburgh (See: W47a), Boston (See: W47b), and New York (See: W47c); the publication of a new edition of *The Jumping Frog of Calaveras County* in Germany; the Columbia recording of *Song of Songs* (See: D23); and the first tour of the Contemporary Improvisation Ensemble.

B19.   Faulkner, Maurice. "Non-Jazz Group Improvisation." *Saturday Review* 42:70 (March 14, 1959)
Review of a concert held in Santa Barbara (no date given) by Foss, Drasnin, Dufallo, DeLancey, William Malm (bass clarinet), and Eugene Wilson (violoncello). As one of the first performances given involving group improvisations, the author describes the procedures used in the music's production. "The tedious score-bound performances, which have become so sterile in our modern concert halls, might be set free if our

contemporary musicians were alerted to group improvisations of this type."

B20.   "Eleventh in Our Series of American Composers." *Music Clubs Magazine* 38:63 (April 1959)
    Chiefly a biographical sketch with major works described, the article announces the commissioning of an orchestral work for the National Federation of Music Clubs.

B21.   Gutekunst, Carl. "New York Concert and Opera Beat: New York Philharmonic." *Musical Courier* 159:17 (May 1959)
    Review of the April 12, 1959 performance by the New York Philharmonic, Lukas Foss, guest conductor. Foss performed and conducted Mozart's *Concerto no. 21 in C major* and Handel's *Harpsichord Concerto in F major.* "His playing possessed not only extraordinary beauty but also an excitement." Also performed was Foss's *Symphony of Chorales* (See: W47c). "There are moments of rhythmic vitality, sonority, and brilliance, and some good ideas, but these are over-long in their development and the general effect is one of diffuseness."

B22.   Foss, Lukas. "On Ensemble Improvisation--A New Way of Making Music Together." *Music Clubs Magazine* 39:4-5 (September 1959)
    Foss explains the differences between jazz improvisation, solo improvisation, and ensemble improvisation. He also notes that there should be no such thing as a composer who does not play an instrument and that through improvisation skills, performers will play music of the masters better.

B23.   Sabin, Robert. "Lukas Foss Appears on Camera 3." *Musical America* 79:25 (November 1, 1959)
    Review of the October 11, 1959 performance by Lukas Foss and the Improvisation Chamber Ensemble on CBS's Camera 3 program. "The ensemble was most impressive in fast, rhythmically incisive passages. The idiom of the improvisations, understandably, tended to resemble that of Mr. Foss's own music, despite the fact that they were free and spontaneous."

B24.   "Improvisation Experiments for Chamber Ensembles Made by Foss." *The World of Music* no. 4:70-71 (December 1959)
    Using prearranged musical guideposts, Foss explains how classically oriented musicians in a chamber setting can break the barrier between composer and performer and create harmony, melody, and counterpoint spontaneously. A textbook by Foss which was to be

published by Schirmer in New York is mentioned. (Article in English, French, and German.)

B25.   Ehrmann, Jacques. "Ein Experiment: Improvisierte Kammermusik." *Musik und Gesellschaft* 9:47-48 (December 1959)
        The article describes the ensemble improvisation that Foss developed through his teaching in Los Angeles and how his modern version of the improvisation techniques of Bach, Mozart, or Handel affect the way we know "classical music."

B26.   Kyle, Marguerite Kelly. "AmerAllegro: Lukas Foss." *Pan Pipes* 52:49-50 (January 1960)
        Listings of the premieres of *Symphony of Chorales* by the Pittsburgh Symphony Orchestra (See: W47a) and a new version of *Ode*, conducted by Eugene Ormandy (See: W41b); Foss's piano solo performances of *Concerto No. 2 for Piano* in Cleveland and Minneapolis; other performances of *Symphony of Chorales* (See: W47b, W47c) and *The Prairie*, and Foss's conducting of his own works and other music at a pair of subscription concerts in Buffalo; and his receipt of a second Guggenheim Fellowship, and commissions from the Ford Foundation and the Fromm Foundation.

B27.   "2 U.S. Composers Will Visit Soviet: Aaron Copland and Lukas Foss to Conduct, Perform During 4-Week Tour." *New York Times* March 8, 1960:38.
        An outline of Foss's and Copland's trip to the Soviet Union under the United States State Department's Cultural Exchange Program which began in 1958. They were to be in the Soviet Union from March 15 to April 11, 1960. From there, Foss continued on to Poland from April 11 to 20.

B28.   "U.S. Musicians in Soviet: Copland and Foss in Meetings With Russian Composers." *New York Times* March 17, 1960:29.
        While in the Soviet Union, Foss and Copland met with Dmitri Shostakovich, Tikhon Khrennikov, Yuri Shaporin, and Antoli Novikov and scheduled visits to Kiev, Leningrad, and Riga to take part in concerts of American music.

B29.   Shneerson, G. "Amerikanskie Kompozitory v Moskve." *Sovetskaya Muzyka* 24:135-137 (May 1960)
        Review of the tour of Russia by Copland and Foss in March 1960. Article in Russian.

B30.   "Return from Russia." *Musical America* 80:6 (May 1960)
        Review of an exchange visit by Foss and Copland to Russia in March 1960. Works by Foss which were performed on this series of four concerts were

Symphony of Chorales, Ode, Concerto No. 2 for Piano, and *String Quartet.* "Members of the [Leningrad Symphony] orchestra told Mr. Foss that his *Symphony of Chorales* was the most difficult score they had ever played, yet the orchestra seemed to like the music, and the audience gave it a rousing ovation."

B31.   Foss, Lukas. "Conductor's Luncheon." *American Symphony Orchestra League Newsletter* 11:5 (July 1960)
Foss discusses his trip to and the musical life of Russia. He felt that he and Copland could not freely exchange ideas with the Russians since they did not accept criticism well.

B32.   Henahan, Donal J. "Caught in the Act: Lucas Foss." *Down Beat* 27:50 (December 22, 1960)
Review of a concert at the Simpson Theater, Natural History Museum, Chicago by the Improvisation Chamber Ensemble and assisted by the Festival String Quartet. "The music that emerged had all the trappings of post-Webern serialism without the compensating logic and mathematical precision of such music."

B33.   Foss, Lukas. "The Myth of Music's Universality." *Saturday Review* 43:15-16 (December 24, 1960)
Foss describes how most music is not universal, and carries any message it has to only a few. He states that Americans think of Stravinsky as a Russian composer, while the Russians think of him as an American composer. "Music is poor propaganda, arouses emotions without stimulating action, and does not necessarily communicate to the people of the world."

B34.   "Lukas Foss." *Composers of the Americas* no. 7:17-23 (1961) Also printed in *Boletin Interamericano de Musica,* no. 25:40-44 (September 1961)
The article in Spanish and English presents a thumbnail biographical sketch of Foss, the reproduction of a page of manuscript from an unidentified work, and a classified catalog of works with publication information.

B35.   Goldberg, Albert. "Versatile New Director." *Musical America* 81:38-39 (July 1961)
Foss was appointed music director for the 15th annual Ojai, California, Festival which was held May 19-21, 1961. "His versatile talents as conductor, pianist and composer, as well as his imaginative and enterprising programming, were responsible for the largest attendance the Festival has ever enjoyed."

B36.   Dumm, Robert. "Lenox, Mass.: Tingles at Tanglewood." *Musical Courier* 163:60-61 (August 1961)

Review of a performance by Foss on piano of Bach's *Brandenburg Concerto No. 5* with Doriot Dwyer, flute, Richard Burgin, violin, the Boston Symphony Orchestra, and Charles Munch, conductor at Tanglewood. "[Foss] is capable of a slow-burning crescendo, which burst into flame at the cadenza and blazed through the finale. People rose and simply shouted."

B37.   Russell, Smith. "Improvisation Ensembles Follow Plans, Called Controlled Chance." *Music of the West Magazine* 17:18-19 (October 1961)

Review of the September 11, 1961 performance of two Improvisation Groups which were "rehearsed" by Richard Dufallo and Charles DeLancey on a Rockefeller Foundation grant. Foss was on hand to give some explanatory remarks on how the pieces were prepared for the performance. "What bothers me most is the creation of so many unmusical sounds in an alleged musical performance. There are enough such things in daily life....Are these musicians really serious?"

B38.   Foss, Lukas. "Über Ensemble-Improvisation." *Melos* 28:312-313 (October 1961)

Foss's philosophies concerning the composer and the performer and their unity through improvisation. "In composition, everything is fate. In improvisation, chance rules...." (translation)

B39.   Kyle, Marguerite Kelly. "AmerAllegro: Lukas Foss." *Pan Pipes* 54:49-50 (January 1962)

Listings of the July 1962 premiere of the chamber version of *Time Cycle* (See: W32a) at Tanglewood; other performances of *Time Cycle* (See: W31c), *A Parable of Death*, *Ode*, and *Symphony of Chorales*; the first staged American performance of *Introductions and Goodbyes* (See: W5c); the publication of the full score of *Time Cycle* by Carl Fischer; the recording and issuance of *Studies in Improvisation* (See: D61; the work is incorrectly identified in the article as *Concerto for Improvising Instruments*), *Time Cycle* (See: D26), and *Song of Songs* (See: D23); the receipt of the New York Music Critics' Circle Award for *Time Cycle*; and lectures given at MIT, Colorado State University, and the New School in New York City.

B40.   Schumach, Murray. "Musical Ad Libbing: Foss Will Demonstrate Improvisations Here." *New York Times* March 4, 1962:II,9.

Foss describes ensemble improvisation in this article which promoted his March 11, 1962 concert at New York's New School for Social Research, sponsored by the Fromm Foundation. On the program were two movements from *Echoi* (See: W74b) and the chamber

version premiere of *Time Cycle* (See: W32c) with Adele
Addison.

B41.   Foss, Lukas. "Improvisation Vs. Composition." *Musical
America* 82:48 (May 1962)Reprinted as "Improvisation
Versus Composition." *The Musical Times* 103:684-685
(October 1962). (See: B43)
       Foss explains ensemble improvisation. He calls it
"performers' music" and refers to his ensemble's
improvisations as "the result of collective planning and
experimentation." He also notes that improvisation
should be used to enhance written compositions.

B42.   Goldberg, Albert. "Mozart and Moderns." *Musical
America* 82:12 (July 1962)
       Review of the 16th annual Ojai, California,
Festival, May 14-20, 1962 at which Foss was musical
director. Foss, Leo Smit, and André Previn performed
Mozart piano concertos on May 18, while Foss
performed and conducted on the other nights of the
festival.

B43.   Foss, Lukas. "Improvisation Versus Composition." *The
Musical Times* 103:684-685 (October 1962) Reprint of:
"Improvisation Vs. Composition." *Musical America*
82:48 (May 1962). (See: B41)
       The article appears here as a prelude to a
performance by the Improvisation Chamber Ensemble,
October 11, 1962, which was broadcast as part of the
BBC Thursday Invitation Concert from Newcastle and a
performance October 13, 1962 at the American Embassy
Theatre, Grosvenor Square.

B44.   Reeves, Jean. "Lukas Foss Is Named by Philharmonic as
Krips' Successor." *Buffalo Evening News* December 28,
1962:1.
       Background article on Foss and his qualifications
for taking on the position of Buffalo Philharmonic
Orchestra director. Foss was told at contract negotiation
time that box office considerations demanded that new
music not be performed as often as the masters. Robert
I. Millonzi is quoted as saying, "He is not here to play
bizarre music or to conduct just his own music."

B45.   "Foss Will Succeed Krips at Philharmonic Helm." *Buffalo
Courier Express* December 29, 1962:11.
       This article details Foss's first appointment as a
full-time conductor. "Foss...signed a two-year
contract...after 42 directors of the [Buffalo Philharmonic]
Orchestra Society unanimously approved his
appointment."

B46.   Machlis, Joseph. "Lukas Foss." In *American Composers
of Our Time.* New York: T.Y. Crowell, 1963:189-200.

A detailed biographical article on the early works
of Foss through his beginnings of improvisation. It gives
plot summaries for his two major operas, *Griffelkin* (See:
W4) and *The Jumping Frog of Calaveras County* (See:
W3) and describes premieres of many of his
compositions.

B47.   Posell, Elsa Z. "Lukas Foss." In *American Composers*.
Boston: Houghton Mifflin, 1963:42-45.
This book is geared toward juvenile readers. It
includes a biographical sketch and a list of major
compositions.

B48.   Foss, Lukas. "*The Prairie, A Parable of Death*, and
Psalms." In: *The Composer's Point of View: Essays on
Twentieth Century Choral Music By Those Who Wrote It*,
ed. Robert Stephan Hines. Norman, OK: University of
Oklahoma Press, 1963:3-13.
Foss outlines his love for setting poetry to music.
He states that he thinks of himself as a vocal composer
and that his choral music is not easy to master
rhythmically. He describes his compositions *The Prairie*
(See: WB58), *A Parable of Death* (See: WB76), and
Psalms (See: WB85).

B49.   Frankenstein, Alfred. "And Now the Atonal Ad Lib."
Horizon 5:76-81 (January 1963)
This article describes in detail the procedures of
the Improvisation Chamber Ensemble in "writing" a
composition and performing it. It gives a history of the
procedure and describes some of the techniques that the
ensemble used in performance.

B50.   Kyle, Marguerite Kelly. "AmerAllegro: Lukas Foss." *Pan
Pipes* 55:50 (January 1963)
Listings of the September 1962 European premiere
of *Time Cycle* by the Berlin Philharmonic Orchestra,
Lukas Foss, conductor (See: W31e); other performances
of *A Parable of Death, Introductions and Goodbyes,
Song of Songs, Griffelkin, Ode*, and *Time Cycle* (See:
W32d); the recordings of *Studies in Improvisation* (See:
D61), *Time Cycle* (See: D26), *String Quartet* (See:
D59), and *Song of Songs* (See: D23); and the
announcement of Foss being elected to the National
Institute of Arts and Letters.

B51.   "Orchestras: East-West Exchange." *Musical America*
83:48 (February 1963)
Announcement of Joseph Krips leaving his post
with the Buffalo Philharmonic Orchestra to conduct the
San Francisco Symphony and of Foss leaving California
to conduct the Buffalo Philharmonic Orchestra beginning
with the 1963-64 season.

B52.   Foss, Lukas. "The Changing Composer-Performer
         Relationship: A Monologue and a Dialogue."
         Perspectives of New Music 1:45-53 (Spring 1963)
         Reprinted in *Contemporary Composers on Contemporary
         Music* edited by Elliott Schwartz and Barney Childs. (New
         York: Da Capo Press, 1978, c1967:325-334). (See:
         B162)
              Foss discusses the evolution of composition from
         Bach's time when composers wrote in figured bass
         shorthand for the performers to interpret as they would,
         to Wagner and Schoenberg when composers wrote
         everything out, and to the present day when composers
         are once again writing in shorthand by outlining the
         important aspects of the piece and allowing the
         performer to fill in the rest.

B53.   Sabin, Robert. "Some Younger American Composers."
         Tempo no. 64:25-28 (Spring 1963)
              A survey of some the American composers of note
         since the 20s and 30s. Foss is briefly described as
         having "achieved supreme skill without being seduced by
         it into academicism or mere virtuosic display."

B54.   "Foss is Eager to Give WNY Joyous Magical Music."
         Buffalo Evening News October 10, 1963:52.
              In a lecture at the State University of New York at
         Buffalo entitled "The Symphony in the 20th Century,"
         Foss said, "'We should play old music as if the ink were
         hardly dry....We should also play the new music with the
         same awe, respect and distance we usually accord to the
         classics.'" He was promoting the October 26, 1963
         Buffalo Philharmonic Orchestra concert which would
         present the Buffalo premiere of Stravinsky's then 50-year
         old *Le Sacre du Printemps*. He mentioned that the
         symphonic orchestra had become a museum, but
         suggested that as any good museum, it must always
         change.

B55.   Dwyer, John. "Bravos, Excitement Greet Foss as
         Philharmonic Season Opens." *Buffalo Evening News*
         October 28, 1963:25.
              Review of Foss's premiere concert as Music
         Director of the Buffalo Philharmonic Orchestra, October
         26, 1963. "A new era in Buffalo music began with the
         debut of conductor Lukas Foss in the season-opening
         Philharmonic program...where an applauding audience of
         2600, rising at the opening, intermission and close in an
         open-handed, open-hearted tribute." The Orchestra had
         been rehearsed "to the limit" and was well-prepared
         through a pre-season tour. Performed were Stravinsky's
         Le Sacre du Printemps, Ives's *The Unanswered Question*,
         and Brahms's *First Symphony*.

B56.   Gill, Kenneth. "Philharmonic Concert Wins Standing
         Ovation." *Buffalo Courier Express* November 18,
         1963:8.
             Review of the November 17, 1963 premiere of
         David Diamond's *This Sacred Ground* by the Buffalo
         Philharmonic Orchestra, Lukas Foss, conductor, in
         Kleinhans Music Hall, Buffalo, New York. "Conductor
         Lukas Foss set forth the work in its proper dignity and
         solemnity while the music shifted in its many moods
         according to the timeless text." The concert was
         concluded with a standing ovation and many curtain
         calls.

B57.   Ericson, Raymond. "Buffalo Takes a Flyer on Foss."
         New York Times November 24, 1963:II,13.
             Describes Foss's reasons for accepting the
         conductor position with the Buffalo Philharmonic
         Orchestra and views from the management that hired
         him. Foss expressed that the position was attractive to
         him because it would allow him time to pursue his
         composing and how he and Allen Sapp had been
         collaborating on the formation of the Center for the
         Creative and Performing Arts at the University of Buffalo.

B58.   Kyle, Marguerite Kelly. "AmerAllegro: Lukas Foss." *Pan
         Pipes* 56:56 (January 1964)
             Listings of the November 11, 1963 complete
         premiere of *Echoi* (See: W74a); other performances of *A
         Parable of Death, Echoi, Ode, Time Cycle, Introductions
         and Goodbyes* (See: W5d), and the march from
         Griffelkin; the publication of the chamber version of *Time
         Cycle*, and the announcement that *Echoi* was in
         preparation for publication by B. Schott Söhne and Carl
         Fischer; the publication of an article in *Perspectives of
         New Music* (See: B52); his appointment as music
         director/conductor of the Buffalo Philharmonic Orchestra
         and his plan to program 50% new music on these
         concerts.

B59.   Davis, Peter G. "Christmas Music Festival." *Musical
         America* 84:48 (January 1964)
             Review of the December 29, 1964 closing concert
         of the New York Christmas Music Festival which was an
         all-Bach program with Lukas Foss conducting a chamber
         ensemble and the Fredonia College Choir at Philharmonic
         Hall in New York City. Foss performed on piano and
         conducted Bach's *D Minor Clavier Concerto* and
         Brandenburg Concerto No. 5. The concert was given in
         memory of Paul Hindemith. "The use of a piano in this
         work would have been more jarring had not Mr. Foss
         played so well."

B60.   "Foss Will Join Summer Faculty at Tanglewood." *Buffalo
         Evening News* January 20, 1964:10.

Announcement of Foss's appointment as one of four composers to teach composition during August 1964 with Copland, Schuller, and Boulez at Tanglewood. All four composers would take part in the Festival of Contemporary American Music, August 9-13, 1964, with the Boston Symphony Orchestra, Erich Leinsdorf, conductor.

B61.   "Orchestra Will Present TV Concert." *Buffalo Courier Express* February 21, 1964:3.

The Buffalo Philharmonic Orchestra was one of five orchestras named to be part of National Education Television (NET) of New York City televised concert series. The concert televised was that of March 1, 1964, which offered the North American premiere of Stockhausen's *Momente*.

B62.   Salzman, Eric. "N.Y. View of Our Premiere: Lots of Life in the Old Town." *Buffalo Evening News* March 4, 1964:67. Reprinted from the *New York Herald Tribune* March 2, 1964.

Review of the March 1, 1964 American premiere of Karlheinz Stockhausen's *Momente* by Martina Arroyo, soprano, the Crane Collegiate Singers (State University of New York, College at Potsdam), Brock McElheran, director, Buffalo Philharmonic Orchestra, and Lukas Foss, conductor in Kleinhans Music Hall, Buffalo, New York. The work was full of clapping, hissing, murmuring, and shuffling sounds by the chorus and was prepared under the direction of Stockhausen. "Stockhausen enlarges our experience and the possibilities of all experience in the world...by the way he creates a new relationship between the audience, performers and composer. (See also: B63)

B63.   Dwyer, John. "Word of *Momente* Rippling Rapidly Around the Globe." *Buffalo Evening News* March 4, 1964:67.

Review of the March 3, 1964 performance of Stockhausen's *Momente* (See also: B62) The reviewer notes the premieres of *Momente* and David Diamond's *This Sacred Ground* as important events in the history of the Buffalo Philharmonic Orchestra since both premieres led to much national and international coverage.

B64.   Gill, Kenneth. "Foss Has Unusual Image Among Conductors." *Buffalo Courier Express* March 8, 1964:19D.

A collection of anecdotes from Foss's travels to Russia and Berlin. It also recounts the fire at his Bel Air (California) home which destroyed all his early manuscripts and recordings, and paintings by Mrs. Foss and other prominent artists.

B65.   Foss, Lukas. "In Memoriam: Paul Hindemith (1895-
       1963)." *Perspectives of New Music* 2:1-4
       (Spring/Summer 1964)
               In this eulogy for Hindemith, Foss sets down into
       words what Hindemith's music was all about, "a genuine
       musical language, solid as a rock, uneclectic" with "tonal
       chromaticism."

B66.   Salzman, Eric. "Far Out in Buffalo." *New York Herald
       Tribune Magazine* May 10, 1964:31.
               Explains how Foss had brought large city avant
       garde musical culture to Buffalo with the help of Alan
       Sapp at the University, and a large Rockefeller
       Foundation grant. His efforts are referred to as a
       "Cultural Peace Corps for underdeveloped artistic areas."

B67.   "Foss Signs 4-Year Contract to Conduct the
       Philharmonic." *Buffalo Evening News* June 22, 1964:30.
               Before Foss left for a music festival in Amsterdam,
       he signed a four-year contract to conduct the Buffalo
       Philharmonic Orchestra through the 1967-68 season.
       Foss said of the agreement, "'[I am] pleased at the
       prospect of spending the next four years building the
       Philharmonic into an even finer orchestra and one which
       will continue to be a front-runner in the music world.'"

B68.   Schlaerth, J. Don. "Foss Takes Viewers On 'An Exciting
       Journey Into Music.'" *Buffalo Evening News TV Topics*
       October 17, 1964:2.
               Foss had a Saturday afternoon, twice monthly
       television program in Buffalo to promote the Philharmonic
       concerts. He compared himself with Bernstein:
       "'Bernstein teaches with clarity, color and flair....He is a
       TV personality and professor, I'm...trying to prepare
       people for the unusual things in music that are going on
       here in Buffalo.'" Before coming to Buffalo, he had
       appeared regularly on Los Angeles television in a series
       on arts and science.

B69.   "Festival Planned by Philharmonic." *New York Times*
       October 21, 1964:54.
               Article which describes the three-week festival of
       French and American music sponsored by the New York
       Philharmonic. Foss was appointed artistic director for
       the festival which would include 10 orchestral concerts
       in July 1965. (See also: B81)

B70.   Schonberg, Harold C. "Music: Handel-Mozart: *Messiah*
       is Presented in Discarded Style." *New York Times*
       December 22, 1964:34.
               Review of the December 21, 1964 performance of
       Mozart's arrangement of Handel's *Messiah* by Bethany
       Beardslee, soprano, Lillian Garabedian, mezzo soprano,
       Stanley Kolk, tenor, William Wolff, bass, the Festival

Chorus of the State University of New York College at Fredonia, Harriet Simons, director, Buffalo Philharmonic Orchestra, Lukas Foss, conductor at Philharmonic Hall, New York City. "[The chorus], more than 300 strong,...sang with delicacy [and] impeccable diction....[The orchestra was] responsive...with superior strings, smooth ensemble and good first-desk players....Mr. Foss appears to be a natural conductor, one with confidence, alertness...and...an ability to transmit, both to orchestra and audience." (See also: B76)

B71.   Mellers, Wilfrid. "Today and Tomorrow: Lukas Foss and the Younger Generation." In *Music in a New Found Land*. New York: A. A. Knopf, 1965:220-235.
        Foss is described as "an eclectic whose career comprises a pocket-history of American music during the twentieth century....[with] a chameleon-like adaptability." Some of Foss's major compositions (*The Prairie*, *Psalms*, *A Parable of Death*, *Time Cycle*) are analysed with regard to Foss's personality and background. (See: WB59, WB77, WB153)

B72.   Foss, Lukas. "Foss." *New Yorker* 40:22-24 (January 30, 1965)
        Staff members from the *New Yorker* got this brief interview with Foss while he was in New York for a lecture-recital at Hunter College. He describes all the new musical events which he was beginning in Buffalo, including the Center for Creative and Performing Arts at the State University of New York at Buffalo. He also described his recent compositions and the reactions Buffalonians had for his Philharmonic programming. "[After premiering Stockhausen's *Momente*] letters just poured in to the newspapers asking what I thought I was doing. I finally had to go on television to defend myself."

B73.   Allen, Jack. "Foss To Be In First of Six Documentaries." *Buffalo Courier Express* February 6, 1965:7.
        The documentary was aired on February 13, 1965 on ABC-TV and was hosted by Van Heflin. It was titled "The Way Out Men," a program featuring trailblazers in the arts and sciences.

B74.   "Baton a Small Part of Foss' Life." *Buffalo Evening News* February 15, 1965:15.
        An overview of a "typical" week in the life of Foss while he was conductor of the Buffalo Philharmonic Orchestra. It outlines rehearsals, concerts, and administrative duties.

B75.   "Festival of Arts Today Very Exciting for Foss--Including Problems." *Buffalo Evening News* February 23, 1965:10.
Description of the events which made up the first Festival of the Arts Today held in Buffalo, New York. The festival was the first time all major arts factors in Buffalo had combined their resources for one project. (See also: B77)

B76.   Stevens, Denis. "A Musical Yuletide in New York." *High Fidelity/Musical America* 15:86H-I (March 1965)
Review of the December 21, 1964 performance by the Buffalo Philharmonic Orchestra, Lukas Foss, conductor in Philharmonic Hall, New York City. A chorus from the State University of New York at Buffalo joined the orchestra on December 23 for Mozart's *Idomeneo* and the chorus from Fredonia State College sang on December 21 and 22 on Mozart's orchestration of Handel's *Messiah*. Also on the 23rd, Foss conducted Mozart's *Piano Concerto*, K.467 from the piano. "The indefatigable Mr. Foss...has not only succeeded in maintaining the excellent level of his orchestra...[but] has noticeably improved it by...giving it one or two hard tasks." (referring to his conducting from the piano) (See also: B70)

B77.   "Avant-Garde: Did You Ever, Ever, Ever." *Time* 85:55 (March 19, 1965)
Review of the first Festival of the Arts Today, held in Buffalo, New York. The festival served as a catalyst to make people take notice of current happenings in art, theater, and music. (See also: B75)

B78.   "33rd Biennial Convention Parade of Stars." *Music Clubs Magazine* 44:60-61 (April 1965)
A brief biography of Foss prepared for the National Federation of Music Clubs program. Foss spoke at the Saturday luncheon as a representative of ASCAP.

B79.   "Foss Explains His Protest During Washington Concert." *Buffalo Evening News* May 13, 1965:55.
Review of a concert by the Buffalo Philharmonic Orchestra, Lukas Foss, conductor, during the 3rd Inter-American Festival in Washington, D.C. Foss staged a protest by refusing to conduct and sitting silently on the podium, when noisy air conditioning equipment wasn't silenced. He didn't want the noise to destroy the musical premieres and had complained beforehand and had been told that it would be turned off during the performance. It wasn't. Foss later remarked, "'My protest was against the careless disregard for the preparation and performance of new music. It deserves the respect, at least of a decent hearing.'" (See also: B80, B82)

B80.   "Buffalo Orchestra Led by Foss Praised by Capital Critic."
        Buffalo Evening News May 13, 1965:55.
            Report by the *Washington Post's* critic Paul Hume
        on Foss's protest at the 3rd Inter-American Festival in
        Washington, D.C. Foss's reason for protest was obvious
        after the intermission when the Orchestra performed the
        work by Carrido-Lecca which with its extreme
        pianissimos, could barely be heard over the fans of the
        auditorium. John Vinton of the *Washington Star* agreed
        with Hume and added that Foss had conducted
        sensitively before the protest and "heavy-handedly"
        after. (See also: B79, B82)

B81.   Ericson, Raymond. "Music: Accent Is American at
        Festival." *New York Times* July 31, 1965:11.
            Review of the July 30, 1965 performance by the
        New York Philharmonic Orchestra, Lukas Foss,
        conductor in New York City as part of the French-
        American Festival. Three works were given their world
        premieres including Charles Ives's *From the Steeples and
        the Mountains* and Charles Wuorinen's *Orchestra and
        Electronic Exchanges*. "For the playing of the orchestra,
        and for Mr. Foss's brilliant conducting, it was a tour de
        force." (See also: B69)

B82.   Lafay, Gloria. "Inter-American Music Festival." *High
        Fidelity/Musical America* 15:124 (August 1965)
            Review of the 3rd Inter-American Music Festival
        held in Washington, D.C. in May 1965. In a period of six
        days and eight concerts, thirty world premieres were
        given. Foss led the Buffalo Philharmonic at some of
        these concerts. He made quite a stir when during the
        final concert, he stopped the orchestra and refused to
        begin again until the air conditioning was shut off. It
        was not, and after an intermission, Foss concluded the
        concert. (See also: B79, B80)

B83.   Kyle, Marguerite Kelly. "AmerAllegro: Lukas Foss." *Pan
        Pipes* 58:61-62 (January 1966)
            Listings of the May 1965 premiere of *Fragments of
        Archilochos* (See: W17a), the March 31, 1966 premiere
        of Beethoven's *Military Marches for Winds* (compiled and
        edited by Foss), and the New York premiere of *Elytres*
        (See: W49b); other performances of *Elytres*, *The
        Jumping Frog of Calaveras County*, *Introductions and
        Goodbyes*, *A Parable of Death*, *Time Cycle*, and *Echoi*;
        the publication of *Elytres* (study score) and *Fragments of
        Archilochos* by Carl Fischer; and Foss's appearances as
        guest conductor of the New York Philharmonic, Toronto
        Symphony, and the Cleveland Orchestra.

B84.   Ericson, Raymond. "Extravagances in Programming."
        New York Times June 5, 1966:II,13.

Promotional article for the Festival of Stravinsky which opened on June 30, 1966 at Philharmonic Hall, New York City by the New York Philharmonic. The music to be performed is mentioned. (See also: B85, B86, WB335)

B85.   Klein, Howard. "Music: Stravinsky's Own." *New York Times* July 16, 1966:15.
Review of the first Festival of Stravinsky concert, July 15, 1966 which included all Stravinsky works. Foss was the developer of the festival. "Hats off to Mr. Foss for his planning and casting..." (See also: B84, B86, WB335)

B86.   Schonberg, Harold C. "Music: *Oedipus Rex* by Philharmonic." *New York Times* July 21, 1966:II,23.
Review of the July 20, 1966 New York Philharmonic Orchestra performance with Lukas Foss, conductor, as part of the Festival of Stravinsky. Performed were works by Gabrieli, Monteverdi, Gesualdo, Verdi, as well as Stravinsky's *Oedipus Rex* with costuming by Larry Rivers. The Camerata Singers performed all the choral works. "In the Verdi *Te Deum*, [Foss] seemed to be emotionally allied to the score." (See also: B84, B85, WB335)

B87.   Klein, Howard. "Philharmonic Festival Offers Music Chosen by Stravinsky." *New York Times* July 23, 1966:13.
(See: WB335)

B88.   Dwyer, John. "The Webern Concert--An Important Event in the Music World." *Buffalo Evening News* October 31, 1966:34.
Review of the International Webern Festival program held in Buffalo. Buffalonians shunned away from the program, however, "scholars and musicians from principal universities and cultural centers of Europe were present." Dwyer points out to the Buffalo readers that Buffalo had gained a place in musical history by being the scene of a Webern revelation.

B89.   Butterworth, Neil. "American Composers." *Music; The Official Journal of the Schools Music Association* 2:38-40 (no. 1, 1967)
In this biographical article which includes eight twentieth century American composers, Foss is mentioned as "the most outstanding composer of the younger generation in America." It describes his early composition *Song of Songs* (See: W29) and how his style developed into the improvisation form used in *Time Cycle* (See: W31) and *Echoi* (See: W74).

B90.   "Lukas Foss." *Current Biography Yearbook* 1966:103-105 (1967)
         A biographical essay outlining Foss's many accomplishments as composer, conductor, and performer. Because of this article's appearance in 1966, emphasis was placed on Foss's accomplishments as conductor of the Buffalo Philharmonic Orchestra and the establishment of the Center for the Creative and Performing Arts at the State University of New York at Buffalo.

B91.   Pisciotta, Louis Vincent. "Texture in the Choral Works of Lukas Foss." Chap. in "Texture in the Choral Works of Selected Contemporary American Composers." Ph.D. diss., Indiana University, 1967:200-233. *Dissertation Abstracts* 28:4658A (May 1968) UMI# 68-7253.
         This chapter discusses and briefly analyses *The Prairie* (See: WB60), *Behold! I Build an House* (See: WB65), *A Parable of Death* (See: WB78), and *Psalms* (See: WB86) with regards to textual and musical texture.

B92.   Klein, Howard. "Opera: Foss and Figaro." *New York Times* February 13, 1967:43.
         Review of Foss's debut as an opera conductor, February 11, 1967, leading the New York City Opera at the New York State Theater, New York City in a performance of Mozart's *Le Nozze de Figaro*. "Tightly knit, stressing clarity and brisk pacing,...Mr. Foss was like a puppet on a string, leaping to his cues, and he did not seem to miss one." (See also: B94)

B93.   Salzman, Eric. "The Many Lives of Lukas Foss." *Saturday Review* 50:73-74+ (February 25, 1967)
         Described as the "eternal Wunderkind" and a "Golden Boy," this article describes Foss's many accomplishments as "composer, conductor, pianist, teacher, impresario-organizer, and tireless proponent of the newest new music." Foss describes himself as a better conductor for having composition skills. The article concludes with a biography of Foss.

B94.   Osborne, Conrad L. "Out of the Wings." *High Fidelity/Musical America* 17:MA13 (May 1967)
         Brief review of the February 11, 1967 performance of the New York City Opera production of Mozart's *Le Nozze de Figaro*, conducted by Lukas Foss. "Sharp, light-textured orchestral playing, good contact with the stage....Regrettably, [Foss] had to pull the whole evening by himself." (See also: B92)

B95.   Foss, Lukas. "Buffalo Is Not a Vacuum." *New York Times* May 28, 1967:II,11-12. Reprinted in *Buffalo Evening News* June 3, 1967:B9 (See: B96)

Foss defends his position in programming and performing new music as well as praising Buffalo for supporting new music through the Evenings for New Music Concerts and the Festival of the Arts Today. He describes the new relationship between performer and conductor, that the two must work together more closely than before if the composition is to receive a fair appraisal. He also is distressed that the performers often receive sparse credit in reviews. (See also: B104, B126)

B96.   Foss, Lukas. "Buffalo's Festival of Arts: The Winds of Change Blow Strongly Here." *Buffalo Evening News* June 3, 1967:B9. Reprint of "Buffalo Is Not a Vacuum." *New York Times* May 28, 1967:II,11-12.
(See: B95; See also: B104, B126)

B97.   Soria, Dorle J. "Artist Life: Interesting and True." *High Fidelity/Musical America* 17:MA4 (July 1967)
This article is a collection of short news items and anecdotes. Mentioned is a four-handed piano recording made by Foss and André Previn of Mozart sonatas in the 1950s that was never released.

B98.   Dwyer, John. "The Maestro Crisis Is National But Not Hopeless, Says Foss." *Buffalo Evening News* December 23, 1967:B7.
Foss remarks on the pressures that are put on conductors of major orchestras and that unless effective assistant and associate conductors as well as guest conductors are employed, the problems will continue to rise.

B99.   Foss, Lukas. "Tendencije Savremene Muzike u SAD." *Zvuk* no. 87-88:401-403 (1968)
Article in Yugoslavian; includes summary in English. This is the same article as "Notes of American Music in the 1960's" presented at the Yugoslav-American Seminar in Music. (See: B124 for details)

B100.   Ewen, David. "Lukas Foss, 1922- ." *World of Twentieth Century Music*. Englewood-Cliffs, NJ: Prentice-Hall, 1968:279-286.
A biographical sketch which includes informational descriptions of major compositions.

B101.   Foss, Lukas. "[Beethoven and Schubert: A Comment]" In *Franz Schubert Symphony in B Minor ("Unfinished") an Autoritative Score, Schubert's Sketches, Commentary: Essays in History and Analysis*. Edited by Martin Chusid. New York: W.W. Norton, 1968:130.
This score includes views and comments by Foss and others about Schubert. This quote by Foss states that Schubert tried to write like Beethoven and created

Schubert. It is reprinted from Smith, Julia. *Aaron Copland: His Work and Contributions to American Music.* New York: Dutton, 1955:288.

B102.   Austin, Larry and others. "Groups: New Music Ensemble, ONCE Group, Sonic Arts Group, Musica Elettronica Viva." *Source* 2:17 (January 1968)
Foss discusses with the authors his five years of improvisational experience and that like the maker of the camera, he is not ultimately responsible for the photograph. "Improvisation that works is improvisation made safe....When I found this out, I dissolved my improvisation ensemble and returned to composition, incorporating techniques I developed during my five years of improvising."

B103.   Putnam, Thomas. "Philharmonic to Go for a Spin." *Buffalo Courier Express Focus* January 21, 1968:20.
Putnam describes the works to be recorded by Nonesuch for three recordings, the first recording contract ever for the Buffalo Philharmonic Orchestra. (See also: D111, D112)

B104.   "Art: Exhibitions: Where the Militants Roam." *Time* 91:74-77 (March 15, 1968)
Review of the 2nd Festival of the Arts Today in Buffalo, New York. It primarily outlines the art works displayed, although theater and musical events are noted. "The theme of the festival in Foss's words, is 'perhaps revolution...meaning that if we don't learn to adapt ourselves to the modern situation now, it's the end--and the artist must show us the way.'" (See also: B95, B96, B126)

B105.   "Contemporary Music for New Audiences." *American Symphony Orchestra League Newsletter* 19:10-11 + (August/October 1968)
The article is taken from a panel discussion held during the 1968 American Symphony Orchestra League National Conference. Foss discussed the good fortune he was having in Buffalo regarding the programming of new music. He stated that orchestras can approach the old symphonic masters better through the performance of new works. "Performances become dusty and unimaginative. After our orchestra has been working on something very different and very new and very difficult...then, we suddenly approach Beethoven's *Fifth* as though the ink were not yet dry."

B106.   Foss, Lukas. "Symphony Women's Associations, the Composer and the Music." *American Symphony Orchestra League Newsletter* 19:21-22 (August/October 1968)

Foss discusses his ideas on contemporary music, audiences, educating listeners, conductors, and programming at the 1968 American Symphony Orchestra League National Conference.

B107. Strongin, Theodore. "Foss In Dual Role for Mozart Work." *New York Times* August 31, 1968:13.
Review of the August 30, 1968 performance by the New York Chamber Orchestra at Philharmonic Hall, New York City with Lukas Foss as pianist and conductor. He performed Mozart's *C Minor Concerto*, K. 491. "His was a personal approach, one of thorough involvement....Mr. Foss's tone is perhaps not the most velvety or silkiest among pianists, but his clear-minded sense of musical direction and the responsiveness of the orchestra together made a lovely performance. Also performed was Mozart's *Mass in C Minor*, K. 427.

B108. Foss, Lukas. "Composition in the 1960s." *High Fidelity* 18:42-43 (September 1968)
Divided into three sections: "Looking Back," "Ballad," and "Looking Ahead," this article by Foss is both a retrospect of his work and a philosophy for composers "not to look back [as] one plunges headlong into a would-be future."

B109. Hamilton, David. "Some Newer Figures in America." *High Fidelity* 18:57 (September 1968)
This issue of *High Fidelity* is entitled "The New Music: Its Sources, Its Sounds, Its Creators." This brief biographical article outlines Foss's accomplishments and describes his music as "a loosely structured music whose final form would be freshly determined in each performance" and "based on distortion and fragmentation...with considerable use of indeterminacy and improvisation."

B110. Hume, Paul. "The Symphony: Is It Alive? Or Just Embalmed?" *New York Times* September 22, 1968:II,25.
Excerpts from a symposium broadcast by the Eastern Educational Network between Elliott Carter, Lukas Foss, and Leon Kirchner. Foss discusses the two alternatives available to symphony orchestras: one, to program only classics, much the way the National Gallery of Art will only hang works of painters who have been dead fifty years; and the other to break up the orchestra into chamber groups.

B111. Fuchs, Harry. "A Mozart-Haydn Festival at Philharmonic Hall." *Music and Artists* 1:30-31 (October 1968)
Review of the August 30, 1968 Mozart-Haydn festival concert in which Foss conducted and performed with the New York Chamber Orchestra. "Happily Lukas

Foss...was the only representative here of the type of younger-generation conductors whose brash, mercilessly theatrical, energetically driving styles render them so patently ill-suited for the eighteenth-century classics."

B112.   *Lukas Foss on the New Lukas Foss.* New York: Carl Fischer, 1969.
        A collection of program notes written by Foss for *Time Cycle, Echoi, Elytres, Fragments of Archilochos, For 24 Winds, Cello Concert, Baroque Variations, Etudes for Organ,* and *Paradigm.* It also includes information on recordings of Foss's works and a catalog of his works available from Carl Fischer. (See: WB92, WB155, WB211, WB213, WB218, WB229, WB341, WB358, WB442)

B113.   Ewen, David. "Lukas Foss, 1922- ." In *Composers Since 1900: A Biographical and Critical Guide.* New York: H.W. Wilson, 1969:207-212.
        A biography of Foss's life from early training to 1969. It follows Foss's composing career as well as his personal life, listing many of his compositions and the situations surrounding their creation. (See also: B172)

B114.   "Composer Briefs." *Pan Pipes* 61:84 (January 1969)
        A listing of premieres and recordings of *Baroque Variations* (See: W52b, D47), the premiere of *Etudes for Organ* (See: W107a), and the publication of *For 24 Winds.*

B115.   Austin, Larry and others. "Events/Comments: Is New Music Being Used for Political or Social Ends?." *Source* 3:90-91 (no. 2, 1969)
        The editors of *Source* collected telephone interviews from many avant garde composers including Foss regarding whether their music was used for political or social ends. Foss replied, "I want my music to change me and to change the minds of others like me. But I consider music incapable of directly stimulating action of any kind."

B116.   Schonberg, Harold C. "Music: Debussy *Fantasy.*" *New York Times* May 8, 1969:55.
        Review of the May 7, 1969 performance by the Buffalo Philharmonic Orchestra, Lukas Foss, conductor at Carnegie Hall, New York City. Performed was the New York premiere of Charles Ives's *Orchestral Set No. 2.* "By now Mr. Foss has created in Buffalo one of the better American orchestras. It is a precision instrument, strong in every department, cohesive in ensemble, supple in rhythm." (See also: B123)

B117.   Putnam, Thomas. "Foss to Leave Philharmonic Director Post." *Buffalo Courier Express* May 13, 1969:1 +

Foss discusses his reasons for resigning his post as musical director of the Buffalo Philharmonic Orchestra. These reasons included the pending merger with the Rochester Philharmonic Orchestra and the low morale of the musicians for not being considered in the negotiations. He mentioned that he would, however, continue his duties with the Creative Associates at the State University of New York at Buffalo.

B118.   Henahan, Donal. "4 Orchestras Play Merger Tune." *New York Times* May 14, 1969:35.
Foss resigned as musical director of the Buffalo Philharmonic because of the affects that talks to merge with the Rochester Philharmonic Orchestra had had on the morale of the Buffalo musicians. Although mergers were familiar in the corporate world, they were foreign to the musical world. Foss felt that it would only be a matter of time before one of the communities involved would dominate the other causing one community to lose its orchestra.

B119.   Henahan, Donal. "Which Runs an Orchestra: The Conductor? The Men? The Dollar?" *New York Times* May 18, 1969:II,19.
Foss speaks candidly in this article on his reasons for leaving the Buffalo Philharmonic Orchestra and his personal musical goals as a composer and conductor.

B120.   Putnam, Thomas. "Orchestra Gives Stirring Concert." *Buffalo Courier Express* May 19, 1969:26.
Review of the May 18, 1969 final concert of the Buffalo Philharmonic Orchestra's 1969 season. Pending meetings with the Rochester (New York) Philharmonic Orchestra to possibly merge the two orchestras, the members of the Buffalo Philharmonic Orchestra and Foss stood silently in protest before performing Beethoven's *Ninth Symphony* to demonstrate their feelings regarding the merger. (See also: B121, B122)

B121.   "Concert Emotion Overflows: Silent Protest, Roaring Ovation." *Buffalo Evening News* May 19, 1969:15.
Review of the May 18, 1969 final concert of the Buffalo Philharmonic Orchestra's 1969 season. "[During the two minutes of silent protest] the audience...buzzed a little and then grew absolutely silent under the dramatic pressure. The whole music hall became a surcharged vacuum, and the two minutes seemed a nerve-wracking eternity." The performance of Beethoven's *Ninth Symphony* was beyond compare for responsiveness and sensitivity on the part of the musicians. (See also: B120, B122)

B122.   Dwyer, John. "Orchestra's Eloquence Hailed by Maestro Foss." *Buffalo Evening News* May 19, 1969:19.

Foss mentions his support for the Buffalo Philharmonic Orchestra's silent protest as a way of showing "protest and a will to live, and not as an acknowledgement of doom." The Philharmonic players association knew that members of the Rochester Orchestra Board would be in the audience and wanted to dramatize their feelings. (See also: B120, B121)

B123.   Lowe, Steven. "Buffalo Philharmonic (Foss)." *High Fidelity/Musical America* 19:MA12 (August 1969)
Review of the May 7, 1969 performance by the Buffalo Philharmonic Orchestra at Carnegie Hall, New York City with Foss conducting. The orchestra performed Ives's *Orchestral Set No. 2* (1st New York performance), Debussy's *Fantasie* for piano and orchestra, and Mahler's *Fourth Symphony*. "Foss drew a torrential outpouring of sound from the orchestra that at times bordered on the terrifying....Foss then directed the cleanest, most transparent account of Mahler's *Fourth Symphony* I could ever imagine." (See also: B116)

B124.   Foss, Lukas. "Notes on American Music in the 1960's." In *Papers of the Yugoslav-American Seminar on Music*, 1970:58-61. Translation of "Tendencije Savremene Muzike u SAD." (See: B99)
A paper presented by Foss at the Yugoslav-American Seminar on Music. Foss discusses philosophies of composition and improvisation. At the end of the article is a list of "personal notes" on what is safe in music. "Show me dangerous music. Music precise like tightrope walking. Music that will stop wars."

B125.   Goss, Madeleine. "Lukas Foss." In *Modern Music-Makers: Contemporary American Composers*. New York: Dutton, 1952; reprint, Westport, CT: Greenwood, 1970:490-499.
A biographical sketch including a chronological chart and a works list.

B126.   Cage, John, Lukas Foss, and Iannis Xenakis. "Short Answers to Difficult Questions." *The Composer (U.S.)* 2:39-42 (no. 2, 1970)
This article is a transcription of a panel discussion held at the 2nd Buffalo Festival of the Arts Today between John Cage, Lukas Foss, and Iannis Xenakis. Each of the three posed questions to the others regarding their philosophies of composition, music of the past, and music of the future. (See also: B95, B96, B104)

B127.   Finn, Robert. "Buffalo: Politics." *American Musical Digest* 1:44-46 (no. 6, 1970) An excerpt reprinted from the *Cleveland Plain Dealer*, March 29, 1970.

The Buffalo Philharmonic Orchestra was near financial collapse in 1969-70 when county government came to the rescue with a one-time grant of $400,000. After seven years under Foss's direction, the Orchestra had gained national and international recognition for adventurous programming of contemporary music. However, with Foss's resignation and the financial status of the orchestra, more conservative programming was mandated to lure audiences back to Kleinhans Music Hall and concerts by the Orchestra.

B128.   Putnam, Thomas. "Foss Changed Musical Tastes." *Buffalo Courier Express Focus* May 31, 1970:28.
Foss discusses his seven years as musical director of the Buffalo Philharmonic Orchestra. He states that his objective was to build the orchestra and "'to serve the de-provincialization of Buffalo.'" Also discussed is Foss's busy itinerary for the summer of 1970 which included the editing of Vox recordings, travel, etc. (See also: WB379)

B129.   Ericson, Raymond. "Music: Spirited *Elijah*: Foss, Disregarding Score Markings, Leads a Memorable Performance." *New York Times* October 30, 1970:31.
Review of the October 28, 1970 performance of Mendelssohn's *Elijah* by Tom Krause as Elijah, Pauline Tinsley, soprano, Joy Davidson, alto, George Shirley, tenor, Westminster Choir, Robert Carwithen, director, members of the the New York Philharmonic Orchestra, Lukas Foss, conductor. "Lukas Foss disregarded probably half the rhythmic and dynamic markings in the score, but he gave it so much dramatic fervor and musical sweep that he realized its potential power....Performances of *Elijah* are seldom memorable. This one was."

B130.   Stevanovitch, Emilio A. "Un Momento con Lukas Foss." *Buenos Aires Musical* 25:3 (December 16, 1970)
Interview with Foss (in Spanish). The article gives a short biographical sketch and asks Foss's opinions on who influenced his music most, advise for a young composer, and why he feels that Bernstein and Boulez are the foundations of conducting.

B131.   Dwyer, John. "Ballet Is Clever Lukas Foss Ode." *Buffalo Evening News* January 30, 1971:B10.
Review of the January-February production of a parody opera by the Company of Man ballet company at the Domus arts center, Buffalo, New York. The company used music from Foss's *Baroque Variations*, *Non-Improvisation*, and *Paradigm* for the live portion of the program and *Echoi* for the filmed ballet portion. All the sections had double meaning titles such as "Meatings of the Executive Bored." The ballet was not very high-

level, but the staging and props were highly imaginative. (See also: WB344)

B132.   Haieff, A. and others.   "Stravinsky: A Composers' Memorial."   *Perspectives of New Music* 9:61-62 (Spring/Summer 1971)
  In this article, Foss writes a "letter" to Stravinsky, fondly remembering all the experiences he had with him, from the first time they met in Boston through a festival of Stravinsky's music Foss planned with the New York Philharmonic Orchestra.   "I always looked at you as a young composer of the eighteenth century must have looked at Papa Haydn."

B133.   "Foss Gets Brooklyn Post."   *New York Times* September 24, 1971:34.
  Announcement of Foss's appointment to the post of conductor and music adviser of the Brooklyn Philharmonia for the 1971-72 season.

B134.   Henahan, Donal.   "Foss Hopes 4 'Marathons' Will Bring Music Lovers to Brooklyn."   *New York Times* October 13, 1971:37.
  Foss describes the marathon concerts that were performed by the Brooklyn Philharmonia in an attempt "to things so fresh at the [Brooklyn] Academy that New Yorkers will feel they must come to Brooklyn."   (See also: B135, B144-B146)

B135.   "Foss Runs 'Marathon'."   *Music and Artists* 4:4 (December 1971/January 1972)
  Foss ran four four-hour no-intermission marathon concerts, one each of all-Bach, all-Mozart, all-American, and all-Beethoven at the Hollywood Bowl and the Brooklyn Academy of Music with the hope of attracting young audiences.   The concerts included chamber, orchestral, and choral works and allowed the audience members to come and go as they wished.   (See also: B134, B144-B146)

B136.   Heinsheimer, Hans.   "Orchesteriana in Amerika Herbst 1971."   *Das Orchester* 19:608-609 (December 1971)
  This article describes the orchestra scene in the United States in 1971.   Heinsheimer "mentioned only briefly the departure of Lukas Foss from Buffalo...where his experimental music gradually got on people's nerves. Foss [was] named conductor, amazingly enough, of a previously insignificant orchestra in Brooklyn, a part of New York City known more for its slums and gangster shootings than for symphony concerts."   (translation)

B137.   "*Music Journal's* 1972 Gallery of Living Composers: Lukas Foss."   *Music Journal* 30:42 (1972 Annual)

Provides a brief biographical sketch with a listing
of major compositions.

B138.   Schefler, Joan K. "Making Music in Israel." *Tarbut* 3
(1972/73)
Foss's association with the Jerusalem Symphony
Orchestra and with the music of Israel is described.
While in Israel, Foss programmed his marathon concerts
on three separate occasions which were met with as
much success as in Los Angeles and New York.

B139.   "Hemidemisemiquaver." *New York Times* March 5,
1972:II,28.
Announcement of Foss's appointment as chief
conductor and musical adviser of the Kol Israel Orchestra
of Jerusalem, Israel's second orchestra, while remaining
as musical adviser and conductor of the Brooklyn
Philharmonia.

B140.   Foss, Lukas and others. "Contemporary Music:
Observations from Those Who Create It." *Music and
Artists* 5:11-12 (June/July 1972)
Foss reflects on himself as conductor, teacher,
and composer and gives his viewpoints on orchestra,
students, notation, and audiences of the contemporary
musical styles.

B141.   Foss, Lukas. "Inaudible Singing." *Choral Journal* 13:5-6
(September 1972)
Foss discusses his emerging and submerging of
sound technique as used in *Geod* (W53), *Elytres* (W49),
Fragments of Archilochos (W17), and *Baroque Variations*
(W52). He describes music as "a continuous
phenomenon" which cannot be heard all the time.

B142.   Hiemenz, Jack. "Mostly Mozart, and Bach at Lincoln
Center: Foss, Raskin." *High Fidelity/Musical America*
22:MA10 (November 1972)
Review of the August 4, 1972 Mostly Mozart
concert conducted by Lukas Foss. Included on the
program were the *Brandenburg Concertos, Nos. 3 and 5*
of J.S. Bach, with Foss performing on piano for No. 5.
Foss also performed on *Elvira Madigan* as a surprise
encore.

B143.   Hart, Philip. "Buffalo Philharmonic Orchestra: Lukas
Foss." In *Orpheus in the New World: The Symphony
Orchestra as an American Cultural Institution*. New
York: W.W. Norton, 1973:216-221.
In this section, Hart focuses on Foss's tenure as
music director and conductor of the Buffalo Philharmonic
Orchestra. He compares Foss's selection of music to
Foss's predecessors and notes the respect that Foss

received from the musicians for their input into musician
and music selection.

B144. Foss, Lukas. "Getting Youth to Face the Music (the
Lukas Foss Way)." *New York Times* April 22,
1973:II,13.
   A letter written by Foss to the music critics of the
New York Times in response to an article by Harris
Green, "If You Want Them to Love the Classics...." Foss
describes his music marathons and how new approaches
to the performances of the classics will bring in new
audiences. "The young adult is ready to embrace all
classical music from Bach to Mahler....He wants to be
enveloped, engulfed, purged, saved, hypnotized, turned
on, rather than entertained." (See also: B134, B135,
B145, B146)

B145. Frankenstein, Alfred. "'Mozart-Marathon' in Jerusalem--
zur Situation des Israelischen Musiklebens." *Musica*
27:282-283 (May/June 1973)
   Foss organized marathons of various composers's
music in Israel as well as in New York and California.
The public in Jerusalem enjoyed the performances in
which Foss conducted and performed. (See also: B134,
B135, B144, B146)

B146. Rockwell, John. "Foss's Marathon." *High
Fidelity/Musical America* 23:MA16-17 (August 1973)
   Review of the April 28, 1973 Romantic Marathon
concert that Foss organized including performances by
the Brooklyn Philharmonia, Concord String Quartet, and
Eleanor Steber held at the Brooklyn Academy of Music.
"The piece-by-piece sequence made pleasurable sense,
particularly with solo, chamber, and orchestral
performances as good as the ones Foss had on hand."
(See also: B134, B135, B144, B145)

B147. Kyle, Marguerite Kelly. "AmerAllegro: Lukas Foss." *Pan
Pipes* 66:52 (January 1974)
   Listings of the premiere of *Orpheus* (See: W54a),
the premiere of *Fanfare* (See: W55a), and the premiere
of the definitive version of *MAP* (See: W80c); and the
many locations where Foss was guest conductor,
lecturer, and teacher for the year.

B148. Kyle, Marguerite Kelly. "AmerAllegro: Lukas Foss." *Pan
Pipes* 67:55 (January 1975)
   Listings of performances of *Time Cycle, The Cave
of the Winds, For 24 Winds, Orpheus, Fanfare, Baroque
Variations*, and *Elytres*; his receipt of the Columbia
University Alice Ditson Award as the "conductor who
has done most for American Music, 1974"; and the
completion of *Concerto for Solo Percussion and
Orchestra* written for Jan Williams.

B149.   Lejtes, Ruf' and Nonna Sahnazarova. *Sovremennoe Burzuaznoe Iskusstvo: Kritika i Razmyslenija = Contemporary Bourgeois Art: Criticism and Reflection.* Moskva: Sovetskij Kompozitor, 1975:389.
Includes an article written by Foss concerning the avant-garde and contemporary society. Book in Russian.

B150.   Christensen, Louis. "An Interview with Lukas Foss." *Numus West* 2:51-55 (Spring 1975)
Includes a list of works and recordings. The interview was given after the December 11, 1974 performance of *Paradigm* by the Vancouver New Music Ensemble. Foss discusses his beginnings of ensemble improvisation and why he left this form of composition in favor of "choice" music and electronic mediums. He relates these aspects to particular compositions and the psychological aspects of his work.

B151.   DeRhen, Andrew. "Brooklyn Philharmonia (Foss)." *High Fidelity/Musical America* 25:MA24 (August 1975)
Review of the April 1, 1975 concert of Latin American music on the series "Meet the Moderns" performed by the Brooklyn Philharmonia, Lukas Foss, conductor. Included on the program were the premiere of *Choro* for viola and orchestra by M. Camargo Guarnieri, *Concerto* for four horns by Carlos Chavez, *Concerto per Cordes* by Alberto Ginastera, and a work by Julian Orbon. A discussion between Foss, Chavez, Ginastera, and Orbon was held during intermission.

B152.   Johnson, Tom. "Lukas Foss Works on the Cathedral." *Village Voice* April 5, 1976:140-141.
Reviews many of Foss's compositions and comes to the conclusion that he has no set style. "Foss is described as a 'musical fashion plate' of 'chameleon-like adaptability' who has written a 'pocket history of American music.'" The gothic cathedral is how Foss refers to contemporary music and that many composers are working on the project at one time with some prominently working on the altar and others on singular pieces that will never be fully appreciated. Foss makes "contributions to the cathedral and, as a conductor, [helps] out other artists."

B153.   Browne, Bruce Sparrow. "The Choral Music of Lucas Foss." Part I of D.M.A. diss., University of Washington, 1976. *Dissertation Abstracts* 37:1287A (September 1976) UMI# 76-20709.
A study of Foss's choral music with a discussion and analysis of his works in regards to "found motivic, melodic, harmonic, and rhythmic characteristics." It traces his choral compositional style from neo-classicism to the avant-garde. (See: WB61, WB64, WB80)

B154.   Hatten, Robert S. "An Evening with Lukas Foss."
        Indiana Theory Review 1:44-47 (no. 1, 1977)
                The article was written as the result of a
        discussion Foss had with the Graduate Theory
        Association of Indiana University on July 27, 1977.
        Foss discussed his compositional styles from his middle
        period, including *Time Cycle* (See: W31, W32), *Echoi*
        (See: W74), *Geod* (See: W53), and *Baroque Variations*
        (See: W52). He mentioned that conducting is his way
        of bridging the present with the past masters and spoke
        of his experimentation with non-improvisational
        techniques.

B155.   Kyle, Marguerite Kelly. "AmerAllegro: Lukas Foss." *Pan
        Pipes* 69:46 (January 1977)
                Listings of the premiere of *American Cantata* (See:
        W20a); other performances of *American Cantata*; the
        publication of *American Cantata* and *Salomon Rossi Suite*
        by Salabert; and the recording of *The Prairie* on the Vox
        label (See: D5).

B156.   Mark, Michael. "New York." *Music Journal* 35:34-35
        (February 1977)
                Review of the December 5, 1976 all-Bach concert
        by the Brooklyn Philharmonia, Lukas Foss, conductor at
        the Brooklyn Academy of Music. "The group and
        soloists were scaled to 'proper' Baroque proportions.
        What the listener heard, however, was an essentially
        romantic approach to the music as surely as a full-scale
        orchestra had been pressed into service."

B157.   DeRhen, Andrew. "Foss, et al.: Louise Talma Works."
        High Fidelity/Musical America 27:MA31 (June 1977)
                Review of the February 5, 1977 concert held at
        Hunter College of works by Louise Talma in which Lukas
        Foss was one of the performers. She and Foss
        reenacted their first meeting 30 years prior by performing
        the same light work "Four-Hand Foolishness" as an
        encore to the program.

B158.   "Conciertos: Lukas Foss." *Heterofonia* 10:37
        (July/August 1977)
                Review of a conference-concert Foss conducted
        with the Brooklyn Philharmonia in Franklin
        Netzahualcóyotl (Mexico). The orchestra performed
        works by various twentieth century composers and Foss
        performed Copland's *El Salón México* on the piano.

B159.   Peterson, Melody. "Foss Ensemble: Malloch's *The Art
        of Fuguing*." *High Fidelity/Musical America* 27:MA27
        (October 1977)
                Review of the May 24, 1977 premiere
        performance of William Malloch's adaptation of J.S.

Bach's *The Art of Fuguing* as performed by forty musicians from the Los Angeles Philharmonic, Chamber Orchestra, Chamber Symphony, and film community with Lukas Foss conducting in the First Presbyterian Church, Hollywood, Calif. (See also: D20, D21)

B160.   Horowitz, Joseph. "Lukas Foss Spans Two Musical Worlds." *New York Times* January 27, 1978:C22.
    Promotional article for the January 28, 1978 "Meet the Moderns" concert by the Brooklyn Philharmonia. Foss explained his reasons for preparing separate concerts of classics and moderns, that "people who pay for a concert want to hear what they want to hear....And if you have the cause in mind, you're going to place the modern work where it makes sense--on a program where the other pieces relate to it in some way." He performs new music because his composer colleagues look to him for understanding, although his heart is really in the classics. He states that the composer/conductor who ignores the past becomes a dabbler.

B161.   Rockwell, John. "Pop Art Is Theme of Concert." *New York Times* February 4, 1979:47.
    Review of the February 2, 1979 "Meet the Moderns" concert by the Brooklyn Philharmonia, Lukas Foss, conductor at the Brooklyn Academy of Music. Included on the program was a symposium including Foss, Kurt Vonnegut, and Leo Castelli (who was substituting for Larry Rivers). Musically, three premieres were presented: Nils Vigeland's *Sisters*, Francis Thorne's *Pop Partita: 'B'Way and 52nd Revisited*, and Charles Zachary Bornstein's *Eight American Dreams*.

B162.   Schwartz, Elliott and Barney Childs, eds. *Contemporary Composers on Contemporary Music*. New York: Da Capo Press, 1978, c1967:325-334. Reprint of Foss, Lukas. "The Changing Composer-Performer Relationship: A Monologue and a Dialogue." *Perspectives of New Music* 1:45-53 (Spring 1963)
    (See: B52)

B163.   Horowitz, Joseph. "His Orchestra Grows in Brooklyn." *New York Times* October 21, 1979, II,25 +
    Foss remarks about his orchestra in Brooklyn and how the "symphony" is no longer a living art form for the orchestra, but a museum. Learning from his tenure in Buffalo, he now divides the concert series in Brooklyn in to Majors and Moderns series, using the full orchestra for the classics and smaller groups (in a smaller concert hall) for the moderns. He speaks of the membership of the orchestra also. Foss notes that he needs to conduct the masters to keep his musical perspective well-rounded while he composes his contemporary music.

B164.   Everett, T. "10 Questions: 270 Answers." *The Composer (U.S.)* 10-11:57-103 (1980)
        Foss and 26 other contemporary composers answer ten questions submitted to them by Everett regarding their compositional techniques, composers' organizations, the state of contemporary music, the use of electronics and computers in music, and the composer's role in academic institutions and society at large.

B165.   Foss, Lukas. "To a Young Composer." *The Composer (U.S.)* 10-11:104-105 (1980)
        This is a response to a letter written to Foss by a composition student in which Foss gives the advise to first follow others, then be brave and experiment. He also advises to use and spoil existing ideas and to always go forward in developing a composition style. This letter was reprinted as a part of "Lukas Foss: New Found Focus for the Composer/Conductor." *Ovation* 1984 (See: B196).

B166.   *Lukas Foss*. Paris: Salabert, 1980.
        List of works issued by Éditions Salabert; the text is in French and English.

B167.   DeRhen, Andrew. "Debuts & Reappearances: Brooklyn Philharmonia." *High Fidelity/Musical America* 30:MA18 (June 1980)
        Review of the February 21, 1980 concert by the Brooklyn Philharmonia, Lukas Foss, conductor, at the Brooklyn Academy of Music. Foss is described as a "livewire music director" and "modern music's answer to P.T. Barnum." The concert was part of the Philharmonia's "Meet the Moderns: Rediscoveries and Revivals" series.

B168.   "Foss, 10 Years at the Helm, Sets Philharmonia Schedule." *New York Times* June 26, 1980:C18.
        Description of the 1980-81 concert season of the Brooklyn Philharmonia which included Foss's arrangement of excerpts from Wagner's *Parsifal* (See: W117), *American Cantata* (See: WB20), and the "Meet the Moderns" series.

B169.   "Foss Is Named Director of Milwaukee Symphony." *New York Times* July 29, 1980:C6.
        Announcement of Foss's appointment as Music Director of the Milwaukee Symphony Orchestra effective with the 1981-82 season.

B170.   "Foss Set to Helm Milwaukee Symphony." *Variety* August 6, 1980:64.

A brief biographical sketch announcing Foss's succession to the post of music director of the Milwaukee Symphony from Kenneth Schermerhorn in the 1981-82 season.

B171.   Potter, Rollin R. "Fritz Reiner, Conductor, Teacher, Musical Innovator." Ph.D. diss., Northwestern University, 1980. *Dissertation Abstracts* 41:2348A (December 1980) UMI #80-26901.
         The section about Reiner's teaching responsibilities at the Curtis Institute includes discussion of Reiner's training of Foss, Bernstein, Boris Goldovsky, and Walter Hendl.

B172.   Ewen, David. "Lukas Foss, 1922- ." In *Composers Since 1900: A Biographical and Critical Guide. First Supplement.* New York: H.W. Wilson, 1981:119-121.
         This article supplements the 1969 edition listing and discussing Foss's works from 1968-1977. It includes biographical facts to 1982. (See also: B113)

B173.   Satz, Arthur. "Lukas Foss: Musician of the Month." *High Fidelity/Musical America* 31:MA5-6+ (January 1981)
         In this interview, Foss describes how his composing and conducting complement each other to satisfy his needs as a musician. He describes his work with both the Brooklyn Philharmonia and the Milwaukee Symphony Orchestra. Foss explains how his programming involves continuity within the concert and his composition style developed within continuity. Foss is described as "one of the most productive musical figures active today."

B174.   Putnam, Thomas. "Foss to Conduct and Play Musical Works by Bernstein." *Buffalo Courier Express* January 9, 1981:9+
         Promotional piece describing his January 10, 1981 performance of Bernstein's *Age of Anxiety* with the Buffalo Philharmonic Orchestra, during which Foss would play and conduct. He describes the difficult task of keeping the cues straight.

B175.   Trotter, Herman. "Foss Excellent in Double Role at Philharmonic." *Buffalo Evening News* January 11, 1981:A9.
         Review of the January 10, 1981 performance as conductor and pianist with the Buffalo Philharmonic Orchestra of an all-Bernstein program. "[Foss's] command of this jazzy pastiche was undeniable."

B176.   Kerner, Leighton. "Lilacs in Bloom." *Village Voice* 26:66 (January 28, 1981)

Review of the January 12, 1981 concert by the Brooklyn Philharmonia, Lukas Foss, conductor in Carnegie Hall. It included the first New York performances of Roger Session's *Rhapsody for Orchestra* and Ives's *Johnny Poe*, a song for male-chorus and orchestra about a popular Princeton man killed in World War I.

B177. Rothstein, Edward. "Silent Films Had a Musical Voice." *New York Times* February, 8, 1981:II,1+
Promotional article for the February 12, 1981 performance by the Brooklyn Philharmonia, Lukas Foss, conductor. Foss conducted music by George Antheil, Fernand Léger, Dudley Murphy, Erik Satie, Arnold Schoenberg, and Darius Milhaud while silent films were projected behind the orchestra. (See also: B185, B186)

B178. "Milwaukee Symphony Plans Ambitious Season under Foss' Direction." *Variety* March 18, 1981:301.
An outline of the programming for Foss's first season (1981-82) with the Milwaukee Symphony Orchestra which included 22 guest artists and conductors.

B179. Orgill, Roxane. "Lukas Foss: Ego Takes Back Seat to Music When He Conducts the Milwaukee Symphony." *Milwaukee Journal/Insight* December 13, 1981:12-17.
Biographical sketch depicting Foss's family and early life. It describes how he is the musician's musician and a "jack of all musical trades" because of his unwillingness to specialize in only playing piano, conducting, composing, or teaching.

B180. Gagne, Cole and Tracy Caras. "Lukas Foss." In *Soundpieces: Interviews with American Composers.* Metuchen, N.J.: Scarecrow, 1982:193-208.
Foss discusses his compositions from the beginning of the Improvisation Chamber Ensemble to the early 1970s in this 1975 interview. The interview was originally published in the *New York Arts Journal*, v. 1, no. 2 (September 1976). It includes a list of works and a short biography.

B181. Dettmer, Roger. "The State of U.S. Conductors." *Fanfare* 6:88+ (no. 1, 1982)
Briefly mentions Foss's conducting career with various orchestras and includes discographical references to two of his recordings as conductor.

B182. Wright, David. "Lukas Foss: The Nimble Prankster at 60." *Keynote* no. 6:9-13 (1982)
"If conductors are gods on a symphonic Olympus, Foss must be Hermes, the nimble prankster and messenger." In this biographical sketch, Foss's

perspectives of his personal, composition, and conducting styles are emphasized. Stravinsky had once told him, "Lukas, be a bad guy." Foss also admits that he will someday have to limit his conducting so that he will have more time to compose.

B183.   Ewen, David. "Foss, Lukas." In *American Composers: A Biographical Dictionary*. New York: G.P. Putnam's Sons, 1982:233-237.
  This biographical sketch discusses and lists Foss's principal works to 1979.

B184.   Orgill, Roxane. "Lukas Foss' 'Other' Band." *Milwaukee Journal* February 7, 1982:5.
  A Milwaukee journalist reports on Foss's tenure with the Brooklyn Philharmonia. She describes how he raised the public's awareness to the orchestra and how his marathon concerts gave way to the "Majors" and "Meet the Moderns" concert series. "Foss' great strength is in putting together exciting, meaningful programs" which is the main difference between Brooklyn Philharmonia and the New York Philharmonic Orchestra.

B185.   Rothstein, Edward. "'Music Plus Film' in Manhattan Plus Brooklyn." *New York Times* April 2, 1982:C4.
  Promotional article for "Music Plus Film, Round II" by the Brooklyn Philharmonia, Lukas Foss, conductor, April 2, 1982. Scores by Henry Cowell, Paul Hindemith, John Cage, David Diamond, Paul Bowles, and John Watts accompanied films by Oskar Fischinger, Laura Foreman, and Kostas Georgiou, among others. (See also: B177, B186)

B186.   Davis, Peter G. "Music." *New York* 15:81 (April 19, 1982)
  Review of a perfomance by the Brooklyn Philharmonia, Lukas Foss, conductor in the "Meet the Moderns" series which consisted of scores composed to accompany films. "Very little in the way of great art emerged from the evening...[but] the event still had the scatterbrained charm that often characterizes an evening with Lukas Foss." (See also: B177, B185)

B187.   Pulido, Esperanza. "Libros: Jose Antonio Alcarez, *Hablar de Musica* (Conversaciones con Compositores del Continente Americano)." *Heterofonia* 15:44-45 (October/November/December 1982)
  Review of the book published by Universidad Autónoma Metropolitana, Coordinación de Extensión Universitaria, Mexico City, which is a collection of conversations which Alcarez had with various composers from the Americas. The interviews provide a very

personal and systematic approach to the study of their music.

B188.   Laine, Barry. "Lukas Foss Still Delights in the Unpredictable." *New York Times* November 21, 1982:II,17+
　　　　　Foss discusses his work as a mature composer and conductor. He describes the gratification of working with the Brooklyn Philharmonic Orchestra because of the virtuosity of the players and the short concert season and the Milwaukee Symphony Orchestra because the musicians initiated his appointment. Having learned from his programming experiences with the Buffalo Philharmonic Orchestra and the "bureaucracy" of the Jerusalem Symphony Orchestra, Foss remarks, "I don't want to shock people anymore," which resulted in the programming of more classics for series subscription concerts.

B189.   Hughes, Allen. Music: Bowery Ensemble in Works by Foss." *New York Times* November 3, 1983:C16.
　　　　　Review of the November 1, 1983 performance by the Bowery Ensemble devoted to works by Foss. "Foss...is a veteran trend-follower, having--seemingly-- tried his hand at virtually every style that has come down the pike in the last 40 years....One could only regret that a musician of Mr. Foss's obvious gifts had not found some style he could believe in completely and into which he could pour his heart and soul when he composes." (See: W33d, W76p, W85f, W103c, W109f)

B190.   "Academy Elects Foss, Gross, Lawrence." *New York Times* December 6, 1983:C15.
　　　　　Announcement of Foss's election to the American Academy of Arts and Letters, replacing the late Gilmore D. Clarke.

B191.   Butterworth, Neil. "Foss, Lukas." In *A Dictionary of American Composers*. New York: Garland, 1984:164-169.
　　　　　A biographical sketch with informational descriptions of major compositions.

B192.   Burbank, Richard. *Twentieth Century Music*. New York: Facts on File Publications, 1984:485.
　　　　　This day-by-day chronology of 20th century musical happenings includes 25 references to significant events in Foss's life including many premiere performance listings.

B193.   Palmer, Virginia. "Composer Survey: Opinions on Solo Vocal Literature." *Perspectives of New Music* 22:631-638 (no. 1-2, 1984)

Results of a selective informal survey conducted between October 1980 and June 1981 of composers regarding their solo vocal music. Foss states that he uses "visually suggestive poetry" and that he will either imitate, contradict, or independently set the poetry to the music.

B194.   Kerner, Leighton. "The Philharmonic at Cross-Purposes." *Village Voice* January 3, 1984:72.
Brief review of a Webern centennial concert by the New York Philharmonic Orchestra, Lukas Foss, guest conductor/pianist. On the program were Webern's *Symphony* and *Five Pieces*, op. 10; Schubert dances; one of the six-voiced *Ricercares* from *Musical Offering*; J.S. Bach's *F minor Keyboard Concerto*, no. 5; and 3 versions of Schumann's *D minor Symphony*. "Foss is still an excellent pianist, but you'd never know it from his slog...on a heavy-sounding piano."

B195.   Varga, Bálant András. "Three Questions on Music: Extracts from a Book of Interviews in the Making." *The New Hungarian Quarterly* 25:197-202 (Spring 1984)
Várga posed three questions to numerous contemporary composers regarding the radical influence another composer has had on their work, how important the sounds of the outside world are to their work, and up to what point can they talk of a personal style and where does self-repetition begin. Presented are the answers from seven American composers, including Foss. He remarks that he is influenced anytime he hears music, always searching for a better way to compose; sounds + noise = music; and image does not allow development, "If you develop, you will not repeat."

B196.   Kupferberg, Herbert. "Lukas Foss: Newfound Focus for the Composer/Conductor." *Ovation* 5:12-17 (April 1984)
This biographical essay on Foss centers around Foss as the conductor of the Milwaukee and Brooklyn Orchestras. He was responsible for a growth in concert attendance in Milwaukee. Of his life, Foss says, "I love both composing and conducting...but composing is like going to a no-man's-land. Conducting is like coming home."

B197.   Trotter, Herman. "Lukas Foss Returns, Reflects, Runs." *Buffalo News* August 12, 1984:E4.
Interview with Foss after a guest conductor performance with the Chautauqua (New York) Symphony. Foss reflects on his work with the Milwaukee Symphony Orchestra, the Brooklyn Philharmonic Orchestra, and his time spent with the Buffalo Philharmonic Orchestra. He mentions that too much of his time was spent on conducting with not

enough time left for composing, but some offers were too good to pass up.

B198.   Belt, Byron.   "A Celebration of American Sacred Music in Milwaukee."   *The American Organist* 19:60-61 (January 1985)
        Review of the third annual salute to American music, September 30-October 3, 1984 in Milwaukee, which featured many religious and philosophical works by 37 composers. (See also: B199)

B199.   Malitz, Nancy.   "Milwaukee: A Festival of Sacred Music."   *Ovation* 5:44+ (January 1985)
        Review of the festival of contemporary sacred music sponsored by Foss and the Milwaukee Symphony Orchestra, September 30-October 3, 1984. "[Religious music today is] just as radical, in its way, as stuffing a Brooklyn program full of classical pieces by jazz musicians." Foss conducted three world premieres with the Wisconsin Conservatory Symphony Chorus: David Del Tredici's *The Last Gospel*; Dane Rudyhar's *Cosmic Cycle*; and John Corigliano's *Creations*.

B200.   Stiller, Andrew.   "Triumph and Tribulation."   In *Buffalo Philharmonic Orchestra: Golden Anniversary Commemorative Book*.   Buffalo: Buffalo Philharmonic Orchestra, 1985:58-65.
        The era of Lukas Foss in Buffalo (1962-1970) was a time of excitement and turbulence. While proponents of the avant garde were reaping the benefits of Foss's talent and experimentation (world premieres, creation of the Center for Creative and Performing Arts, a world-reknowned orchestra), other local figures were dismayed at the new programming for the orchestra and blamed Foss for the eminent financial troubles of the orchestra. This article chronologs this historic time for the Buffalo Philharmonic Orchestra.

B201.   Page, Tim.   "Foss and the Brooklyn Philharmonic Innovate and 'Have a Grand Time.'"   *New York Times* November 3, 1985:86.
        Foss discusses the work of the Brooklyn Philharmonic Orchestra and how such a group would only be possible in New York. "We thrive on a lack of routine....We are a genuine orchestra...not just a pick-up ensemble....But we want to work a little bit differently."

B202.   Davis, Peter G.   "Masterpiece Theater."   *New York* 19:64-65 (February 10, 1986)
        Review of the concert at Cooper Union, New York City by Michael Barrett, piano and the Brooklyn Philharmonic Orchestra, Lukas Foss, conductor. The performance included the revival of Marc Blitzstein's *Piano Concerto*. "Foss, Barrett, and the Brooklyn

> Philharmonic deserve all praise for rediscovering a valuable score, as well as for giving it such a zestful performance."

B203.   Davis, Peter G. "Good Things in Small Spaces." *New York* 19:110 (March 3, 1986)
>   Review of the concert at the Brooklyn Academy of Music by the Brooklyn Philharmonic Orchestra, Lukas Foss, conductor. The mediocre concert included unknown works by Sibelius. "As with so many Foss projects, the idea turned out to be more appetizing in theory than in practice."

B204.   Porter, Andrew. "Discourse Most Eloquent." *New Yorker* 62:96-99 (April 28, 1986)
>   Review of the April 1986 concert at the Brooklyn Academy of Music by the Brooklyn Philharmonic Orchestra, Lukas Foss, conductor. The concert included György Kurtág's *Messages of the Late R. V. Trussova*, op. 17. "A choice program had been assembled. The artists had worked hard. The performances were accomplished. But the presentation was poor."

B205.   Chute, James. "Milwaukee Symphony." *High Fidelity* 36:MA44 (June 1986)
>   Review of the January 31, 1986 concert in Milwaukee by the Milwaukee Symphony Orchestra, Lukas Foss, conductor. Performed was the premiere of John Adams's *The Chairman Dances* which was composed for the orchestra. "The orchestra sounded uncomfortable with Adams' rhythms and syncopations, and the playing was uneasy and hesitant....Still, it was evident that *The Chairman Dances* can prove to be an attractive work."

B206.   Shuman Associates, Inc. *Lukas Foss: Long Biography.* New York: Shuman Associates, 1987.
>   Biography of Foss that is supplied by his agent.

B207.   Shulgasser, Mark. "Eareviews: Meet the Moderns: Music from the West Coast." *Ear* 12:24 (no. 4, 1987)
>   Review of the March 20, 1987 performance by the Brooklyn Philharmonic Orchestra at Cooper Union with Foss conducting. "There was little evidence of the new, relaxed West Coast sound in Lukas Foss' selection of mostly old-school academic composers from California."

B208.   Rockwell, John. "Foss to Offer Nietzsche Composition." *New York Times* January 2, 1987:15.
>   Promotional article for the United States premiere performance of Friedrich Nietzsche's *Hymn to Life* by the Grace Choral Society of Brooklyn, the Brooklyn Philharmonic Orchestra, Lukas Foss, conductor on January 2, 1987. It explains how Nietzsche came to

compose the work using Lou Andreas-Salomé's poem as text. (See also: B215)

B209.   Rockwell, John. "Music: Bolcom's Rendering of Blake's Songs." *New York Times* January 11, 1987:42.
Review of the January 9, 1987 New York premiere performance of William Bolcom's *Songs of Innocence and of Experience* performed by the Sine Nomine Singers and Brooklyn College Chorus, Cathedral Choristers, various soloists, Brooklyn Philharmonic Orchestra, and Lukas Foss, conductor at the Brooklyn Academy of Music's Opera House. (See also: B210, B211)

B210.   Davis, Peter G. "Forces of Nature." *New York* 20:71-72 (January 26, 1987)
Review of the January 9, 1987 concert at the Brooklyn Academy of Music which premiered William Bolcom's *Songs of Innocence and of Experience*. Foss conducted the performance by the Brooklyn Philharmonic Orchestra, a large chorus, and several soloists. "Foss [coordinated] the various elements crisply and efficiently." (See also: B209, B211)

B211.   Porter, Andrew. "Voice of the Bard." *New Yorker* 62:70-73 (February 2, 1987)
Review of the January 1987 New York premiere of William Bolcom's *Songs of Innocence and of Experience* at the Brooklyn Academy of Music, New York City by the Brooklyn Philharmonic Orchestra, Lukas Foss, conductor. This lengthy work (two hours and twenty minutes) took Bolcom twenty-six years to compose. "The Brooklyn performances were not very good. Mr. Foss did not seem to know the work well." (See also: B209, B211)

B212.   Brody, Meredith. "Lukas Foss..." *L.A. Weekly* February 27-March 5, 1987:47+
Interview with Foss before his performance with Tashi at the New Music Los Angeles festival on March 1, 1987 (See: W95h). Foss speaks of his musical training and of his time at UCLA in the 1950s as well as his schedule for composing.

B213.   Porter, Andrew. "Exuberant Inventions." *New Yorker* 63:97 (June 1, 1987)
Review of the May 1, 1987 concert at Cooper Union, New York City by the Brooklyn Philharmonic Orchestra, Lukas Foss, conductor, as part of his "Meet the Moderns" series. The concert included the New York debut of Pierre Boulez's *Mémoriale*, the world premiere of Alan Hovhaness's *Partita for Piano and Strings*, Giacinto Scelsi's *Natura Renovatur*, Karl Aage Rasmussen's *Pianissimo Furioso*, and Takashi Yoshimatsu's *Threnody to Toki*.

B214. Blau, Eleanor. "Lukas Foss to Conduct a Manuel de Falla Oddity." *New York Times* October 9, 1987:C3.

Promotional piece for the October 9, 1987 opening concert of the Brooklyn Philharmonic Orchestra's season. Performed was de Falla's *Fuego Fatuo*, "an orchestral suite based on bits of mazurkas, scherzos and whatever else in Chopin's oeuvre struck the fancy of the Spanish composer."

B215. "Thus Composed Nietzsche." *Ovation* 8:10 (December 1987)

Listing of the first United States performance of Nietzche's choral cantata *Hymn to Life* performed by the Brooklyn Philharmonic Orchestra and the Grace Choral Society of Brooklyn, Lukas Foss, conductor. Also on the program were New York premieres of Webern's *Three Orchestral Studies on a Ground* and Felix Mottl's orchestral arrangement of Beethoven's song *Die Ehre Gottes aus der Natur*. (See also: B208)

B216. Bassin, Joseph Philip. "An Overview of the Third Period Compositional Output of Lukas Foss, 1976-1983." Ed.D., Columbia University Teachers College, 1987. *Dissertation Abstracts* 48:1573A-1574A (January 1988) UMI# 87-21079.

Bassin conducted two interviews with Foss regarding his nineteen Third Period works composed from 1976-1983. Each of these pieces is discussed with regards to Foss's commentary of specific details of individual works and general insights to his way of thinking. (See: WB109, WB110, WB169, WB170, WB287, WB292, WB302, WB305, WB306, WB393, WB395, WB400, WB404, WB410, WB412, WB446, WB450)

B217. Waleson, Heidi. "A Many-Sided Maverick." *New York Times Biographical Service* 19:9-10 (January 1988) Reprinted from *New York Times* January 3, 1988:II,17+

Foss remarks on his composer/conductor career in this biographical article. Although he tries to split his time for both activities equally, he hopes to be remembered best for his compositions. He takes back his statement about composers "working on a cathedral" and complains that since media and music discovered each other, "hype has raised the second-rate to prominence." Included in the *New York Times* article is a brief discography.

B218. Behr, Michael. "Lukas Foss am Pult und am Flügel." *Das Orchester* 36:1047 (October 1988)

Review of a performance by Lukas Foss with the Duisberg Symphony. "His program offered him the opportunity to shine in three different roles--as director, composer, and pianist and it's hard to say which is his

best role. With Tschaikovsky's *Fifth Symphony*, he
proved himself to be an orchestra conductor of
international repute....The performance was dynamic,
poetic, sensitive....Bravo to the Symphony."
(translation)

B219.   Rockwell, John. "Lukas Foss to Leave Brooklyn
        Philharmonic." *New York Times* January 5, 1989:C14.
        Announcement of Foss's retirement at the end of
        the 1989/90 series of the Brooklyn Philharmonic
        Orchestra after 20 seasons as director. He was
        responsible for evolving the orchestra "from essentially a
        community ensemble to a highly visible part of New
        York's musical life." He will continue as conductor
        laureate and devote more time to composing.

B220.   Foss, Lukas. "From Ojai: Lukas Foss on Music
        Programming." *OnAir* 11:22 (February 1989)
        Foss describes various types of music
        programming for concerts, ranging from variety and unity
        to trying to cater to everyone. The most important
        aspect for programming is that the performer play music
        he likes. It is only then that the performance will be
        convincing and fulfilling to the audience.

B221.   Campbell, Karen. "New Horizons for an Avant-Garde
        Classicist." *Symphony Magazine* 40:14-19 (May/June
        1989)
        A retrospective of Foss, primarily as conductor, in
        the light of his retirement from the Brooklyn Philharmonic
        Orchestra after 20 years of service to the orchestra. It
        relates his work as conductor to that as composer by
        mentioning some of his most recent premieres. He will
        continue to conduct but will concentrate more on
        composition and giving opportunities to the young as
        Koussevitzky, Fritz Reiner, and Hindemith gave to him.

B222.   Ruff, Mark E. "Composers Should Write What They
        Love." *UB Today* 7:14 (Winter 1989)
        Foss discusses his viewpoints on his composition
        career, describing his four style periods: neo-
        classical/Hindemith; Stravinsky/American; avant-garde/
        experimental; American/adventurous. He also expresses
        concern about contemporary composers and their need
        to be "popular."

B223.   Foss, Lukas. Interview by author, March 22, 1990, New
        York City. Tape recording.
        Interview conducted by the author in preparation
        of this book. Topics covered included biographical
        information and clarification of composition questions.

APPENDIX A:
AWARDS AND HONORS

1942 Pulitzer traveling scholarship for music awarded for his suite to *The Tempest*.

1944 New York Music Critics' Circle Citation awarded for *The Prairie* as the most important new American choral work.

1945 Guggenheim Fellowship. Foss, at the age of 23, was the youngest composer to ever receive this award.

1948 Citation from the Society for the Publication of American Music for *String Quartet in G*.

1950-51 Prix de Rome. Fellow of the American Academy in Rome.

1950-52 Fulbright scholarship.

1952 Mark M. Horblit Award awarded for *Concerto No. 2 for Piano*.

1953 Becomes youngest full professor at the University of California at Los Angeles.

1954 New York Music Critics' Circle Citation awarded for *Concerto No. 2 for Piano* as the best instrumental work of the season.

1956 Honorary LL.D. from the Los Angeles Conservatory of Music.

1957 Creative Music Grant from the National Institute of Arts and Letters.

1957 Naumburg Recording Award for *Song of Songs*.

1960   First American to conduct the Leningrad Symphony.

1960   Second Guggenheim Fellowship.

1961   New York Music Critics' Circle Citation awarded for *Time Cycle*.

1962   Elected to the National Institute of Arts and Letters.

1964   New York Music Critics' Circle Citation awarded for *Echoi* as best new chamber music work.

1965   Added to the Walter W. Naumburg Foundation, Inc.

1968   Buffalo Philharmonic Orchestra awarded $2,000 from ASCAP for "distinguished performance of American Music written since 1940" in June at the American Symphony Orchestra League Conference.

1974   Alice Ditson Award for "conductor who has done the most for American music."

1976   New York City Award for special contributions to the arts.

1979   Award from the American Society of Composers, Authors, and Publishers (ASCAP) for "adventurous programming."

1980   American Composers Alliance Laurel Leaf Award.

1982   Brandeis University Creative Arts Award in Music.

1983   Elected to the Academy of American Academy and Institute of Arts and Letters.

APPENDIX B:
CHRONOLOGICAL
LIST OF COMPOSITIONS

Numbers following each title, e.g. W20, refer to the "Works and Performances" section of this volume.

1937	Violin Sonata, W96
1938	Four Two-Part Inventions, W97
	Grotesque Dance, W98
	Wanderer's Gemütsruhe (Song for a Wanderer), W24
	Three Songs on Texts by Goethe, W25
1939	Sonatina, W99
1939-40	Two Symphonic Pieces, W35
	Incidental Music for Shakespeare's Tempest, W1
1940	Cantata Dramatica, W9
	Four Preludes for Flute, Clarinet, and Bassoon, W70
	Melodrama and Dramatic Song of Michelangelo, W27
	Passacaglia, W100
	Set of Three Pieces, W71
	Where the Bee Sucks, W26
1941	Concerto No. 1 for Clarinet, W37
	Duo, W101
	Two Pieces for Orchestra, W36
	We Sing, W10
1943	Concerto No. 1 for Piano, W38
1944	The Prairie, W11
	The Prairie. Symphonic Suite, W40
	Fantasy Rondo, W102
	The Heart Remembers, W6
	Ode, W41

	Symphony No. 1 in G Major, W39
	Three Pieces, W103
	Within These Walls, W7
	Gift of the Magi, W8
1945	Pantomine, W42
	Song of Anguish, W28
	Tell This Blood, W12
1946	Song of Songs, W29
1947	Adon Olom, W13
	String Quartet No. 1 in G, W72
1948	Capriccio, W104
	Concerto for Oboe, W43
	Recordare, W44
1949	Elegy, W45
	The Jumping Frog of Calaveras County, W3
	Prelude in D, W105
1949-51	Concerto No. 2 for Piano, W46
1950	Behold! I Build an House, W14
1952	Concerto No. 2 for Piano; revised version, W46
	A Parable of Death, W15
1953	Scherzo Ricercato, W106
1953-55	Griffelkin, W4
1955	For Cornelia, W30
1955-56	Psalms, W16
1956-58	Symphony of Chorales, W47
1958	Concerto for Oboe; revised version, W43
	Ode; revised version, W41
1959	Introductions and Goodbyes, W5
	Studies in Improvisation, W73
1959-60	Time Cycle (orchestral version), W31
1960	Concerto for Improvising Instruments, W48
	Time Cycle (chamber version), W32
1961-63	Echoi, W74
1964	Elytres, W49
1965	Fragments of Archilochos, W17
1966	For 24 Winds, W50
1967	Baroque Variations, W52
	Cello Concert, W51
	Four Etudes for Organ, W107
	Non-Improvisation, W75
1968	Paradigm, W76
1969	Paradigm; new version, W76
1969	Geod, W53
	Waves, W77
1970	MAP, W80
1972	The Cave of the Winds, W78
	Ni Bruit Ni Vitesse, W79
	Orpheus, W54
	Three Airs for Frank O'Hara's Angel, W18
1973	Divertissement Pour Mica, W81
	Fanfare, W55
	Lamdeni, W19
1974	Concerto for Solo Percussion, W56
1975	Chamber Music, W82

	Salomon Rossi Suite, W58
	String Quartet No. 3, W83
1975-76	Folksong for Orchestra, W57
1976	American Cantata, W20
1977	American Cantata; revised version, W20
	Curriculum Vitae, W108
	MAP; revised version, W80
	Music for Six, W85
	Quartet Plus, W84
1978	Folksong for Orchestra; revised version, W57
	Music for Six; revised version, W85
	Brass Quintet, W86
	Then the Rocks on the Mountain Begin to Shout, W21
	Thirteen Ways of Looking at a Blackbird, W33
	Music for Antigone, W2
1979	Round a Common Center, W87
	Quintets for Orchestra, W59
1980	Curriculum Vitae With Time Bomb, W88
	Measure for Measure, W34
1980-81	Night Music for John Lennon, W60
1980-82	Exeunt, W61
1981	Solo for Piano, W109
1982	Solo Observed, W89
1983	Curriculum Vitae Tango, W110
	For 200 Cellos, W90
	Horn Trio, W92
	Percussion Quartet, W91
	Orpheus and Euridice, W63
1984	De Profundis, W22
1984-85	Embros, W94
1985	Saxophone Quartet, W93
1985-86	Renaissance Concerto, W63
1986	Griffelkin Suite, W64
	Tashi, W95
	Three American Pieces, W65
	Three Early Pieces, W111
1987	Central Park Reel, W112
	Chaconne, W113
1988	Concerto No. 2 for Clarinet, W66
	For Lenny, W67
	With Music Strong, W23
1989	For Anne Frank, W68
	Guitar Concerto, W69

APPENDIX C:
ALPHABETICAL
LIST OF COMPOSITIONS

Numbers following each title, e.g. W20, refer to the "Works and Performances" section of this volume.

Adon Olom, W13
Airs for Frank O'Hara's Angel, Three (See: Three Airs for Frank O'Hara's Angel)
Airs Pour l'Ange de Frank O'Hara, Trois (See: Three Airs for Frank O'Hara's Angel)
American Cantata, W20
American Landscapes (See: Guitar Concerto)
Ariel's Song (See: Where the Bee Sucks)
Baroque Variations, W52
Behold! I Build an House, W14
Brass Quintet, W86
Cantata Dramatica, W9
Cantata for Children (See: We Sing)
Capriccio, W104
Cave of the Winds, The, W78
Cello Concert, W51
Central Park Reel, W112
Chaconne, W113
Chamber Music, W82
Concerto for Improvising Instruments, W48
Concerto for Oboe, W43
Concerto for Solo Percussion, W56
Concerto No. 1 for Clarinet, W37
Concerto No. 1 for Piano, W38
Concerto No. 2 for Clarinet, W66

INDEX

Numbers preceded by "p" refer to page references in the "Biography" section, numbers preceded by "W," "WB," or "W" with a number and a lower case letter refer to item numbers in the "Works and Performances" section, numbers preceded by "D" refer to item numbers in the "Discography" section, numbers preceded by "DB" refer to item numbers in the "Discography Bibliography" section, and numbers preceded by "B" refer to item numbers in the "General Bibliography."

About the Author

KAREN L. PERONE is Systems Librarian at Canisius College Library. She has contributed to *The Clarinet.*